Becoming a Synthesizer Wizard: From Presets to Power User

Simon Cann

Course Technology PTR
A part of Cengage Learning

COURSE TECHNOLOGY
CENGAGE Learning·

Australia • Brazil • Japan • Korea • Mexico • Singapore • Spain • United Kingdom • United States

COURSE TECHNOLOGY
CENGAGE Learning

Becoming a Synthesizer Wizard: From Presets to Power User
Simon Cann

Publisher and General Manager, Course Technology PTR: Stacy L. Hiquet

Associate Director of Marketing: Sarah Panella

Manager of Editorial Services: Heather Talbot

Marketing Manager: Mark Hughes

Acquisitions Editor: Orren Merton

Project Editor/Copy Editor: Cathleen D. Small

Technical Reviewer: Gino Robair

Editorial Services Coordinator: Jen Blaney

Interior Layout Tech: Macmillan Publishing Solutions

Cover Designer: Luke Fletcher

Indexer: Sharon Shock

Proofreader: Kate Shoup

For product information and technology assistance, contact us at
Cengage Learning Customer & Sales Support, 1-800-354-9706

For permission to use material from this text or product, submit all requests online at **www.cengage.com/permissions**
Further permissions questions can be emailed to
permissionrequest@cengage.com

All trademarks are the property of their respective owners.

Library of Congress Control Number: 2008902399

ISBN-13: 978-1-59863-550-8

ISBN-10: 1-59863-550-6

Course Technology, a part of Cengage Learning
20 Channel Center Street
Boston, MA 02210
USA

Cengage Learning is a leading provider of customized learning solutions with office locations around the globe, including Singapore, the United Kingdom, Australia, Mexico, Brazil, and Japan. Locate your local office at: **international.cengage.com/region**

Cengage Learning products are represented in Canada by Nelson Education, Ltd.

For your lifelong learning solutions, visit **courseptr.com**

Visit our corporate website at **cengage.com**

Printed in Canada
1 2 3 4 5 6 7 11 10 09

Acknowledgments

There are many people who have helped with this book who I would like to thank.

First, there are the guys behind the software that is featured in this book:

- Martin Fay at Software Technology (VAZ Modular)

- Urs Heckman (Zebra 2)

- Jeff McClintock at SynthEdit

- Kasper Nielsen at KarmaFX (KarmaFX Synth Modular)

Without these individuals' singular vision, the world of software synthesis would be a much duller place.

I would also like to thank everyone involved with the production of this book, especially Orren Merton, Cathleen Small, Gino Robair, Stacy Hiquet, and Mark Hughes, as well as the good people at Course Technology PTR.

Thank you all.

About the Author

Simon Cann is a writer based in London. He is the author of a number of music-related and business-related books.

His music-related books include: *How to Make a Noise, Cakewalk Synthesizers: From Presets to Power User, Building a Successful 21st Century Music Career, Sample This!* (with Klaus P. Rausch), *Project5 Power!*, and *Rocking Your Music Business*. His business-related books include the *Made It In...* series of books (madeitin.com), which feature the experiences of international entrepreneurs who have built successful companies in the hottest business locations around the world.

You can read more about Simon at his website, simoncann.com, and check out his other music-related books at his Noise Sculpture website, noisesculpture.com.

Contents

Introduction xiii

Chapter 1
An Introduction to Digital Audio and Software Synthesis   1

Problems? 1
Music-Making Computer 1
Software Synthesizers 3
     Synthesizer Accompanying This Book 3
     Formats and Compatibility 4
MIDI and Human Input Devices 5
     MIDI Channels 6
     Splits and Layers 7
Plug-In Host 8
     Free/Low-Cost Hosts 9
     Setting Up the SynthWiz Simple Synth in a Host 9
A Bit of Know-How 15
     Understanding Digital Audio 15
     Latency 17
     Audio Drivers 20
     Aliasing 21
Moving On 22

Chapter 2
Getting a Grip on Synthesizer Programming   23

Synthesizer Basics 23
Getting Started with Synthesis 25
How to Use SynthWiz Simple Synth 26
     Waveform Selector 28
     Sliders 29

Direct Text Entry 29
Output Meter 29
The Elements of Synthesis 30
Sound Sources 30
Filter 31
Modulation 33
Volume Envelope 33
Filter Envelope 35
Filter Key Tracking 37
Output Level 37
Making Sounds 38
Soft Bass 39
Pad 40
Filtered Noise 41
Squelch 43

Chapter 3
Synthesizer/Patch Construction Basics   45

Audio Path and Non-Audio Path 45
Audio Path 45
Control Elements 46
Modulation Elements 46
Modulation: The Concept 47
Modulation Sources and Modulation Control Sources 48
Modulation Destinations 50
CPU Considerations 52
Synthesizer Construction Basics 52
Reconstructing SynthWiz Simple Synth 53
Audio Path 53
Inputs and Outputs 54
Basic Controls 54
Modulation Envelopes 54
Modulation Envelope Controls 56
Volume 57
The Finished Synthesizer 57
Construction with Zebra 2 58
Loading Modules in Zebra 2 58
Hooking Up the Audio Path in Zebra 2 58

Attaching the Modulators in Zebra 2..59
Saving in Zebra 2..62
Construction with VAZ Modular..63
Loading Modules in VAZ Modular 64
Hooking Up the Audio Path in VAZ Modular..66
Attaching the Modulators in VAZ Modular..73
Saving in VAZ Modular..74
Construction with KarmaFX Synth Modular 75
Loading Modules in KarmaFX Synth Modular 76
Hooking Up the Audio Path in KarmaFX Synth Modular 78
Attaching the Modulators in KarmaFX Synth Modular 80
Saving in KarmaFX Synth Modular 81
Construction with SynthEdit 83
Saving in SynthEdit 83
Loading Modules in SynthEdit..84
Hooking Up the Audio Path in SynthEdit 86
Attaching the Modulators in SynthEdit 90
Adding the Controls in SynthEdit 91
Adding the Finishing Touches in SynthEdit..94
Interface Building in SynthEdit..98
Exporting a VSTi from SynthEdit 102
About the Rest of the Book..107

Chapter 4
An Introduction to Sound Sources   109

Basic Wave Shapes 109
Sine Wave 109
Sawtooth Wave 110
Square and Pulse Waves 111
Triangle Wave..112
Noise 112
Complex Wave Shapes: Combining Sounds 112
Doubling Oscillators 113
Combining Oscillators..116
Sample-Based Synthesis 118
What Is Sampling? 119
What Is a Sample? 121
Deploying Samples 121

Additive Synthesis 124
   Additive Synthesis: Basic Principles 126
   Additive Square Wave 126
   Additive Sawtooth Wave 126
   Additive Triangle Wave 127
   Difficulties with Additive Synthesis 128
Frequency Modulation (and Other Sorts of Modulation) Synthesis 128
   Operators 128
   Getting a Grip on FM Programming 129
   Controlling FM Sounds 131
   Quick and Dirty Guide to FM Synthesis 133
   Ring Modulation 134
The Available Sound Sources 136
Sound-Creation Modules in Zebra 2 136
   Osc: Oscillators 136
   FMO: Frequency Modulation Oscillators 142
   Noise: Noise Source 145
Sound Creation Modules in VAZ Modular 146
   Common Controls 146
   Oscillator 147
   MultiOscillator and Multi-Saw Osc 149
   Cosmo A Oscillator 150
   Comso B Oscillator 150
   Noise Source 151
   Sample 152
   Sine Oscillator 152
   Wavetable Oscillator 153
   WTVoice 154
Sound Creation Modules in KarmaFX Synth Modular 155
   Osc 1 155
   Osc 2 156
   Sampler 158
   Additive 159
   Pad 162
   Noise 163
Sound-Creation Modules in SynthEdit 163
   Oscillator 164
   Phase Distortion Oscillator 165
   SoundFont Oscillator 166

Chapter 5
Filters   169

Filter Types 169
   Low-Pass 169
   High-Pass 170
   Band-Pass 171
   Notch (Band-Reject) 171
   Peaking 171
   All-Pass 172
   Formant 172
   Comb Filters 172
Filter Parameters 173
   Cut-Off Frequency 173
   Resonance 173
   Bandwidth 174
   Drive 174
   Filter Slopes 174
   Moog, SVF, 303, Zolzer, and So On 175
Controlling Filter Parameters 175
   Controlling Filter Cut-Off 176
   Key Tracking and Filters 176
   Controlling Resonance 176
The Available Filters 177
Filter Modules in Zebra 2 178
   VCF Filter 178
   XMF: Cross-Modulation Filter 180
   Shaper 181
   Comb Filter 182
Filter Modules in VAZ Modular 183
   One-Pole Filter 184
   The Filter 184
   Filter K 186
   Filter R 186
   Filter S 188
   SVFilter 189
   Comb Filter 190
   Vowel Filter 191
   Waveshaper 192

Filter Modules in KarmaFX Synth Modular..192
      Low-Pass/High-Pass/Band-Pass/Notch Filters................................192
      Comb Filter and All-Pass Filter 195
      Formant Filter 195
Filter Modules in SynthEdit 196

Chapter 6
Modulation and Control   199

Introducing Envelopes..199
      ADSR Envelopes 201
      DAHDSR Envelopes 204
      Multi-Stage Envelopes..205
      Other Envelope Controls..207
Envelope Followers 209
Low-Frequency Oscillators (LFOs)..210
      Main LFO Controls 211
      LFO Modules..214
      Creating an LFO in SynthEdit..216
Step Generators 217
Synthesizers in Real Time: Control and Automation................................220
      XY Pads 221
      MIDI Learn 226
      Automation 226

Chapter 7
Global Controls and Other Modules   233

Global Controls 233
      Polyphony 233
      Portamento..234
      Pitch Bend Range 235
Amplifiers 236
Switches, Mixers, and Splitters..238
Inputs and Outputs 241
Inverters, Multipliers, Mathematics, and Logic... 246
      Clever Stuff in VAZ Modular 246
      Clever Stuff in SynthEdit..248
Visualization Modules..250
      Volt Meters 250
      Level Meters 250

Frequency Analyzer 251
Oscilloscope 252

Chapter 8
FX Units   255

Deployment of FX 255
   Insert FX 256
   Send FX 256
   Using FX in Practice 256
Distortion and Overdrive Units 257
   "Analog" Distortion 257
   "Digital" Distortion 258
Compression 260
EQ 263
   Parametric EQ 263
   Shelf EQ 265
   Graphic EQ 265
Delay 266
Modulation Delay Effects 269
Reverb 272

Chapter 9
Creating Sounds   275

Synthesizer Architecture: Initial Considerations 276
Sonic Considerations 276
Filter Configuration and Signal Routing Options 277
   Straight Series 279
   Straight Series with Feedback 280
   Filtered Feedback 280
   Parallel Filters 282
   Half Waveshaping 282
CPU Considerations 283
Design Philosophy 284
   Programming with a Purpose 284
   Arrangement of the Track 285
   Can't I Just Go and Buy Something? 285

Principles of Sound Design 286
    Main Food Groups 287
    Getting the Combination Right 288
    Playability 289
Building Blocks 289
Building Sounds 292
    Noisy Synth 294
    Organ-Like 296
    Pseudo Echo 300
    Human Choir 305
    Rough and Ready FM 307
    Bass 313
    Synth Brass 318

Index. 323

Introduction

I would like to start with an apology to any Harry Potter fans who have accidentally stumbled across this book. If you're looking for a guide to magic and spells, then I'm afraid you've come to the wrong place. However, if you're looking for the place to get a firm grasp on sound design and using synthesizers, then you have come to the right place.

About This Book

This book is intended for:

- People who are new to synthesis and who want to understand the basics, taking their first steps in creating and controlling sounds with synthesizers.

- Musicians who are familiar with synthesis, but who want to solidify or expand that knowledge so they can use their tools more fully.

The book covers four main areas:

- **Getting started with synthesis and digital audio.** The early chapters introduce you to the world of digital music creation. We then move to an introduction to synthesizers and sound creation.

- **Modules.** The second section of the book looks at the modules that are available to create and shape sounds. In short, this is the palette from which you can create your sounds.

- **Synthesizer architecture.** As we look at the modules, we will start to think about synthesizer architecture and how the elements of synthesis—in other words, the modules we are looking at—can be put together. Partly this is a matter of structure, but it also has a significant effect on the sound, and as you will see, the architecture is inextricably linked with sound design.

- **Sound design.** Once you have a grasp of synthesizer basics, the elements of synthesis, and synthesizer architecture, you can start putting the pieces together to build the sound that you hear in your head, but which you may not have been able to realize. You can then apply these principles to any synthesizer in your arsenal.

As you can see, this is not about how to be creative. Instead, it's about the process for understanding the mechanics behind sound creation and giving you a firm grasp of the building blocks. With this knowledge, you can then use your own creativity and take control of your sounds, creating the tones that are right for you. In working through this book, it might be useful to understand my intentions:

- First, I do not try to emulate specific sounds, so I have not attempted to show you how to perfectly re-create, say, a violin or a specific synthesizer tone. Where I have made reference to specific sounds (such as a violin), the purpose has been to offer a point where we can have a common understanding of a sound (otherwise, it can get quite difficult to try to describe sounds on the printed page). My intention in not looking at specific sounds is to help you find how to create your own sound, not how to create someone else's sound. Added to which, as I will mention in the sound design chapter (Chapter 9), there are logistical impracticalities associated with replicating highly nuanced tones (not least that each different articulation has to be programmed, and you then have to record the MIDI tracks playing the different sound for each articulation).

- Second, this is not a manual for any synthesizer, and it is in no way intended to replace the guidance that is provided by the developers for the featured synthesizers. While I will illustrate my points with specific synthesizers—and you can learn a lot about using those synthesizers—my aim is to show general principles that can then be widely applied to as many different synthesizers as possible. As you will see, this means I will ignore some of the modules from the featured synthesizers, and equally, I'm not intending to illustrate all of the potential functionality that is available in all of the featured synths.

- This book is about picking up skills, attuning your ears, and getting your hands dirty. This book is not intended to be read from cover to cover before you go near a synthesizer—read a bit, then try out what you have read. Then read some more. Ideally, read the book while you are sitting next to your synthesizer so you can try things immediately.

- As a follow-up to the previous point, there are only a few presets that accompany the book (after all, it's called "*From* Presets...," as in getting away from). I talk you through a number of sounds in the book—I have not included presets because I want you to follow what I am doing and create sounds for yourself by listening and using your own sense of what sounds good. I don't want you to become skilled at loading presets. Also, as you work through a particular sound, you may decide you don't like the course I'm following with that sound, in which case you can take the sound in the direction you want. And if you do, that's fine with me.

After reading this book, the only limitations to your sound design skills will be your imagination and your computer's CPU (and you can always get a new CPU).

One last point before we move on—I talk in terms of *patches* and *sounds*, as well as *presets*. Generally, all three terms are interchangeable. With patches and presets, all I am referring to is a combination of settings that make a sound.

A Short History of Synthesizers

Before we go too much further, it might be useful to have a bit of synthesizer history that can help to give some context to the tools and techniques featured in this book. For the detail freaks, please be aware that this is only a very brief history, just to give a bit of context to the position we have reached today—it is not intended to mention every synthesizer that has ever been made available. If you're after further information and detail, then I suggest you start with an internet search and follow that with a look at the books that have been published on the subject.

Synthesizers can be traced back to the 19th century, when early telephone technology could be applied to create sounds. Arguably, the first practical synthesizers that were available to musicians were organs that offered a wide range of tones, such as the Hammond Organ (see Figure I.1). However, I don't want to argue... so let's start by looking at the first beasts that resemble what we might think of today as a synthesizer.

The earliest synthesizers that we would recognize today as synthesizers were essentially boxes for creating noises—some didn't even have keyboards attached, which could make pitch control something of a challenge. These devices were collections of what might now be seen as old-fashioned electronics: resistors, transistors, and diodes. There were no chips or integrated circuits like you may find today. This was true handcrafted analog electronics, which lent these

Figure I.1 A software incarnation of the Hammond B3 Organ—in this case, the B4 organ from Native Instruments (native-instruments.com).

Figure I.2 A software incarnation of the Minimoog—in this case, the minimoog V from Arturia (arturia.com).

synthesizers a warm sound but also made them susceptible to atmospheric conditions (so if the temperature in a room changed, then the synthesizer could go out of tune).

One of the first widely available synthesizers was the Minimoog. (See Figure I.2—again, I'm showing a software implementation of the original hardware because these pictures let us see more detail.) When this synthesizer was released in 1970 (as in when the hardware was first released), it cost $1,495 (which would be around $8,500 if you take account of the change in consumer prices to January 2009). While it was phenomenally expensive, the Minimoog could only play one note. If you listen to any records made during the 1970s that feature a synthesizer, then there is a very strong chance that you are hearing a Minimoog (or one of the Moog Modular synthesizers).

Perhaps the next highly significant synthesizer was the Prophet 5 from Sequential Circuits (see Figure I.3). The Prophet 5 took two important steps forward (when compared with the Minimoog). First, it was polyphonic. The Moog was monophonic—that is, it only allowed one note to be played. By contrast, the Prophet 5 could play up to five notes simultaneously. Second, the Prophet 5 had a patch memory—very often people would take Polaroid snaps of a Minimoog sound in order to remember the correct settings.

In the early 1980s, the Prophet 5 was eclipsed (no space pun intended) by the Roland Jupiter-8 (see Figure I.4). On paper, this shared many features with the Prophet 5, but it had a larger patch memory and was generally felt to be more reliable than the Prophet. Both the Prophet 5 and the Jupiter-8 can be heard on many records released during the 1980s.

Figure I.3 A software incarnation of the Prophet 5—in this case, the Pro-53 from Native Instruments (native-instruments.com).

Figure I.4 A software incarnation of the Jupiter-8—in this case, the Jupiter-8V from Arturia (arturia.com). By the way, this is a software rendering intended to make the instrument look three-dimensional—the actual virtual instrument (if that's not too much of a contradiction) shows as a two-dimensional representation on the screen.

Figure I.5 A software incarnation of the DX-7 synthesizer—in this case, the FM7 from Native Instruments (native-instruments.com).

In the 1980s, things got digital.... For the first time, sounds were created without using analog components. One of the first digital synthesizers was the Fairlight CMI (Computer Music Instrument)—the first sampler. At the time, the introduction of sampling was revolutionary and profound. With sampling, a note could be digitally recorded and then replayed at any pitch. For the first time, this meant that a real instrument could be "perfectly" reproduced on a machine. Suddenly, it was no longer necessary to hire an orchestra to record a piece; instead, you just needed to hire one keyboard player with a Fairlight.

Needless to say, the Fairlight was eye-wateringly expensive (although there were even more expensive digital synthesizers available). However, one cheaper digital synthesizer (which didn't offer sampling) was the Yamaha DX-7 (see Figure I.5). The DX-7 was the first synthesizer to widely employ the use of *frequency modulation* (or FM) synthesis to create its sound. For the moment, don't get too hung up on not knowing what FM synthesis is all about—by the time you have finished this book, you will know a lot about it.

The DX-7 was also radical for another reason: It was the first mainstream synthesizer to do away with knobs on the synthesizer. Instead, its sound control interface was accessible through a menu-driven system. Although this kept costs down, it also stopped many people from tinkering—the combination of the extreme complexity of FM programming, lack of access to the controls, and lack of knowledge about FM synthesis was enough to deter all but the very brave. However, in terms of numbers sold, the DX-7 is perhaps the most popular hardware synthesizer ever.

The synthesizers we have looked at so far were all self-contained instruments where everything that you could need to create sounds was included within the instrument, and if you wanted anything else—such as another oscillator or another filter—then you were out of luck. Before these self-contained instruments, and in parallel with them, several manufacturers—including Moog, ARP, Roland, and Buchla, to name a few—produced modular synthesizers. Take a look at Figures I.6 and I.7.

Modular synthesizers were so named because they included modules that the musician could wire together to make sounds. Some of these synthesizers were produced as individual modules so musicians could buy what they wanted. Others came as a number of modules that were physically grouped together—these could then be wired up, and additional modules (outside of the framework) could also be hooked up.

While modular synthesizers were—and are—hugely powerful, they do have a number of significant downsides:

- First, they are (and always have been) expensive. These synthesizers are usually handmade and use many high-quality and expensive components. The designs are highly specialized and they are made in extremely small numbers, meaning that the notion of making these instruments in a low-cost manufacturing location is simply not practical.

- Manufacturing takes a long time. As a corollary to the small numbers manufactured, the high price, and the impracticability of manufacturing through a conventional factory process, manufacturing usually has to be undertaken by highly skilled individuals. The combination of these factors means that costs remain high, and manufacturing takes a long time.

- They are complicated and impractical. Whereas the functions of most self-contained synthesizers could be accessed from the front panel, modulars are more complicated. You cannot get any sound out of the synthesizer until it has been connected up. In practice, this means that a number of patch leads have to be plugged in to attach the keyboard, the sound generators, the filters, the amplifiers, and the envelopes. While this could be fun and allows lots of room for experimentation, it also makes these synthesizers anything but simple and straightforward to use.

- They are large, cumbersome, and fragile. This (coupled with the complication and lack of patch memory) makes them impractical for use on the road. However, that is not to say that these tools have never been on the road. Some people have been that brave.

The combination of these factors made the wide-scale adoption of modular synthesizers highly limited. Often they would only be found in universities and in the studios of musicians with large incomes.

Figure I.6 A software implementation of the Moog Modular synthesizer—in this case, the Moog Modular V from Arturia (arturia.com).

Figure I.7   A software implementation of the ARP 2600 modular synthesizer—in this case, the ARP 2600 V from Arturia (arturia.com).

The 1990s saw a new and revolutionary development: software instruments. These offered some huge advantages over their hardware counterparts, including:

- **Price.** The physical costs of software are much lower than the costs associated with hardware.

- **Interface.** Most software synthesizers have a much more accessible interface than their digital hardware counterparts. This is because there is no cost associated with adding lots of knobs to a piece of software. By contrast, each hardware knob and hardware switch has a direct cost.

- **Try before you buy.** With software you can try a demo version of a synthesizer before you lay down your money. With hardware, you might try the synthesizer in a store, but generally you will only get to find out how good it is after you have paid.

- **Upgradeable.** Software can be easily upgraded. Some hardware can be upgraded (or rather, the computer software within the hardware can be upgraded), but proper analog hardware cannot be changed (except with a soldering iron). Also, as software can be upgraded, this means that synthesizers can be released at a much earlier stage in their development (because developers know they can work out the problems/add features easily).

Some of the earliest software instruments were modular-like synthesizers. In many ways the combination of software and modular synthesis gave the perfect combination.

However, there were (and remain) some problems with software-based instruments:

- **Power.** The synthesizer is only as powerful as the computer on which it is running. So, if your computer is dedicated to doing other things (such as running other software instruments, recording audio, processing software effects units, and so on), then there may not be much grunt left for your synthesizer, and so the sound could be degraded or the whole computer could become sluggish.

- **Audio quality.** Very often, computers are not optimized for audio, which could lead to poor sound quality. A second factor affecting sound is the lack of experience of many programmers—it has taken a long time for people to understand how to create pleasing digital audio in the software realm.

Synthesizers in the 21st Century

While synthesizer history is superficially interesting, you're probably reading this book because you want to know more about how you can create sounds with the tools that are available today, so let's move on.

Unless you want to invest several thousands of dollars, then the synthesizer you are most likely to come into contact with is a software synthesizer—in other words, a synthesizer that comes as a piece of software that will run on your computer. As I have mentioned, there are advantages and disadvantages to software, but unless you want to invest thousands of dollars, you will probably reach the conclusion that the advantages of software outweigh the disadvantages.

This is a sensible conclusion, and given that this book features software synthesizers, it is quite advantageous for me.

Most software synthesizers that are available today have a fixed architecture—in other words, the modules are routed together in a certain way, and you (as the user/musician) have few options to change these routings. The four main synthesizers mentioned in the last section (Minimoog, Prophet 5, Jupiter-8, and DX-7) all have fixed architecture. For many synthesizers, the architecture is one of the key design decisions that will affect the sound of the synthesizer.

Another feature of virtually all software synthesizers is that they are totally contained—in other words, you cannot add other modules to them, and if you don't like certain features, you can't make any changes. However, one of the platforms in this book (SynthEdit) does allow for the inclusion of external modules, and another—VAZ Modular—allows external effects.

In addition to the sound, the architecture has an influence on every aspect of a synthesizer, including:

- Its interface

- Its simplicity (or otherwise) from a user's perspective

- Its CPU load

Let's have a look at some of the features of these different types of synthesizers.

Fixed Architecture

With a fixed-architecture synthesizer, the number of modules, the number of filters, the number of envelopes, the number of low-frequency oscillators, and so on is fixed. In addition, the path of the audio signal through the synthesizer is fixed. Some synthesizers offer flexibility—for instance, an option to set up modulation or audio routing changes (perhaps offering a series or parallel filter option)—and others have a very large number of modulation sources, but in essence, there are limits to the synthesizer.

But these limits are not necessarily a bad thing. Indeed, they generally give many advantages:

- Usually the synthesizer's interface will be clear and intuitive from the user's perspective. This will make the synthesizer easy to learn so the musician can focus on creating sounds, not on reading the manual.

- Generally, the synthesizer designer will have built the synthesizer in such a way that the features the user would want most frequently will be in place or easily called up. Again, this makes using a synthesizer a more intuitive/organic process and not one where the musician has to fight against the synthesizer.

- Assuming that the synthesizer has been built by a good software engineer, there will have been extensive amounts of optimization, giving the very lowest CPU hit. That isn't to say

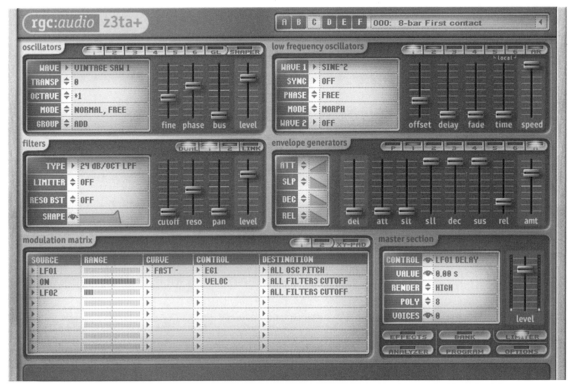

Figure I.8   Z3TA+ from Cakewalk.

that there will be no CPU hit, simply that the engineer will have been able to design the synthesizer so that it is optimized, which allows the key elements (the sound-generation parts and the filter) to use more CPU to give the very best sound.

Although fixed architecture may seem limiting, you can have two synthesizers that on the face of it have very similar features, but due to the architecture are very different beasts. As an example, take two leading software synthesizers: Z3TA+ (see Figure I.8) and Rapture (see Figure I.9), which are both made by Cakewalk (cakewalk.com). These synthesizers both have six oscillators, but after that they are very different:

- Z3TA+ mixes the six oscillators together and then passes the mixed signal through the filter and processing block. Although it is possible to set up two separate busses (in other words, two separate audio channels), you are essentially dealing with one sound.

- By contrast, Rapture operates like six separate single-oscillator synthesizers strapped together. Each separate oscillator has its own filters and digital signal processing blocks and a wide variety of modulation options. Only after each oscillator has been fully processed are the sounds mixed, immediately before the output.

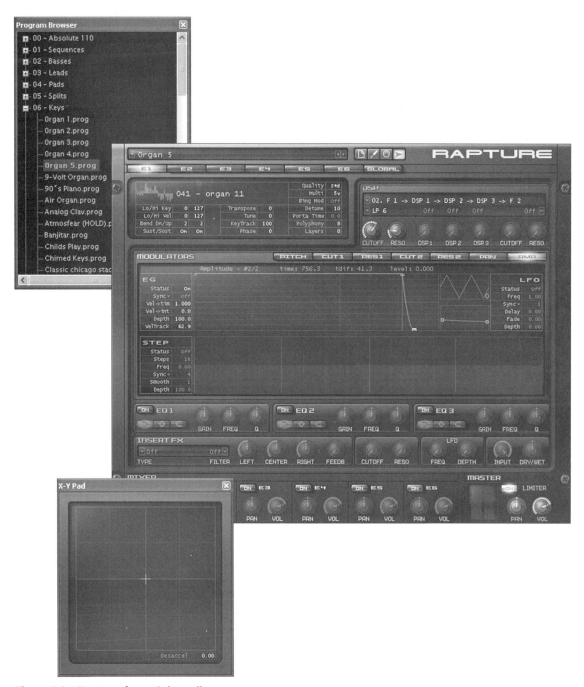

Figure I.9 Rapture from Cakewalk.

Neither approach is better or worse—they are just different and achieve different results in different circumstances.

As a side note, you can read more about Z3TA+ and Rapture in my book *Cakewalk Synthesizers: From Presets to Power User* (Course Technology PTR, 2006).

Synthesizer Building

There are two main forms of software modular synthesizers. The first contains what I am categorizing as "synthesizer-building" programs.

With these programs you are given a bunch of modules that can be hooked up. You can then build an interface to access some or all of the controls in the modules. Once you have hooked up the modules and created the interface, you save the result as a synthesizer, which can then be loaded into your audio program. For all intents and purposes, this synthesizer is then treated like any other fixed-architecture synthesizer, and so, for instance, you can build a set of presets to accompany it.

Two examples of this type of synthesizer are:

- SynthEdit (synthedit.com), which is one of the synthesizers I will be featuring in this book

- Reaktor from Native Instruments (native-instruments.com), which is one of the most well-established modular environments, being the successor to Generator, which was both one of the earliest software synthesizers and one of the first modular software synthesizers

Modules and Wires

The other form of modular synthesizer is the more commonly understood implementation, which could be characterized as a "modules-and-wires" approach. With this approach, the software offers a bunch of modules that can be hooked up with software "wires." Each patch (in other words, each sound) will have a different set of modules and routings. This approach has several key differences from the synthesizer-building approach:

- The interface will show the modules and the wiring (depending on the particular synthesizer and whether individual modules have been hidden).

- Within each patch you can edit every parameter—nothing is hidden behind the interface.

- Each patch is different—there is no freestanding synthesizer with its own range of associated sounds.

From a sonic perspective, there is no difference between the synthesizer-building approach and the modules-and-wire approach. However, there is clearly a huge difference between the two when you look at workflow. In addition, different synthesizers will sound different (and I will explain some of these differences later in the book).

All of these factors make any meaningful comparison of the two approaches somewhere between very difficult and pointless, so I won't attempt such an exercise.

Different Synthesis Techniques

Irrespective of which synthesizer you use, you will have a range of different sound-creation techniques on hand. I will talk about these in much greater detail later in the book, but for the moment, let me give you a brief introduction. All of the synthesizers covered feature several of these synthesis techniques. You should note that these techniques are not mutually exclusive—you could (as you will see later in the book), for instance, create a sound using FM and subtractive techniques at the same time.

Subtractive ("Analog") Synthesis

Subtractive synthesis is perhaps the most common form of synthesis. It is the process of taking a sound source that is rich in harmonic content and then reducing and shaping those harmonics with a filter. This technique is available in most synthesizers and was the main synthesis technique in the Minimoog, Prophet 5, and Jupiter-8.

FM/PM (Frequency Modulation/Phase Modulation or Phase Distortion) Synthesis

I'm sorry to throw a whole range of terms at you, but unfortunately, while frequency modulation and phase modulation/distortion are technically different techniques:

- They can give similar sounds, and

- People tend to use the terms interchangeably (or incorrectly, if you want to be a stickler).

This is the technique that was first widely used in the DX-7. It is the process by which one wave will modulate another wave, thereby distorting its waveform. Now, this may sound horrible—and sometimes it is—but when done properly, it can give a pleasing and broad range of tones, allowing sounds with very detailed and delicate nuances to be created.

This technique is most commonly used to create metallic tones (such as bells and electric pianos) and also to create quite "hard" sounds (for instance, very "in your face"-type bass sounds).

Additive Synthesis

Additive synthesis is in some ways the opposite of subtractive synthesis. With additive synthesis you take individual sine waves and add them together to create a new sound.

Sampling

Sampling is the process by which a note can be digitally recorded and then replayed. This allows real instruments to be "perfectly" reproduced by a synthesizer as well as giving a very wide range of sound sources for more creative forms of synthesis.

The Featured Synthesizers

I've already briefly mentioned some of the synthesizers that will be featured in this book. Let's look at them in a bit more detail.

Each of the four synthesizers has slightly different features and may be more or less preferable as a tool in different situations. I see the different flavors as being a good thing—I don't want this book to be about the one and only way to do things. Instead, I'm aiming to illustrate different options and different colors/techniques.

I have chosen these four because (a) they are good and (b) they are popular. Hopefully, many of you reading this book already own one or more of these synthesizers. In case it's not clear, then let me be clear—I like all of the synthesizers and think they're all good. You will not make a bad decision by getting hold of any of these synthesizers. The developers all offer demo versions, which I recommend you check out, and if you've got the cash, then I suggest you invest in one or more of these synthesizers to support the developers (and to get your hands on a top-class synthesizer).

While this book does feature four synthesizers, it is intended to illustrate techniques that can be applied to these synthesizers and to other synthesizers, too (including fixed-architecture synths). The book uses specific synthesizers to illustrate specific points because you cannot illustrate with generic synths (since there is, by definition, no such thing as a generic synthesizer).

SynthEdit

Developer: Jeff McClintock

Website: synthedit.com

Price: Free (shareware). There is a paid option (£47.54/$49.95) if you want to redistribute your creations.

Platform: Windows

SynthEdit (see Figure I.10) is a synthesizer (and effects) building program. It allows for synthesizers and effects to be created and for an interface to be added to control the synthesizer/effects unit. These creations can then be exported as VST/VSTi-format effects/synthesizers. (VST will be explained in Chapter 1.)

On its own, SynthEdit is highly powerful. However, that power is then multiplied, and the whole product has been taken forward by the range of additional modules that have been developed by external programmers who are part of an impressive SynthEdit community. This facility to add third-party modules has meant that programmers can create singular, highly-specialized modules, focusing on their programming strength without having to create a whole synthesizer.

At the time of this writing, there is one problem with SynthEdit: Plug-ins created with the software do not play nice with multi-core systems, with the result that you cannot use more than one instance of any SynthEdit plug-in (without some behind-the-scenes kludging). However, hopefully by the time you read this book, that issue will have been addressed.

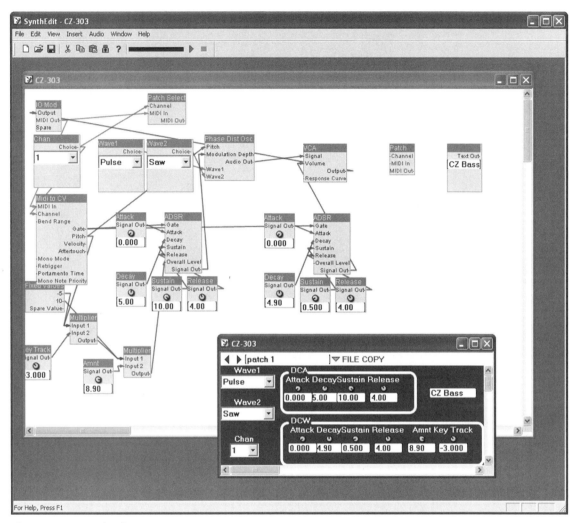

Figure I.10 SynthEdit.

KarmaFX Synth Modular

Developer: Kasper Nielsen/KarmaFX

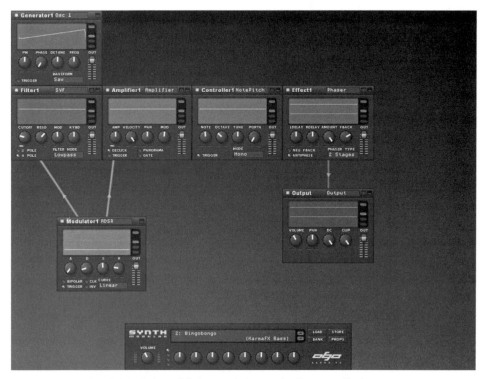

Figure I.11   KarmaFX Synth Modular with its modules and wires on display.

Website: karmafx.net

Price: €95 (including VAT)/$96

Platform: Windows VST

The KarmaFX Synth Modular (see Figure I.11) is a modules-and-wires type of program—indeed, of all the featured synthesizers, the KarmaFX Synth Modular's interface is probably the closest to a hardware-based modules-and-wires approach. The synthesizer comes with a large array of modules, including many sound-creation modules and many different types of filters.

KarmaFX Synth Modular is © Copyright KarmaFX 1998–2009. All rights reserved. The KarmaFX logo is a registered trademark of KarmaFX.

VAZ Modular

Developer: Martin Fay at Software Technology

Website: software-technology.com

Price: A downloadable version of VAZ Modular costs £199.95/€236.90/$298.29, and a retail boxed version with a CD is available for £249.95/€296.14/$372.88.

Platform: Windows (stand-alone, VST, and DXi). While it is a Windows-based synthesizer, Martin has suggested that it will also run under OS X. If this is of interest to you, I suggest you chat with him before you purchase.

VAZ Modular is a well-established synthesizer that Martin continues to develop (see Figure I.12). It is a modules-and-wires type of program that has an incredibly wide range of modules, including many specialized modules.

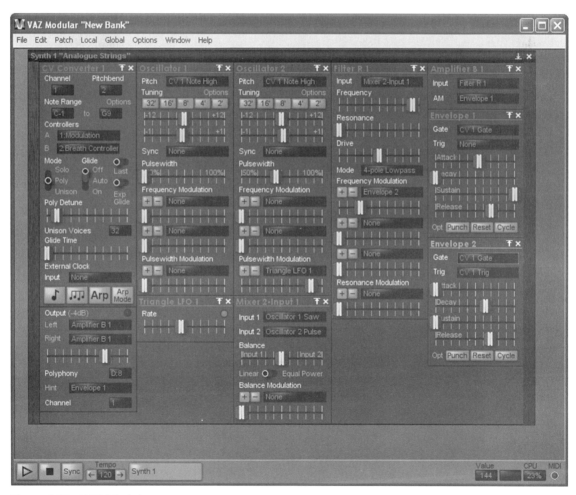

Figure I.12   VAZ Modular.

Zebra 2

Developer: Urs Heckman

Website: u-he.com

Price: $199

Platform: Windows VSTi, Mac (AU, VST, and RTAS)

Zebra 2 (see Figure I.13) is an incredibly popular cross-platform (Windows and Mac) synthesizer that is described as a wireless modular. In practice this means that it is a modules-and-wires design, but the wires bit is handled very elegantly. (Then again, the whole interface is quite elegant.)

One factor that sets Zebra 2 apart from the other synthesizers is that there are limitations to this synthesizer. There are a limited number of sound generators, a limited number of filters, a limited number of envelopes, and so on. However, it's flexible enough and has sufficient power to justify its place in the book, so I decided to let Zebra 2 in.

Figure I.13 Zebra 2.

A Quick Word to Mac Users

Throughout this book, I will be using the Windows versions of these pieces of software, so don't get too discouraged if the screenshots don't show the signs of running on a Mac. Also, the mouse-click commands listed here are for PC users. If you're using a Mac, you might want to spend a moment or two checking the Mac-equivalent clicks.

So Which Synth Should I Choose?

So which synth should you choose? Now *that* is a really tough question—they're all great synths, and I suggest you get them all. However, that advice may not be practical, so here are a few thoughts:

- If you've already got one of the synths, then stick with it through this book. You will get much further much sooner with your understanding of how to use synthesizers and to create sounds with synthesizers if you focus. If you try them all, you will get lost with learning the basics and comparing/contrasting each synth. Don't be a jack of all trades—be a master of one, the synthesizer that you own.

- If you want the cheapest option, then SynthEdit can't be beaten. The downside to SynthEdit is that you have to create a synthesizer in order to play your sounds in a host. This is not the end of the world, but it is not the most flexible option.

- If you are using a Mac, then the choice is pretty limited, so go with Zebra 2 (or perhaps see how well VAZ Modular will run on a Mac at the point you are looking to buy).

- If you are after a modules-and-wires modern re-creation of analog, then you have two choices: KarmaFX Synth Modular and VAZ Modular. My feeling—and it really is a feeling on my part and most definitely not a recommendation—is that if you're after a re-creation of an analog modular, then VAZ Modular may be the place to start looking, but if you're after something more modern, then KarmaFX Synth Modular is the place to start.

All of the synths have demos, so do take some time to check these out to see what sounds good to you and works in a way that feels right for your purposes.

Further Reading

As its title suggests, this book is intended to take you from your first steps with a synthesizer through to an advanced level of proficiency. However, that is not the end of the story as far as synthesizer programming goes. There will always be more to learn about the subject, and so it is quite lucky for me that I am able to suggest some of my other books for your consideration once you have finished this one.

I have written a number of music-related books, but let me recommend two:

- *How to Make a Noise* (Coombe Hill Publishing, 2007). This book looks at creating sounds with six specific synthesizers. Whereas the book in your hands looks at general principles that can be applied to a range of specific synthesizers, *How to Make a Noise* takes a much closer look at what can be achieved with a number of today's leading software synthesizers and looks at the details of creating some very specific sounds with those synthesizers. It also looks at creating a much wider range of sounds than are created in this book.

- ■ ***Cakewalk Synthesizers: From Presets to Power User*** (Course Technology PTR, 2006). This book looks at the Cakewalk/rgcaudio synthesizer range and how to create sounds with these synthesizers. It also details the SFZ format (which is a sample format that is mentioned later on in this book that can be loaded into KarmaFX Synth Modular), as well as other sample-based synthesizers not featured in this book.

You can check out details of all my music-related books at noisesculpture.com (where you can also download the materials mentioned in the next chapter).

1 An Introduction to Digital Audio and Software Synthesis

To get started with software synthesis, you will need:

- A computer. Your computer will then need to be attached to some speakers so you can hear the output from your synthesizer.

- A software synthesizer.

- A "host" for the software synthesizer.

- A (musical) keyboard, if you want to play your synthesizer.

- A bit of know-how to understand what's going on.

We'll look at these elements in a bit more detail, but before we do that, let me suggest where you can get help if you run into trouble.

Problems?

If you are having trouble setting up your computer or running your software, there are many forums filled with eager and knowledgeable people who are willing to share their experience and help you get up and running. One of the best groups of forums can be found at KVR (kvraudio.com/forum). If you have any problems, I suggest you start there. After that, check out the support forums for the people who supplied your software and/or your hardware.

Music-Making Computer

Any modern computer—whether Windows-, Mac OS-, or Linux-based—is capable of functioning as a music-making computer. From a practical perspective, (virtually) all commercial software is produced for either the PC or the Mac (or both), and so, if you want some real choice in the tools you use, you'll want a PC or a Mac. As I've already mentioned, I'm a PC guy, so I'll be relying heavily on PC examples throughout this book; however, the principles I have set out here apply equally to the world of Macs.

There are certain prerequisites that are necessary for any music-making computer:

- **Hard disk space.** You need sufficient space to install your software synthesizer and any associated files. For most software synthesizers, this usually isn't a problem. However, sample-based synthesizers will often come with very large sample libraries that can take up a lot of disk space, so the larger your hard drive, the better.

- **Sound card.** A sound card is the device that converts internal digital audio into analog audio. (If you're concerned about the difference, it's this: You can hear analog, you can't hear digital…but sound needs to be stored in a digital form in order to be processed within a computer.) Most modern computers come with a sound card of some variety—generally, these are consumer-quality cards and are of an acceptable quality. (However, I wouldn't wish to use one of these cards in a professional recording environment.) Some sound cards also allow you to convert external audio sources to digital audio—if they do, then that sound can usually be recorded or processed through your synthesizer.

- **Speakers.** Your sound card will need to be attached to some sort of speakers. The quality of your speakers will have a huge influence on the perceived quality of sound created by any synthesizer, so cheap computer speakers (or speakers built into your screen) may not give great results. You can use headphones instead of speakers, but you are unlikely to achieve satisfactory results, because these have limited bass range.

- **MIDI input device.** If you want to play your synthesizer, then you will need some sort of input device, such as a keyboard (as in a piano-style keyboard, not a QWERTY-style keyboard).

- **Sufficient processor power.** In an ideal world, we would all have a computer dedicated to music production. However, this is not an ideal world—it is the real world, and so if your computer is used for other things (surfing the net or typing documents, and so on), then it is important that sufficient processor power is available to run any synthesizers. The amount of power needed will depend on the synthesizer you are using and the number of things you are trying to do with that synthesizer. (Each module will take more power.) Ideally, when you use your computer for music, it should be doing as few other things as possible. So, for instance, if you can switch off the virus checker, stop browsing the internet, and disconnect any peer-to-peer downloads while you are making music, then you will find that your software runs much more smoothly.

As a general rule of thumb, if your computer only uses a few percent of its processing power when the computer is idling, and it can play music (such as an MP3 file or a CD), then it will be suitable to run synthesizers.

If you're not happy with your music-making computer, there are a lot of things you can do. Of course, these all cost money…. The most obvious thing is to get a better computer, and ideally a computer dedicated to making music—preferably with lots of processing power, lots of memory (RAM), lots of hard disk space (ideally, separate drives for your system files and your data), and a high-end sound card.

Software Synthesizers

I have already introduced the four software synthesizers that I will be using for most of the book: SynthEdit, KarmaFX Synth, VAZ Modular, and Zebra 2. Apart from the four featured synthesizers, there are many other synthesizers, many of which are free—spend five minutes with Google, and you will find lots. However, there is one other synthesizer that I would like to introduce now.

Synthesizer Accompanying This Book

May I introduce you to SynthWiz Simple Synth (see Figure 1.1)—a free synthesizer that you can download from my music-related website.

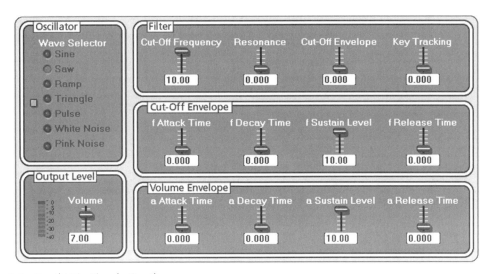

Figure 1.1   SynthWiz Simple Synth.

You can download the synthesizer from noisesculpture.com/synthwiz-downloads.html.

This synthesizer is offered "as is" and is intended purely to illustrate some of the points raised in the next chapter. No warranty is offered or implied by either me or the publisher of this book. Equally, no support is offered by either of us. So if you can't get this working, then I'm afraid you're on your own.

This synthesizer has been built using SynthEdit. There are two implication of this:

■ First, it is available in Windows VST format only, so if you're a Mac person, then you won't be able to run the synthesizer (unless you get it running under some form of Windows emulator). However, there are other Mac-related options in the next chapter, so all is not lost.

■ There are limitations with the current incarnation of SynthEdit: Specifically, in certain circumstances you cannot run more than one instance of the same synthesizer at one time.
Given that I only want you to run a single instance, this should not be a problem. At the time
of this writing, there were beta versions of an upgrade to SynthEdit available—this upgrade
is intended, among other things, to address this specific issue.

This synthesizer has been produced for a specific purpose: to illustrate certain points in the next
chapter. It has been designed to be as straightforward to operate as possible—it has not been
designed to be a full-featured (or even reasonably well-featured) synthesizer, and I have not
undertaken any work to optimize its sonic qualities. I would not expect anyone to use this synthesizer except in connection with the next chapter. After you have learned and understood the
principles there, you will find there are much better synthesizers out there (such as the other
synthesizers featured in this book).

By the way, this lack of features/functionality is not a reflection on SynthEdit. You can build
wonderful rich and complex synthesizers with SynthEdit—I have just chosen to build something
very simple with no distractions.

Later in this chapter, in the "Plug-In Host" section, I will explain how to set up SynthWiz Simple
Synth so that you can make sounds with it.

Formats and Compatibility
One of the key issues for any software synthesizer is its format. This is beyond simple PC/Mac
compatibility. Unfortunately, there are several different formats you may need to be aware of,
which include VST/VSTi, DX/DXi, Audio Units, and RTAS. Let me explain…

Most synthesizers come as plug-ins. This means that they can't work on their own; instead, they
plug into another piece of software (often called a *host*—these are described in greater detail in
the next section). For a plug-in to work with a host, the plug-in needs to be available in a format
that is compatible with the host.

VST/VSTi
The VST/VSTi (Virtual Studio Technology) format was created by, and can be licensed from,
Steinberg (steinberg.net) and is incredibly popular, with thousands of free and paid effects and
instruments available in this format. As far as formats go, this is as close as there is to a *lingua
franca* of plug-in formats, and you will find that most synthesizers are available in VSTi format.

VST format is used for effects, and VSTi format is for instruments; however, some effects
(mostly involving tempo-synchronization features) are created in VSTi format.

The format is Windows, Mac, and Linux compatible; however, the majority of VST plug-ins are
only available for Windows.

SynthWiz Simple Synth is available in Windows VSTi format.

DX/DXi

DirectX was developed by Microsoft to handle various multimedia functions, especially relating to game programming and video. As such, it is exclusive to Microsoft-based computers. The format has been quite widely adopted—especially by Cakewalk for their SONAR and Project5 programs—however, where it may have once had technical advantages, VST/VSTi seems capable of matching these advances and has eclipsed DX/DXi.

Like for the VST format, DX format is used for effects, and DXi format is for instruments; however, some effects (mostly involving tempo-synchronization features) are created in DXi format.

RTAS

Real-Time AudioSuite (RTAS) is the plug-in protocol developed by Digidesign for Pro Tools.

AU (Audio Units)

Audio Units is Apple's plug-in architecture, which is provided by Core Audio in Mac OS X. To a great extent, this format has displaced Mac VST format for Apple-compatible software.

Stand-Alone

In addition to these plug-in formats, many synthesizers are also available as stand-alone synthesizers, which are (in essence) plug-ins with a host wrapped around the synthesizer to manage the audio in/out and MIDI in/out relationships. VAZ Modular will run as a stand-alone synthesizer, and SynthEdit (when you are constructing synthesizers/modules) will run as a stand-alone.

MIDI and Human Input Devices

MIDI (Musical Instrument Digital Interface) is the industry-standard protocol by which electronic musical instruments, such as keyboard controllers, computers, and other electronic equipment, communicate.

MIDI is the communications protocol, and a MIDI keyboard would be a hardware keyboard that is equipped with a MIDI port.

The power of MIDI is its standardization—it has been around for more than 25 years, and it is a standard that all hardware manufacturers have adopted. It allows devices to communicate, control, and synchronize with each other, all in the digital domain. However, MIDI should not be mistaken for an audio signal—it is a digital communication, which could be a message from a keyboard to a synthesizer to say "play this note, *now*," or which could be a message to adjust a control on a synthesizer.

If you want to play your (software) synthesizer (in the same way that you play a piano), then you will need a MIDI keyboard that is attached to your computer. There are many of these keyboards on the market. All MIDI keyboards will have a MIDI out port; most will also have a USB connection to send MIDI directly to a computer via a USB cable. If your keyboard does not have a USB connection, then you will need a MIDI interface to connect your keyboard to your computer.

Figure 1.2 shows my MIDI interface in my home setup. This is an eight-in/eight-out device that can also act as a patch bay to connect various devices together.

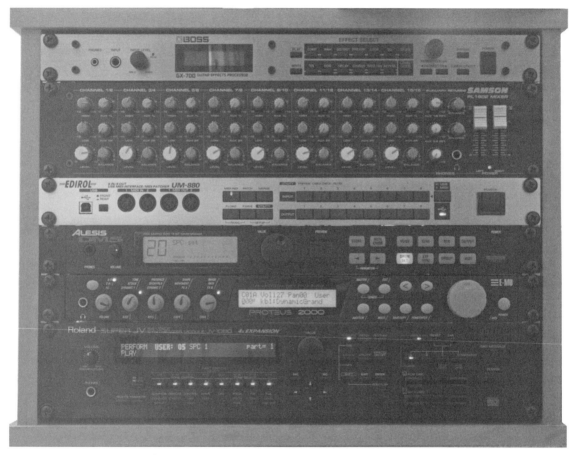

Figure 1.2   The MIDI interface in the author's home setup—it is the third unit from the top (the Edirol UM-880).

There are many different types of MIDI input devices. The most obvious is the MIDI keyboard; however, you will also find drum pads, MIDI guitars, wind controllers, and mixer-styled interfaces, to mention a few of the other sorts of MIDI/human interface units.

MIDI Channels

It would be wrong to give the impression that any MIDI connection is simply a straightforward one-to-one connection. A single MIDI connection can include 16 MIDI channels, and several MIDI devices can be hooked together (either in series or parallel).

Sixteen MIDI channels means that you can send 16 separate parts down one MIDI cable—so for instance, you could send your bass part on Channel 1, your violin part on Channel 2, your trumpet part on Channel 4, and your piano on Channel 13. At the other end of all this data you will need either:

- A multi-timbral instrument that is capable of receiving several different MIDI channels simultaneously and playing each different part with a separate sound. (Think of a multi-timbral instrument as being like several synthesizers in one box, and you'll get the idea.)

- A mono-timbral instrument that can receive only one channel of MIDI data, provided this instrument then has a MIDI output port so that the data for the other channels can be forwarded to other instruments that are set to receive the other channels of MIDI data.

You can, of course, have a combination of multi-timbral and mono-timbral instruments connected.

Most hosts (which we will look at in the next section) are capable of handling all of this MIDI data.

For our purposes, looking at software synthesizers, if you want to play a synthesizer that is running on your computer, you will often have a single keyboard and a single instance of the software running, so MIDI channels may not be a big issue. However, you may want to do something more complicated—for instance, you may have two keyboards (one for each hand) and some foot pedals. In this case, you would need to set each input device (the two keyboards and the foot pedals) to a separate MIDI channel so that each part is processed separately.

Splits and Layers

This approach in MIDI allows you to get into the world of splits and layers.

- A layer is the term when two instruments respond to the same MIDI part (and so the part is played by two instruments). This is generally used to thicken or add texture to a sound.

- A split occurs when one instrument is playable over part of a keyboard and another is playable over another part of the keyboard, with neither part overlapping. So in this situation, you might have a bass guitar sound on the lower range of your keyboard and a trumpet sound on the higher range.

Many software synthesizers are mono-timbral—in other words, they can play only one sound at once. All of the featured synthesizers in this book are effectively mono-timbral. This should not be seen as a limitation. In the world of software, you can open several instances of a synthesizer simultaneously, so in practice you can circumvent this apparent limitation (but you may need to do some MIDI and audio routing in your host). However, as noted earlier, with the incarnation of SynthEdit that is available at the time of writing, there may be some challenges in running multiple instances of the same synthesizer in certain circumstances.

If you are in a situation in which you have one keyboard attached to a computer and you want it to talk to the computer without any messing about, then Omni mode may be useful for you. With Omni mode, your MIDI data is transmitted over all channels. The clear advantage of this approach is that you don't have to ensure that your sending and receiving devices are set to the same channels; instead, you accept that whatever data is transmitted will be the right data (which it will be if there is only one device connected). Many MIDI devices transmit data in Omni mode by default.

Plug-In Host

As I mentioned, most synthesizers come as plug-ins—in other words, they plug into another piece of software. This other software is called a *host*.

At its most basic, a host will manage the relationship between the synthesizer (or other plug-in, such as an effects unit) and the computer. The main tasks that this involves are:

- Routing MIDI inputs from MIDI hardware attached to the computer to the plug-in. A host will also handle the output of any MIDI data.

- Managing the audio output of the synthesizer and connecting it to the computer's hardware. A host will also handle the input of any audio data.

- Displaying the plug-in's interface.

At its most basic, a host doesn't make any sound or add to the music creation process—it is simply there to manage the ins and outs and to open the plug-in's interface. However, there are hosts that do a lot more than that.

Many hosts are complete audio production suites that do the hosting as just one of the related tasks. Examples of these complete production suites include SONAR and Project5 from Cakewalk, Logic from Apple, Live from Ableton, Nuendo and Cubase from Steinberg, and Pro Tools from Digidesign. They will all facilitate:

- Recording, editing, and playback of MIDI data

- Recording, editing, and playback of audio

- Hosting and running multiple plug-ins, including synthesizers and effects units

- Automation of the controls of the synthesizer and effects on playback

- Mixing the separate audio channels

In short, these tools will run your whole musical life—for many people, these tools are all they need to create a professional audio recording. If you're serious about making music on a computer, you will need to get this sort of software to use in conjunction with your synthesizers.

Free/Low-Cost Hosts

I'm not going to recommend anything I haven't tried for myself, so I'm afraid that when it comes to recommendations for hosts that are available for free or at a very low cost, I can only recommend Windows hosts. The two that I use and recommend for handling VSTs are:

- SAVIHost (hermannseib.com/english/savihost.htm), which was created by Hermann Seib.

- Tobybear MiniHost, which was created by Tobias Fletcher (tobybear.de). Unfortunately, at the time of this writing, the Tobybear website had been down for some months—I don't know whether this is permanent. However, you can download the host from www.dontcrack.com/freeware/downloads.php/id/4228/software/MiniHost/#.

There is one other host that many people say good things about, but which I have not tried myself. It is called Cantible, and you can download a free version (Cantible Lite) from www.cantabilesoftware.com/download. However, as I say, I haven't tried it, so I can't recommend it.

The two hosts that I can recommend both handle the basic relationship between the plug-in and the computer. They deal with MIDI in/out and audio in/out, but they do not perform any sort of MIDI sequencing/audio recording–type functions. They are both very light on system resources and straightforward to use.

If you're looking for a low-cost host that will also do MIDI sequencing and automation and handle audio including mixing, then you might want to check out Project5 from Cakewalk (project5.com). There's also a good book that tells you how to use Project5—it's called *Project5 Power* (Course Technology PTR, 2008). You can check out details here: noisesculpture.com/p5p.html. I will use Project5 to illustrate a few points in this book. In addition, some lite (in other words, lower-specified) versions of the more popular hosts are offered for free with some audio interfaces. These are often upgradable to the full version for a very reasonable fee.

Setting Up the SynthWiz Simple Synth in a Host

If you haven't done so already, you can download SynthWiz Simple Synth—the free synthesizer that is used in the next chapter—from noisesculpture.com/synthwiz-downloads.html. The download comes as a zip file, which contains two files (see Figure 1.3):

- **simple.dll.** This is the plug-in synthesizer.

- **Read This First.** This is a PDF with a few notes to accompany the synthesizer.

Installing the Plug-In

Installation of the SynthWiz Simple Synth plug-in is very straightforward: Unzip the zip file you downloaded and then copy the simple.dll file to anywhere on your system that is convenient for you. However, I would suggest:

- You create a subfolder in a convenient location on your hard drive and place simple.dll into that folder.

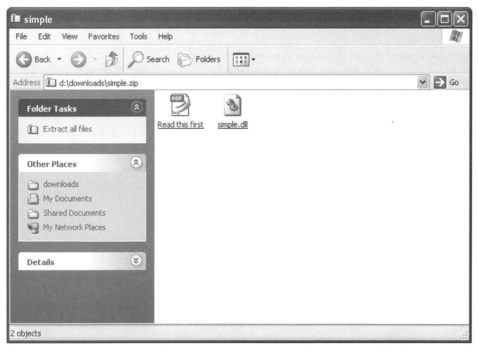

Figure 1.3   The opened zip file with the download package including SynthWiz Simple Synth.

- If you have a number of other VSTs that your host scans—and if the notion of VST scans doesn't make sense, don't worry; I will explain it further in a moment—then locate simple.dll in its own subfolder within your VST folder.

I have put simple.dll into the folder c:\vsti\SynthWiz (because that's an easy place for me to remember).

Running SynthWiz Simple Synth under SAVIHost

If you don't already have another host, then you can run SynthWiz Simple Synth under one of the free hosts listed earlier. The hosts come with documentation—and this section should in no way be seen as replacing that documentation—but I want to show you how to set up a synthesizer plug-in within a host, so I'll show you what to do with SAVIHost. (Clearly the process will be different for other hosts.) Please ignore the remainder of this section if you already know what you are doing.

1.   First (obviously), download SAVIHost.

2.   From the SAVIHost download, copy the file called savihost.exe into the folder where simple.dll is located.

3.   Rename savihost.exe as simple.exe.

4.   Run the newly renamed simple.exe file (by double-clicking on it).

All being well, you should have something that looks like Figure 1.4.

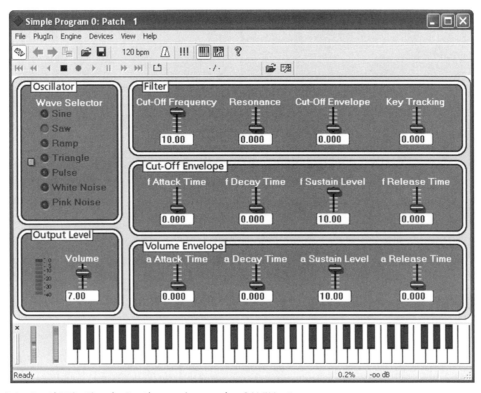

Figure 1.4   SynthWiz Simple Synth running under SAVIHost.

You will notice that at the bottom of the interface, there is now a keyboard underneath the synthesizer. If you click on the keyboard (assuming your speakers are switched on), you should hear a sound coming out of the synthesizer. If you don't have your speakers attached—or you have another problem with your audio (which I will come to in a moment)—then you should still see the movement with the output meter in the Output Level section (bottom left of the synthesizer, to the left of the Volume slider).

Setting Up the Audio under SAVIHost

If you don't hear anything, but the output meter is working, or the output is coming out of the wrong speaker, then you can select the appropriate audio output.

To change the audio output in SAVIHost, select Devices > Wave, and that will bring up a dialog box that looks something like Figure 1.5.

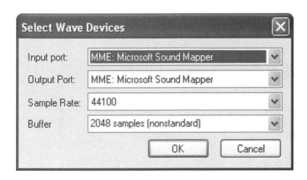

Figure 1.5 The Select Wave Devices dialog box in SAVIHost, from which you can choose the appropriate audio output.

From the Output Port drop-down, choose the appropriate device that is attached to your speakers. (If you don't know which the right one is, then you're in for some trial and error.) Once you have selected the appropriate output port, then click on OK, and you should hear sound when you mouse-click on the SAVIHost keyboard.

SynthWiz Simple Synth doesn't accept audio in, so there's no need to worry about the Input Port setting in the Select Wave Devices dialog box.

If you want to improve the quality of your audio output, then check out ASIO4ALL, which is mentioned later in this chapter, in the "ASIO for Windows" section.

Setting Up MIDI under SAVIHost

If you have an external MIDI device (such as a keyboard) that is connected to your computer, then you can play SynthWiz Simple Synth while it is running in the SAVIHost host. To do this, select Devices > MIDI, which will bring up the Select MIDI Devices dialog (see Figure 1.6).

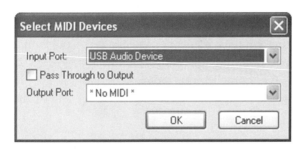

Figure 1.6 In the SAVIHost Select MIDI Devices dialog, you can set the MIDI Input Port from which MIDI messages will be sent to SynthWiz Simple Synth.

In the Select MIDI Devices dialog box, you can select the appropriate MIDI port from the Input Port drop-down. Once you have selected the input port and clicked on the OK button, then incoming played MIDI notes will show on the SAVIHost keyboard (and hopefully you should hear sounds from the synthesizer as you play the keyboard).

VSTi Scanning: Running SynthWiz Simple Synth under Project5

SAVIHost and the like are designed as small, lightweight hosts that can run a single synthesizer, and against that ambition, they are very successful. Most hosts function as part of a larger piece of music software that is a complete music production suite. As I've already mentioned, these suites include SONAR and Project5 from Cakewalk, Logic from Apple, Live from Ableton, and Nuendo and Cubase from Steinberg.

These pieces of software have the facility to run many VSTs/VSTis simultaneously. Rather than setting up each VST/VSTi individually, these hosts will often scan for new and changed plug-ins on startup. Figure 1.7 shows Project5 undertaking its startup scan (and yes, I would have liked it to show SynthWiz Simple Synth being scanned, but the scan moved a bit too quickly for my screen capture).

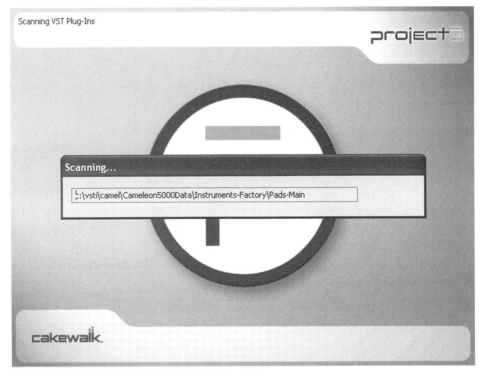

Figure 1.7 Project5 undertaking its VST scan on startup.

The exact process for scanning varies from host to host—you will need to check the documentation that comes with your favored piece of software. Figure 1.8 shows the VST Plug-Ins dialog in Project5, which sets the scan options.

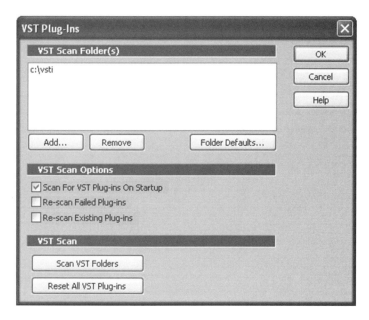

Figure 1.8 Project5 VSTi scan options.

Project5 is not atypical—in most hosts:

- You set a folder (or folders) where your plug-ins are located. (For most synthesizers, the .dll file will be placed in that folder during installation.)

- This folder can be accessed by different software. (So if you are using more than one host, you only need to install the synthesizer once—as long as each host knows where the synthesizer files are located, then the synthesizer can be shared.)

- There is usually an option to scan on startup. This ensures that all of your synthesizers are always available. Most hosts allow you to disable the auto-scan or to manually scan. The advantage of disabling the auto-scan is that it saves time when your host is opened.

You should check the documentation for any host you are using to find the procedure to follow to scan for synthesizers.

As you read earlier, I placed the SynthWiz Simple Synth simple.dll in the folder c:\vsti\SynthWiz. This is a subfolder of c:\vsti, which (as you can see from Figure 1.8) is the folder that is automatically scanned on startup. Therefore, for me, Project5 found SynthWiz Simple Synth when I first started Project5, and so the synthesizer was available to me with no further work (see Figure 1.9).

One of the other advantages of these integrated suites is that once you have set up your audio ins and outs and your MIDI ins and outs, then you don't need to set them up again when you add a new synthesizer. I will therefore assume that if you are using one of these more sophisticated hosts, you have a grasp on how to set up the MIDI and audio (or that if you do not, you know where the manual is).

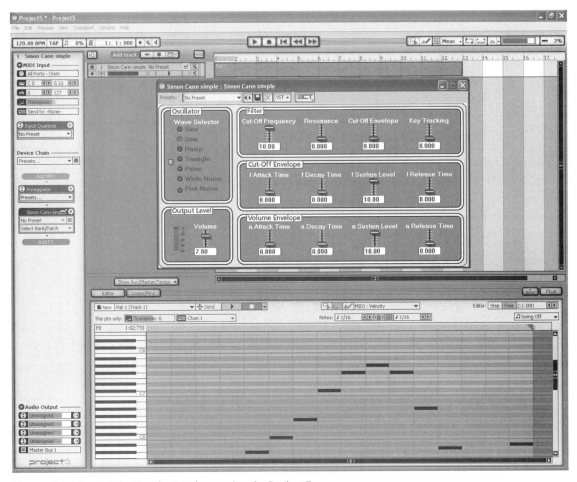

Figure 1.9   SynthWiz Simple Synth running in Project5.

A Bit of Know-How...

As well as understanding how to set up a synthesizer in a host, it's also useful to have a bit of understanding about how digital audio works. This will help you understand how the sound quality of your system can be tweaked and optimized.

Understanding Digital Audio

Audio waveforms are created in a digital format. Once the audio is in a digital format, there are two key factors you need to think about:

- Bit depth
- Sample rate

There are other factors (such as the quality of the digital-to-audio converter), but let's start with these two concepts.

Bit Depth

The bit depth determines how many different levels of loudness a digital waveform can have. The minimum standard for audio creation is 16-bit, with 24-bit being the norm. Sixteen-bit means there are 65,536 (2^16) possible levels of loudness for a waveform. Twenty-four-bit gives 16,777,216 (2^24) possible values for loudness.

Sample Rate

The second factor determining the quality of digital waveforms is the sampling rate, which is the number of slices a waveform is cut into. A sampling rate of 44.1 kHz would mean that the waveform is cut up into 44,100 snapshots of the wave each second. This is the rate used for audio CDs and is the default value for high-quality audio.

The significance of 44.1 kHz is explained in greater detail under the "Aliasing" section at the end of this chapter.

Interaction between Sample Rate and Bit Depth

As you can see in Figure 1.10, a higher sampling rate and a higher bit depth will give greater resolution—in other words, there will be a finer "grid." From the listener's perspective, greater

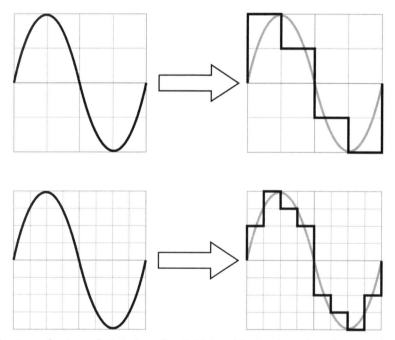

Figure 1.10 The imperfection of digital audio. A higher bit depth and an increased sample rate can give a more detailed digital representation of the sound. By increasing the resolution of the digital wave, the sound will be closer to the analog signal, giving a more natural (or less distorted) sound.

resolution means better sonic fidelity, and many people claim this gives a more analog-like sound (if that is the result they are after).

Apart from the most basic models, most audio interfaces can convert to and from both 16- and 24-bit digital formats and can cope with a wide range of sample frequencies. At the moment there are no mass-market digital interfaces with a bit depth above 24-bit.

Unless you have a good reason not to, I would suggest you always work at 24-bit because it will give you the highest audio fidelity. As far as sample rates go, I tend to stick with 44,100 Hz, since that is the CD standard. Any variation that will require the sample rate to be converted may introduce unwanted side effects on the material when it is converted for CD output. Some people also favor 88,200 Hz, as it converts (comparatively) smoothly to 44,100 Hz.

By the way, CDs are produced at 16-bit. It is easy to export a 24-bit wave in 16-bit format without loss of quality (since in effect all you will be doing is changing the volume level of a wave). This is very different than the issue with the sample rate, where any conversion requires throwing away data and interpolating the results—which, as noted earlier, can give unwanted side effects.

Latency

When you start working with digital audio, you will hear the word *latency* a lot. Latency means delay, and you are likely to find this is a problem in two areas:

- First, there is the delay between hitting a key on your keyboard (or other MIDI input device) and the time when you hear the sound coming out of your speakers.

- While a less frequent problem, there will also be a delay between the input of any audio to the computer and the time you hear the sound come out of your speakers. This may occur if you are running an external audio source through your synthesizer. Although this is a less frequent problem, it is often a more pronounced problem because you are experiencing two conversions (as I will explain in a moment), and therefore you will encounter double latency.

In the world of music and audio, latency is a bad thing. However, in the world of digital audio, latency cannot be avoided. Latency arises in many places in the audio chain. It is the unfortunate combination of several latency-inducing devices that can lead to significant problems.

Audio Conversion

The most noticeable form of latency arises when analog audio is converted to digital, and vice versa. When analog audio is converted into digital, the analog signal passes through an analog-to-digital converter (often called an *ADC*) in the sound card. The ADC cuts the audio into slices and takes a snapshot of each slice. The number of slices is determined by the sampling rate (which, as mentioned earlier, is usually 44,100 Hz). The ADC outputs digital data, which is then recorded or processed in the computer. This can be recorded in some software (such as

Project5) and/or processed through a synthesizer or an effects processor. For the purposes of this book, our main focus is on processing through a synthesizer.

So, to summarize, there are two phases to the sampling process:

- Taking the snapshots

- Passing the digitized data

ADCs work by taking the snapshots and then passing a bundle of data representing several snapshots to the synthesizer (see Figure 1.11). Because a number of snapshots are passed at once, there is an inherent delay in the processing of the data—the first snapshot is not passed until the last snapshot in the bundle is also passed. This delay is the input latency.

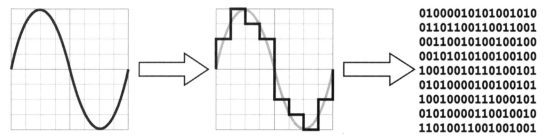

Figure 1.11 The operation of an analog-to-digital converter. First it converts the analog signal into digital format, and then it passes the data to a synthesizer for processing.

You may have already figured out a straightforward solution: Pass the snapshot immediately, or if you can't pass the data immediately, pass fewer snapshots more frequently.

This is the root of finding a workable solution. However, the more frequently that data is passed, the more CPU-intensive the process becomes, and hence the less CPU that will be available to run your synthesizers. Accordingly, you must strike a balance between reducing the CPU hit and the delay caused by waiting for the converted data to be passed.

When audio leaves a computer, there is a similar issue. The data is passed through a digital-to-audio converter (called a *DAC*) within the sound card, which then outputs an analog signal. A DAC will deal with bundles of data, which are then converted to analog audio. The size of the bundle that is converted will determine the latency, and the number of bundles will have CPU implications.

If you are using a modest amount of CPU with your synthesizer, then you might feel happier decreasing the latency (thereby decreasing the delay) and so increasing the CPU hit. However, when you start working with large projects, you may find that you run up against your system's limitations, so you have to increase the latency to drop the CPU hit.

Dealing with Latency

If you are simply recording an audio source, then input latency is unlikely to be an issue because it won't matter when the digital data is actually recorded in the computer. Equally, if you are listening to the output audio that has already been created, there will not be a problem because most hosts can adjust the timing to take account of latency. However, there are two places where latency is a particular issue:

- When a musician is playing a software instrument—it can be quite disconcerting to hit a key and not hear a sound for a fraction of a second.

- When a musician is making music that is being processed and/or recorded, and the musician is listening to the track that has been processed (for instance, if a guitarist is listening to his or her performance processed through a synthesizer).

The difficulty when a musician is trying to play (and perhaps record) a software instrument is that the output of the synthesizer has to pass through a DAC, which introduces latency. Since this is a live performance, the host cannot compensate for the latency, although it can compensate when the recorded performance is played back.

When a musician's audio output is recorded and the musician is listening to the recorded signal (perhaps after the processing by a synthesizer has been added), then the audio signal must pass through an ADC, be processed, and then pass back through a DAC before the musician can hear the signal. This double conversion will lead to a delay that can be annoyingly noticeable—for many players, it is perceived as an echo.

There are two common solutions for these issues:

- If you are a musician playing a software synthesizer, then the latency in your host should be reduced as far as possible. (Check your host's user manual for details.) This will ensure that as the keyboard (or other MIDI controller) is struck, the note is heard immediately without delay. If there is a delay between when you trigger the note and when you hear the note, then your playing will be (adversely) affected.

- If you are recording an audio source, the most practical solution is to split the audio signal. One part is then fed into the ADC, and the other is fed to the musician's audio monitor (in other words, the musician is listening to his or her own performance). This is the solution I have adopted in my setup because it means there is no audio delay for the musician. Alternatively, there are several audio interfaces that provide hardware monitoring for this purpose. There is, of course, an obvious downside to this approach—the musician cannot hear the audio signal that is being processed through the synthesizer. If the musician wants to hear the processed signal in real time, then the only option is to reduce latency as much as possible.

Audio Drivers

Different hosts address sound cards using different protocols. For high-quality audio, there are three audio driver standards that you are likely to come across:

- ASIO (Audio Stream Input/Output)

- WDM (Windows Driver Model, which is applicable to Windows-based computers only)

- Core Audio (which is for Apple computers only)

The difference between ASIO and the other formats is comparatively irrelevant, since they can all produce high-quality, low-latency results. What matters is which standard your audio card supports. If your card supports one standard, then the matter is decided for you. If your card supports both standards, then you can try each and see which works best for you. You may, for instance, find that one standard gives you a glitchy result with audio problems. Equally, you may find that one standard gives you much lower latency without problems than the other does.

As long as you are using a reputable brand of audio interface, you have a computer with a reasonable amount of power, and you are working with ASIO or WDM/Core Audio, then you are likely to be able to achieve acceptable results. If you want spectacular results (which typically means latency under 1.5ms), then you may be able to achieve this on a regular computer. However, if you really want the best results, then you need a dedicated audio computer (that doesn't run office programs, virus programs, or any of the other junk that is likely to slow your computer's performance).

ASIO for Windows

If you a running a Windows machine with a lower-grade audio interface, then you may find that the driver is insufficient for your needs. In particular, you may find that:

- The audio quality is degraded (often this will manifest as a lot of crackling).

- The latency is unacceptable.

- Both of the above.

If you have any of these problems, then you might want to check out ASIO4ALL (asio4all.com); see Figure 1.12.

ASIO4ALL works with all recent flavors of Windows. It is described as a hardware-independent low-latency ASIO driver for WDM audio devices. What this means is that it will use ASIO drivers to address your sound card, and in so doing it may:

- Increase the quality of your sound (by reducing the crackling and so on)

- Reduce the latency

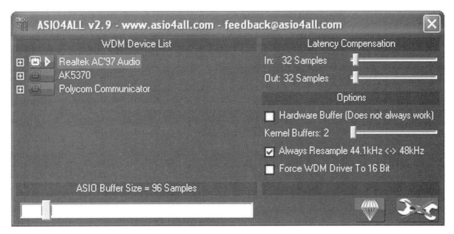

Figure 1.12   The advanced view in ASIO4ALL.

It's free, so if you've got a problem, try it. At the time of writing, it was up to version 2.9 and has a deserved reputation for quality and stability.

Once installed on your system, you can select the ASIO4ALL drivers from your host.

Aliasing

Aliasing is most prominent when a sample is played above the pitch at which it was sampled. This can be significant in many synthesizers where the sound source is a sampled waveform. Whether aliasing is an issue for you—and if so, the extent to which it will be a problem—is dependent on the synthesizer you are using. Some synthesizers are designed to eliminate aliasing completely.

Aliasing is a side effect of digital sound creation. To understand aliasing, you need to understand the Nyquist point. The Nyquist point is one-half of the sample rate (described earlier in this chapter). So, if the sampling rate is 22,050 Hz (which is quite a low rate), then the Nyquist point will be at just over 11,000 Hz, which is well within the audio spectrum. Any sound (or element of a sound) that has its frequency (pitch) above the Nyquist point will lead to digital distortion or aliasing.

With the sample rate set at 44,100 Hz (in other words, the usual rate for CDs), the Nyquist point is 22,050 Hz, which is above the threshold for human hearing. Therefore, you can filter out any sounds that may lead to aliasing without affecting the sound that is heard. Well, theoretically you can…. In practice, sometimes sounds above the threshold of human hearing can have an effect on sounds below the threshold. However, you will usually need highly sensitive ears to notice this effect, and the science behind it is outside the scope of this book.

When we start looking at additive synthesis, you will see how a waveform with a low pitch can still contain high-frequency elements, and it is these elements that may lead to aliasing.

Moving On

That has been a very quick introduction to digital audio. Let's move on and start to think about how to make sounds. I suggest that, at least initially, you focus on how to make sounds and don't worry about audio fidelity. You can improve your audio quality as your synthesizer sounds improve.

2 | Getting a Grip on Synthesizer Programming

When looking at modular synthesizers, there's a real chicken-and-egg situation: Do you learn how to make sounds first, or do you learn what the modules are? I've decided to start with creating sounds, which means that we need a synthesizer...

To bring things full circle, the synthesizer I am going to use is SynthWiz Simple Synth, a synthesizer that I have created in SynthEdit. This is intentionally a very simple synthesizer so that I can illustrate a few points.

I do realize that there will be a number of readers—specifically Mac users—for whom a Windows-based VSTi will not be good news. For you people, I have a patch to re-create the SynthWiz Simple Synth using Zebra 2 so that you can follow this chapter (and I've also made a patch using VAZ Modular and KarmaFX Synth Modular available, too). However, Zebra 2 is inherently more complicated than SynthWiz Simple Synth, so there may be a bit of head-scratching here and there, for which I do apologize. You can download the emulation patches from noise-sculpture.com/synthwiz-downloads.html (which is the same web address from which you can download SynthWiz Simple Synth).

In the next chapter, I will look at synthesizer/patch construction using all of the featured synthesizers. Once we have a handle on how to create sounds—both in terms of putting modules together and in terms of how to then control the sound created by those modules—then we will look at the basic elements in more detail. The introduction to creating sounds in this and the next chapter will give the background, putting the detailed look at the modules into context.

Synthesizer Basics

There are two elements that both need to be considered when creating a sound with a synthesizer:

- The audio path—in other words, the processing that is applied to the audio signal as it passes through the synthesizer.

- The control and modulation path. (I will look at these elements separately in the next chapter.) The control and modulation path include changes that are applied to the elements

23

that affect the audio signal. One key factor to remember is that nothing on the control path makes a sound.

We are going to look at both the audio and the control/modulation path, starting with the audio path. In a basic synthesizer, there are many factors in a sound's design, but in essence a sound will usually have three main elements (see Figure 2.1):

- The sound generator, usually an oscillator

- The filter, which is like a complex tone control that shapes the tone to give the timbre of the sound

- The amplifier, which controls the volume of the sound

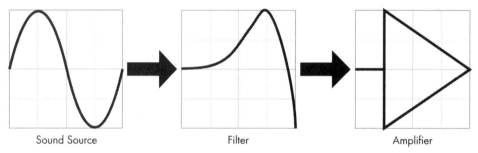

| Sound Source | Filter | Amplifier |

Figure 2.1   The basic audio path in a subtractive synthesizer.

Most of this book is dedicated to looking at these three elements in various combinations.

This form of synthesis is often called *subtractive synthesis*, because you start with a sound source that is then shaped—in other words, elements are subtracted by the filter, much like a sculptor removes elements in creating a piece of art.

All synthesized sounds emanate from a sound generator of some sort. Most of today's synthesizers are software instruments—even those that may be wrapped in a hardware box—and so the sound source is usually some form of computer code. The five synthesizers (four, plus SynthWiz Simple Synth) are all software synthesizers.

Once the sound has been created, it is then "shaped"—in terms of both the tone and the volume over time—to provide a (hopefully) pleasing tone, or if not a pleasing tone, then hopefully the unpleasant tone that the programming was intending to create. It is quite possible that the pitch of the sound may be changed over time, too. The main tools that are used to shape the sound are the filter (which controls the tone) and the amplifier (which controls the level).

The settings on a filter and an amplifier do not need to be static—they can change over time, in the same way that the volume and tone of a note played on a real musical instrument will change over time. There are tools that can be used to control the filter and envelope to shape the sound. The two main tools are:

- Envelopes

- Oscillators (often low-frequency oscillators, or LFOs)

We will look at these in a lot more detail later in the book, but for now, think of them as levels that change over time, and you'll understand.

Getting Started with Synthesis

Let's have a look at the various elements in more detail. Once we understand what each element is and how it works, we can look at how they interact to create a sound that can be controlled by a musician.

For the remainder of this chapter, there will be no presets for you to download. This part is not about sonic accuracy—it's about laying your hands on a synthesizer and getting a feel for what does what and how things interact. There are no more diagrams to represent sounds and functions; instead, I want you to use your ears and listen to how things sound, however rough they sound. Also, listen to how the sound changes as you move the controls around, and listen to the nuances of sounds that these changes create.

If you can't run Windows VSTis (or if you just don't like SynthWiz Simple Synth), then use Zebra 2 for this section. You can download the starting patch (which is called *SSS Emulation*) from the Noise Sculpture website at the same place that you downloaded SynthWiz Simple Synth. If you are going to use Zebra 2, then you should be aware that:

- There is a much broader choice of waveforms than is available in SynthWiz Simple Synth, and those waveforms may not obviously have the exact same name or timbre as the waves in SynthWiz Simple Synth.

- The controls work differently in Zebra 2. Specifically, there are knobs rather than sliders, and the range that these controls may work over is different from the ranges in SynthWiz Simple Synth.

As I said before, this section is about getting used to using a synthesizer and understanding the basics, so don't worry if you don't feel you are precisely replicating the SynthWiz Simple Synth patches in Zebra 2.

If you are confused or don't understand at any point—irrespective of which synthesizer you are using—then don't worry. For the moment, the important thing is that you start using the synthesizers and not that you understand what you are doing. Follow along, and I'll explain everything later.

So, to get going, open up SynthWiz Simple Synth. It should look something like Figure 2.2.

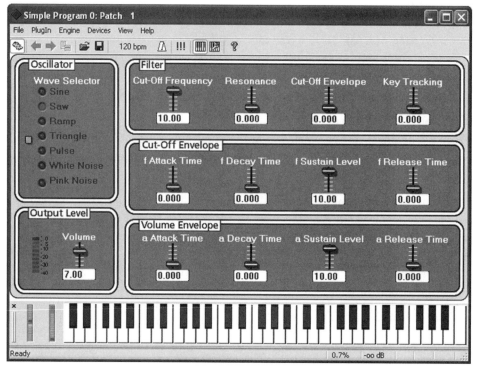

Figure 2.2 SynthWiz Simple Synth running in SAVIHost. Check back in Chapter 1 for details of how to get hold of these two free tools and how to open SynthWiz Simple Synth in SAVIHost.

If you're running Zebra 2, then open it and open the SSS Emulation patch, which is available for download from the Noise Sculpture website. Figure 2.3 shows the controls that are equivalent to those in SynthWiz Simple Synth when the SSS Emulation patch is loaded. By the way, I will explain the construction of this patch in the next chapter.

How to Use SynthWiz Simple Synth

There are five sections in SynthWiz Simple Synth:

■ The Oscillator—the sound source

■ The Output Level, which, unsurprisingly, controls the output level

Figure 2.3 A patch in Zebra 2 to replicate the functionality of SynthWiz Simple Synth. The equivalent control labels are marked.

- The Filter, which has many of the filter settings
- The Cut-Off Envelope, which sets the parameters that control the filter cut-off frequency over time
- The Volume Envelope, which sets the parameters that control the volume level over time

Figure 2.4 shows these modules, which will be explained in the upcoming "The Elements of Synthesis" section.

Let's have a look at how to use SynthWiz Simple Synth in a bit more detail.

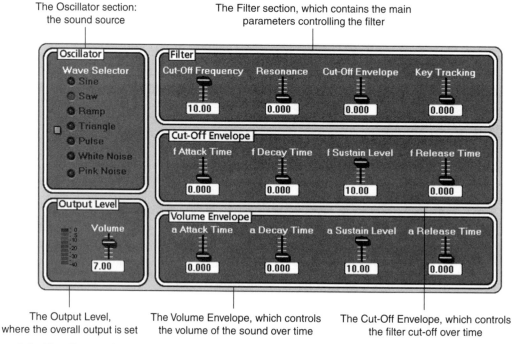

Figure 2.4 The five sections in SynthWiz Simple Synth.

Waveform Selector

To select a waveform, click on the button to the left of the waveform list (see Figure 2.5). With each click you will step in sequence through the available waves. (There is no facility to step backward.) The selected wave is indicated by a lit red LED (which doesn't show up very well in the grayscale image of Figure 2.5).

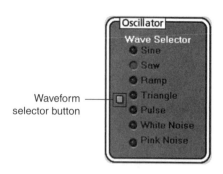

Figure 2.5 The waveform selector in SynthWiz Simple Synth.

Sliders

The sliders (see Figure 2.6) can be adjusted by clicking and dragging (up or down) to the appropriate setting. As you adjust a slider, its value will be displayed in the text box immediately below the slider.

Figure 2.6   You can adjust a slider (in this case, the Resonance slider) by clicking and dragging to the appropriate setting.

As you will read later in this chapter, there is a high degree of interaction between some of the sliders, so you may occasionally find that sliders appear not to work.

Direct Text Entry

Instead of moving a slider, you can directly enter a value into the text box below the slider. To directly enter a value:

1. Double-click on the value you want to change—the text will be highlighted.

2. Hit the Delete button to delete the current value.

3. Enter the new value.

4. Click outside of the text box (or hit the Tab key).

The corresponding slider will then move to indicate the input value.

You can input a number greater than the maximum allowed for any slider, but this has no additional effect. (In other words, the value will be set to the minimum or the maximum. You can set the volume to 11, but all you will hear is 10.)

Output Meter

The output meter (see Figure 2.7) in the Output Level section gives a rough idea about the level of a sound. Its main purposes are:

■   To give you an indication when the synthesizer is creating a noise. This can be helpful if you are not sure whether the synthesizer is routed to an audio output.

■   To give you an idea about the level of the sound that is being created.

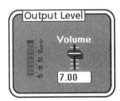

Figure 2.7   The output meter in the Output Level section

The Elements of Synthesis

That's your introduction to the synthesizer. Now, let's start making some noise!

Sound Sources

When you open SynthWiz Simple Synth, the synthesizer has been set to play a very simple but uninteresting sound. This is an unfiltered sawtooth wave. Although this may sound uninteresting, this wave is the basis for many (perhaps most) synthesized sounds.

You will notice that as you hold the key down (whether on a MIDI keyboard or if you mouse-click on the keyboard in a host running the VSTi), the sound can be heard. As you release the key, the sound stops.

As you can see in Figure 2.8, the Oscillator section offers a choice of seven different waveforms:

- Sine

- Saw (sawtooth)

- Ramp (reverse sawtooth)

- Triangle

- Pulse

- White Noise

- Pink Noise

Figure 2.8   The waveform options in SynthWiz Simple Synth.

Take a moment or two to step through the sounds and listen to the characteristics of the raw waveforms. You will hear:

- The Sine wave has a very pure tone and seems to lack strength. (It doesn't really lack strength—it just seems to.)

- The Saw and the Ramp sound the same, which is not surprising because they are effectively the same wave. These waves are very useful general-purpose waves that will be used frequently throughout this book.

- The Triangle has a characteristic somewhat like the Sine wave, but with a slightly brighter sound. In the real world, where very delicate nuances can get lost, these two waves can often be interchangeable. However, as you get more confident in designing sounds, you will find many occasions when you don't want to change one wave for the other.

- The Pulse wave (which in this case is effectively a square wave) has a very reedy tone with something of the characteristic of a woodwind instrument.

- The noise waves are just that: noise. The White Noise is brighter, whereas the Pink Noise has a darker characteristic.

If you're using Zebra 2 rather than SynthEdit Simple Synth, you will have found that Zebra 2 has a lot more wave choices and that the tone of these many other waves is quite varied.

Filter

When you have finished listening to the waveforms, select either the Saw wave or the Ramp wave and then let me direct your attention to the Filter block (see Figure 2.9)—and in particular, the Cut-Off Frequency slider.

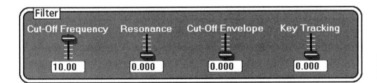

Figure 2.9 The Filter block in SynthWiz Simple Synth.

A filter is a very sophisticated and controllable tone control. The filter in SynthWiz Simple Synth is what is called a *low-pass filter*. This works by cutting the high-frequency elements of a sound, allowing the low-frequency elements to pass through unaffected.

If you hold a note and drag the Cut-Off Frequency slider, you will notice:

- The sound will get duller (or less bright). Not only does the tone change, but the characteristic of the sound changes, too. If you listen you will hear that the sound is far less aggressive and could perhaps be regarded as being warmer.

- The sound gets progressively quieter as more of the waveform is filtered out. Toward the bottom of the range, you may have difficulty hearing any sound.

The cut-off frequency is the point above which frequencies are attenuated. As you moved the slider, you changed the point at which the filter's cut-off frequency has effect.

Now push the Cut-Off Frequency slider up to 10 and (while still holding a note) push the Resonance slider all the way to the top. (The value under the slider should show 9.00—this is one that would get dangerous if we went to 10.)

As you push the Resonance slider, you will hear the tone change quite noticeably. The sound will be brighter and sharper. With the Resonance slider kept at 9, now listen to the sound as you move the Cut-Off Frequency slider again.

Now, sound is a highly subjective issue, but this is what I heard when I moved the Cut-Off Frequency slider (with the Resonance slider set to the maximum):

- Most obviously, the sound was brighter. It started brighter, and it stayed brighter.

- The sound was also more aggressive and kept that edge. Without the Resonance slider, the sound became warmer or mellower as I pulled the Cut-Off Frequency slider down. With the Resonance slider up, the tone changed, but the sound still kept a certain aggressive characteristic.

- The Cut-Off Frequency slider seemed to be more sensitive to movement, and there seemed to be a wider range of nuances of tone uncovered as the Cut-Off Frequency slider moved. In particular, there was a noticeable nasal tone as I moved the slider.

- At the top of the range, the Cut-Off Frequency slider seemed to have less effect on the overall volume of the sound (which did seem to start from a louder volume).

This is what *I* noticed—as I said, sound is highly subjective, so you may not hear all of these. Equally, you may hear other characteristics and changes that I haven't noticed. Also, you may express what you hear with different words—for instance, you may not regard what you heard as "aggressive."

Anyway, that's enough about words. This is a book about sounds, so what just went on there?

The Resonance control is an interesting one. Where the filter cuts the sound, the purpose of the resonance is to boost the sound at the cut-off frequency. So if you heard the sound as brighter or louder when the resonance was boosted, that would be fully expected—the sound was brighter and louder due to the resonance boost.

By the way, the reason the Resonance control only goes up to 9 and not 10 is that at 10 the resonance boost is so significant that the filter *self-oscillates*—in other words, it starts creating sound on its own rather than simply filtering the sound.

Now that you know what the filter cut-off does and what the resonance does, take some time to:

- Listen to how the two interact.

- Listen to how they affect the other waveforms. Some waveforms react in a better way (in other words, in a more sonically pleasing way) than others when pushed through a filter.

As a side issue, if you're using SAVIHost and don't have a MIDI keyboard, you can hold a note (so that it continues to sound) by right-clicking on one of the keys. To release the held note, right-click again on the note.

Modulation

At this point, I think it would be sensible to introduce the notion of modulation. The concept of modulation in a synthesizer is simple—something is changed by something else, usually in real time.

Conventionally, a *source* will modulate a *destination*. So if we think about the volume of a sound (which we will look at in the next section), an envelope would act as the source, and the volume would be the destination.

Modulation does not make a sound, but it does affect things that do, and it affects modules that contour the sound.

We'll look at modulation in greater detail in Chapter 6, "Modulation and Control." As you will see, it is fundamental to all aspects of sound design because it is the process that allows sounds to change over time.

Volume Envelope

The filter changes the tone and the volume. However, it is not the ideal choice for dealing with volume in a musical way—for that, you need a volume envelope. A volume envelope is a level control that controls the level of volume over time.

Think of a piano note and an organ note. Clearly, these are both different sounds, not least of all due to the different tones they create. However, think about their volume for a moment.

- If you strike a piano note, there is an immediate impact as the hammer hits the string. After this impact, the sound then decays rapidly.

- By contrast, an organ note may not have quite the same impact (although it does start very quickly). However, after an organ note is triggered, provided the key is held, the note will sustain. Theoretically, it could sustain indefinitely (although if it's your finger holding the note, you may get bored and want to release it at some point).

An organ and a piano have different volume envelopes. With a synthesizer we can replicate this behavior through the use of envelopes, although we can't always replicate the natural tone of an instrument. With SynthWiz Simple Synth, we can control the volume of a sound over time with the Volume Envelope (see Figure 2.10).

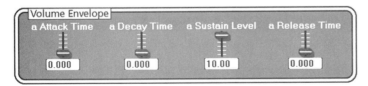

Figure 2.10 The Volume Envelope in SynthWiz Simple Synth.

The function of the Volume Envelope is to control the amplifier in the SynthWiz Simple Synth. There are four controls in the Volume Envelope block:

- **a Attack Time.** The a Attack Time control governs the time it takes for the sound to reach its maximum volume after a note is triggered. Using the example of a piano, the attack time would be zero—in other words, it would take no time for the sound to go from nothing to the maximum volume.

- **a Decay Time.** The a Decay Time control governs how quickly the sound drops (to the sustain level) after it has reached its maximum volume. Again, using the example of the piano, the decay time would be fast, but it would be longer than the attack time.

- **a Sustain Level.** The a Sustain Level control sets the volume of the sound (or the level of the envelope) while a key is held. This level stays constant until the key is released.

- **a Release Time.** The a Release Time control governs the time it takes the sound to decay to zero after a key is released.

The letter "a" preceding each function is there to differentiate between a similar function in the filter envelope (which I am calling the Cut-Off Envelope in this synthesizer). The Cut-Off Envelope is discussed in the next section.

This form of envelope—often referred to as an ADSR (attack, decay, sustain, release) envelope—is very prevalent in synthesizers. All of the synthesizers featured in this book have ADSR envelopes.

Let's try this in practice. Go to SynthWiz Simple Synth and set the Oscillator to Saw, the Cut-Off Frequency to 10, and the Resonance to 9. We're now going to set an envelope so that you can hear it work. To do this, set the controls as follows:

- a Attack Time: 7
- a Decay Time: 10
- a Sustain Level: 3
- a Release Time: 9

Now play and hold a note. You should hear:

- The note will slowly fade in. The volume will increase over time and then it will suddenly start getting quieter. The time while it was getting louder is the a Attack Time.

- After reaching the loudest point at the end of the a Attack Time phase, the note will get quieter. At the end of the a Decay Time, it will reach the a Sustain Level. When it reaches this point, the volume will remain constant while the key is held.

- When you release the key, the note will fade from its volume at the time that the key was released, to zero, over the time set by the a Release Time slider.

Take some time to play with this and then reset the envelope as follows when you're ready to move on:

- a Attack Time: 0

- a Decay Time: 0

- a Sustain Level: 10

- a Release Time: 0

Filter Envelope

Whereas the Volume Envelope controls the volume over time, the Cut-Off Envelope (see Figure 2.11) controls the filter cut-off frequency over time. By the way, people often call a cut-off envelope a filter envelope—usually the terms are interchangeable, but I am specifying cut-off envelope here so that there is no confusion about which function within the filter is being controlled.

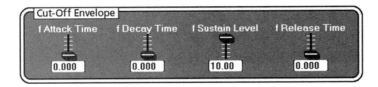

Figure 2.11 The filter Cut-Off Envelope.

The controls on the Cut-Off Envelope are the same as on the Volume Envelope—as you will see, we have an ADSR envelope again. However, the functions of the Cut-Off Envelope are subtly different because the filter's cut-off frequency is being controlled over time.

- **f Attack Time.** The f Attack Time governs the time it takes for the cut-off frequency to open fully after a note is triggered.

- **f Decay Time.** The f Decay Time controls how quickly the filter cut-off drops (to the level set by the sustain level) after it has reached its maximum frequency.

- **f Sustain Level.** The f Sustain Level is the cut-off frequency while a key is held. This level stays constant until the key is released.

- **f Release Time.** The f Release Time is the time it takes the filter to close after a key is released.

So far, so good... However, I'm afraid things are a bit more complicated—we've got a bit of interaction to deal with....

- The Cut-Off Envelope will only function if the filter Cut-Off Frequency is set at less than its maximum amount. If the Cut-Off Frequency is set to the maximum (10), then it can't be opened any further, and so the envelope can have no effect.

■ We also want to keep some control over the extent to which the Cut-Off Envelope can mess with the filter's cut-off frequency. To do this, we've got another slider—go back to Figure 2.9, and you will see that there is a slider labeled Cut-Off Envelope in the Filter block. This slider controls the extent to which the Cut-Off Envelope will affect the filter.

I think an example may help. Take a look at Figure 2.12 and copy those settings onto your SynthWiz Simple Synth.

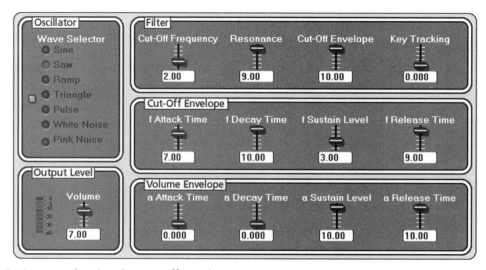

Figure 2.12   A patch using the Cut-Off Envelope in practice.

This is often called a *filter sweep* because the filter's cut-off frequency is being swept (or changed) as the note is held.

Let me point out a few things about this sound:

■ First, notice that the Cut-Off Frequency is set to 2. Without the effect of the Cut-Off Envelope (which is set to its maximum, 10) this sound would be virtually inaudible, so in large part, the character of this sound is controlled by the Cut-Off Envelope.

■ Resonance has been added (set to the maximum, 9) to make the change in the cut-off frequency more pronounced.

■ The Cut-Off Envelope is quite slow. In other words, you can hear it changing the filter over time. Very often the change will be so swift that you can perceive it, although you can't hear it as a separate event (much in the same way that you can hear a chord, but you may not perceive the individual notes).

■ The Volume Envelope still has effect. In particular, you will notice that the a Release Time has been set to its maximum, 10. Without this setting, it would be much harder (and at some settings, impossible) to hear the effect of the f Release Time setting.

Once you have listened to the effect of the Cut-Off Envelope:

- Experiment with the Cut-Off Envelope slider. Notice how it changes the effect of the Cut-Off Envelope.

- Balance the Cut-Off Envelope slider and the Cut-Off Frequency slider to see how these two controls interact.

- Adjust the controls in the Cut-Off Envelope block to gain a greater understanding of how these times and the level have an effect on the sound.

Filter Key Tracking

Acoustic instruments exhibit a behavior where, as higher notes are played, the sound becomes brighter. This sounds very natural to the human ear. If you've got an acoustic instrument around, play it and listen as you play higher notes. We can reproduce this behavior with synthesizers.

Look back again at Figure 2.9. You will see that to the right of the filter block is a slider labeled Key Tracking. As you increase the Key Tracking slider, the filter's cut-off frequency will automatically open as you play higher notes. As with the Cut-Off Envelope, the Key Tracking function will only have effect if the filter Cut-Off Frequency is set at less than its maximum amount. If the Cut-Off Frequency is set to the maximum (10), then it can't be opened any further, and so the Key Tracking can have no effect.

To try this out, set:

- Cut-Off Frequency: 1

- Resonance: 7

- Key Tracking: 1 (maximum)

Play low notes, and the sound will be quiet and muffled. Play high notes, and the sound will be loud and bright.

Set Key Tracking to zero, and the whole keyboard range will be quiet and muffled.

Key tracking isn't just used with filters. For instance, you might want to make an oscillator quieter as the pitch gets higher. Anything that can be modulated can be controlled by key tracking.

Output Level

The Volume slider (see Figure 2.13) in the Output Level section controls the volume of the synthesizer. While the Volume Envelope has an effect on the volume, this level is not controlled by another envelope (so, for instance, you cannot override it with an envelope or the like).

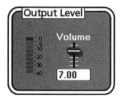

Figure 2.13   The Output Level block in SynthWiz Simple Synth.

This meter is there to give you an idea about the relative loudness of a sound; it is not intended as an accurate gauge. As a general rule of thumb, you should try to ensure your sounds do not hit the red indicator (as this can lead to digital distortion, which is a very ugly sound).

You will find that the output level in any particular patch depends on many factors, including:

- The number of notes being played. More notes equals greater level.

- The selected waveform. Some waves are inherently louder than others—for instance, a sawtooth wave is louder than a sine wave.

- The amount of filtering. Since the filter is subtractive, greater filtering will see a reduction in output level.

Making Sounds

That's the theory and the introduction to how to use synthesizers. Shall we make a few straight-forward sounds?

The following sounds are all straightforward, lacking ornamentation, sophistication, and animation. However, they will give you an idea about the basics of creating specific sounds. Later in the book, we will look at creating far richer, more elegant sounds.

For these sounds, instead of listing the settings or giving you patches to download, I'm going to include a screenshot, and I will explain the key features of the sound in the text. There is no need to precisely replicate these sounds (and indeed, there is little value in doing so). Instead, I would like you to focus on:

- The general structure of the sound and the process by which I took a raw wave and made it sound like something else.

- The interaction between the various elements in the synthesizer.

- The differences between each of the sounds that are created in the rest of this chapter. Sure, there are certain characteristics that have similarities, but I want you to focus on the differences and what makes each sound unique.

Soft Bass

Let's first look at a soft bass sound; see Figure 2.14.

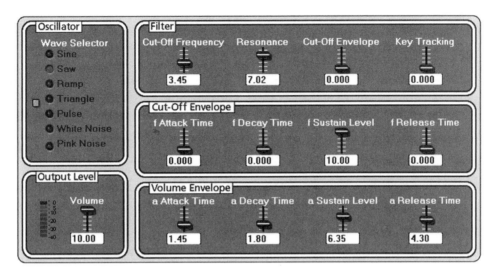

Figure 2.14   A soft bass sound.

There are times when you need a flashy bass sound, which can become a feature within your track. There are other times when you need a sound that is unobtrusive but that serves a function (that function being to add low-end weight and sit perfectly in a mix). This sound has been designed for that latter category—it is purely functional and has no flash.

As you can hear (if you create the sound or a similar one), this bass sound is soft, both in terms of level and in terms of the quality of the sound. The softness—in terms of the sound quality—is largely due to the filter settings. The Cut-Off Frequency has been set quite low, although there is quite a bit of resonance, and the Cut-Off Frequency is not then controlled by the Cut-Off Envelope. (The settings in the Cut-Off Envelope block have not been changed, and the Cut-Off Envelope slider has been set to zero.)

The sound has also been made softer—or if you prefer, less aggressive—through the use of the Volume Envelope, where the hard edges have been filed off the sound. There are a few things I have done here:

- First, the a Attack Time has been slowed slightly. This softens the initial impact of the note.

- The a Decay Time is fairly quick, but not too quick. This allows the start of the note to have some shape but doesn't allow it to predominate in the way that a pluck-type sound would have its impact predominate.

- The a Sustain Level has been set at a reasonably high level. If this setting were set at a lower level, then the change between the maximum volume reached after the a Attack Time phase and the level set by the a Sustain Level would be too extreme, adding too much emphasis to the early part of the note. You could set a faster a Decay Time and a lower a Sustain Level in order to give a sound more of a "plucked" character.

- Finally, the a Release Time has been set to allow the note to naturally decay after the key is released. This ensures that there is not too much of a staccato effect when the note is released.

To my ear, this sound works best as a soft bass sound (hence, I called it soft bass). You could, of course, play chords with this sound or play it in a higher range than would be appropriate for bass. However, to my ear—and you may take a different view—this sound is just plain dull when used for those other duties.

Pad

I want to stick with the softer side of sound creation and create a pad-type sound. A pad is a sound that can be used for background chords within a track, so again, you probably don't want anything that will be too much of a feature. This sound is illustrated in Figure 2.15.

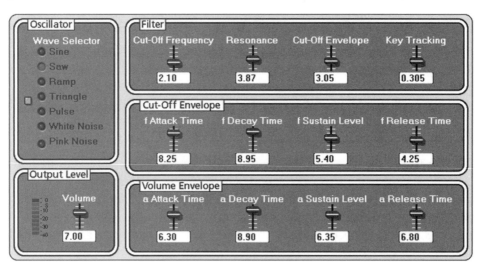

Figure 2.15 A pad sound.

There are certain similarities between this sound and the soft bass sound. However, in this sound there is a lot more going on, and several different aspects are interacting. Let's look at the Filter block first:

- You will see that the Cut-Off Frequency has been set at quite a low level. This would make the sound quite dull and quiet. There is some resonance, but not enough to add much brightness to the sound, nor enough to add much volume.

- The Cut-Off Envelope slider has been set to a modest level. This allows the Cut-Off Envelope to give the sound some movement—in other words, the character of the sound can change over time. This is important for a pad: A static sound will grate in the context of a track. The modest Resonance setting gives slightly more emphasis to the filter movement introduced by the Cut-Off Envelope.

- The Key Tracking slider has also been set to a moderate amount. This means that the sound will get brighter in higher ranges. This is good, but to my ear, the sound does get too bright at a certain point.

As you can see, while the filter Cut-Off Frequency has been set at a low level, it is then worked on by two other factors. The change in the filter's cut-off is then controlled and allowed to evolve by the Cut-Off Envelope, which has been set so that:

- The a Attack Time is quite slow. This allows the sound to become progressively brighter as it sustains. The effect is subtle, but the movement in the sound is noticeable.

- After reaching a peak of brightness at the end of the a Attack Time, the sound then becomes less bright, thereby maintaining some movement (over the f Decay Time) until it reaches the level set by the f Sustain Level.

- When a key is released, the filter closes over the time set by the f Release Time slider. You will notice that this closes the filter more quickly than the sound decays as set by the a Release Time slider. The effect here is to take the brightness out of the decaying sound, giving an effect rather like a single echo.

Lastly, you will see that the Volume Envelope has been set to allow the sound to fade in and fade out gently. Like soft bass, there are no sharp edges here.

Filtered Noise

We used the Key Tracking facility in the last patch, pad. This patch (filtered noise; see Figure 2.16) uses Key Tracking in a much more extreme manner, but still in a highly musical way.

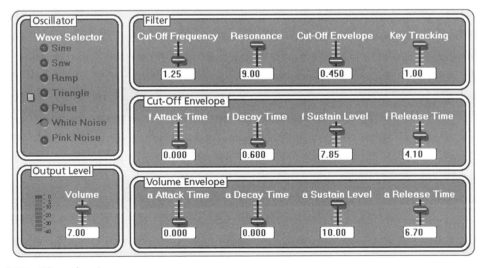

Figure 2.16   Filtered noise.

As you would expect given the name, this patch filters noise. However, what it does is slightly more interesting than making hiss less annoying than it could be—the filter cut-off frequency is linked to the pitch of the key you press, so what you are doing is playing "pitched" noise. Try playing a simple melody with this sound, and you will hear that you can play noise and create a tune.

You're not going to want to do this every day, but this technique is very useful, so let me talk about how you can create it.

First, you will notice that White Noise has been selected in the Oscillator. This gives us a very bright sound source. The effect would be the same if you were to use the Pink Noise source, but then the overall tone would be darker. Now let's look at the Filter block:

- You will see that the Cut-Off Frequency has been set to a very low level—were it not for the other settings in the block, the sound would be completely cut—and the Resonance has been set to its maximum. The interaction of these two controls gives a very pronounced resonance boost at the cut-off frequency. It is this boost peak that we are exploiting in this sound.

- The Key Tracking slider has been set to its maximum. At this level, there is a 1:1 correlation between the cut-off frequency in the filter and any incoming note (for instance, played on a MIDI keyboard). Therefore, if you play one note, the filter will adopt a certain cut-off frequency. If you then play a note an octave higher, the filter cut-off will be an octave higher (and the sound will be correspondingly brighter).

These three sliders—Cut-Off Frequency, Resonance, and Key Tracking—are the essential part of the sound. I've then added a few other tweaks that don't change the effect but that, to my ear, improve the sound:

- You will see that the a Release Time slider has been set in the Volume Envelope. This allows the sound to gently decay after a key is released, giving a less abrupt sound.

- The Cut-Off Envelope in the Filter block has been given a very low value. While this is low, it does still mean that the Cut-Off Envelope has a noticeable effect on the sound. If you set the slider to zero, you will hear the sound without the envelope. If you listen as the note decays, then you will particularly hear the effect. If you set the slider to too high of a level, then you will get an unwanted effect (which, coincidentally, I will be taking advantage of in the next sound).

- The Cut-Off Envelope has been set to give effect in two places. The combination of the f Decay Time and f Sustain Level settings mean that there is a very slight peak when a note is first triggered. This gives a subtle effect on the impact of each note. More importantly, the f Release Time slider has been set so that the filter closing can be heard. However, this closing is faster than the setting for the a Release Time slider, so you can clearly hear the effect as the sound decays.

You may not use this sound every day, but the principle of key tracking—in other words, linking a control to pitch—is regularly used.

Try changing the waveform for this sound. You will hear that this sound works with Pink Noise; however, it may not be quite as good. Equally, this sound works with the other waveforms, but the effect of the filter key tracking is not so noticeable. Instead, there is a peak at the cut-off point, which is more likely to lead to distortion.

Squelch

We're now going to create a classic synthesizer sound where you can hear the effect of the filter cut-off moving, even if the movement is too fast to be able to actually identify that there is filter movement.

The squelch sound (see Figure 2.17) sounds best when played at lower registers. This could be the kind of bass sound you use when you want to make a feature of the sound.

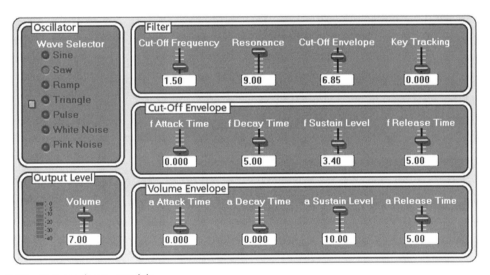

Figure 2.17   Get ready to squelch.

The squelch characteristic in this sound is created by the filter's cut-off frequency moving. This means the filter needs to do two things simultaneously:

■ Shape the tone of the sound

■ Create the squelch

As with many sounds, there is a balance to be struck. Sometimes there will not be enough squelch, and the only way to get more squelch is to compromise the resulting sound. At other times, there will be too much squelch, and the only way to remove the squelch is to compromise the resulting sound. As you may have guessed, at times the only real option is to accept more or less squelch than you may otherwise want.

However, there is another option—choose a different filter. Each filter has a different characteristic, and some squelch better than others. This is one of the key advantages of modular synthesizers: You can choose the right components for a very specific sound.

Anyway, moving back to the squelch at hand, you will see that in the Filter block, the Cut-Off Frequency is set quite low, and the Resonance is set high. We know that this setting will emphasize the sound around the cut-off frequency. The squelch is then created by the Cut-Off Envelope working on the filter cut-off—it is the movement in the cut-off that gives the squelching sound.

If you look at the Cut-Off Envelope block, you will see:

- The f Sustain Level is set quite low. This means that there is a peak at the start of the envelope. The amount by which this peak affects the cut-off frequency is then set by the Cut-Off Envelope in the Filter block. (As you can see, this is set at a reasonable level.)

- The f Decay Time slider is set halfway, which is not particularly fast. It is fast enough that it is hard to identify the changes, but the effect is noticeable.

The key to the sound is the interaction between the f Decay Time and the f Sustain Level. There is an interesting relationship between the two. Both controls on their own make significant changes to the sound, but when used in combination, the effect is very powerful.

- The f Decay Time slider may perhaps have the greatest influence over the characteristics of the squelch. If you set the time to be too fast, then you add more of a "click" to the start of the note. Set the time to be too slow, and the squelch disappears and is replaced by an open filter, giving a rather unpleasant sound.

- The f Sustain Level sets the depth of the squelch. If the level is too high, then there is no squelch because the filter doesn't move. Most lower settings increase the squelch; however, this then has an effect on the sustained sound while a key is held.

- The Cut-Off Envelope slider in the Filter block obviously has an effect, too. Again, this affects the characteristic of the squelch sound.

Take some time to play with the three sliders and listen to their interaction. Then let's move on to the next chapter.

3 Synthesizer/Patch Construction Basics

In the last chapter, we looked at creating sounds with a synthesizer—specifically, we focused on how the movement of parameters could have an effect on the resulting sound. This chapter moves forward to look at the mechanics of constructing a synthesizer/patches in a modular environment using the four featured synthesizers.

With each synthesizer I will re-create the SynthWiz Simple Synth that we used in the last chapter. Having re-created the synthesizer with Zebra 2, VAZ Modular, and KarmaFX Synth Modular, I will then show you exactly how I created the synthesizer in SynthEdit.

While we are only looking at creating a simple synthesizer, the build (and for that matter, the architectural) principles are the same whether you are dealing with a single oscillator device or the largest synthesizer imaginable—all that changes are the scale and complication. So, once you can create a simple synthesizer in all of these tools, you can then do anything, provided you have an understanding of what modules are available to you. We will look at the available modules in detail in the next chapters.

Audio Path and Non-Audio Path

If you look back at the SynthWiz Simple Synth, you will see that there are elements that have a direct effect on the sound (such as the filter), and there are elements that don't change the sound but do have an effect on parts that change the sound. (An example of this would be the Cut-Off Envelope.) Okay, this is getting a bit cryptic—let's have a look at some detail.

Audio Path

The audio path contains elements that create sounds, carry sounds, and modify sounds. There are three main elements that fall into this category (and these elements are likely to be used many times within a single sound):

- **Sound sources.** Sound sources include oscillators (and there are many types of oscillators) and devices for playing back samples. In SynthWiz Simple Synth, there is one sound source: the oscillator. This has a number of waveform choices to create the basic sounds that are then processed by the synthesizer.

- **Filters.** Filters are the main tools that are used to shape sounds. At their most basic, filters may be thought of as simple tone controls. However, as you will see when we get further into the book, filters can do much more than make minor tonal changes. In SynthWiz Simple Synth, there is a single low-pass filter.

- **Amplifiers.** Amplifiers carry sounds and make them louder or softer. Ideally, they do not affect the tone of the signal (since that is the purpose of a filter); however, when used in conjunction with envelopes and other modulators, an amplifier can have a significant effect on the perceived sound, lending much to its character. In SynthWiz Simple Synth, there is a single amplifier to control the sound, which is controlled by:

  - The Volume Envelope
  - The Volume slider

Control Elements

If you look at SynthWiz Simple Synth, you will see that in the Filter section, there is a slider labeled Cut-Off Frequency. As you drag that slider up and down, you will hear the cut-off frequency of the filter change, making the sound brighter or duller.

All of the sliders on SynthWiz Simple Synth are examples of control elements. They all allow you to access and directly control certain parameters.

With SynthEdit, all of the control elements need to be specified. With the other three synthesizers, many of the control elements are already available on each module's face. However, you may still want to attach other control elements in order to control the function in another way. (This may be the case for SynthEdit synthesizers, too.) For example, if you look at Zebra 2, you will see that on the Perform page, there are three XY pads. You could, for instance:

- Set the vertical axis on one pad to control a filter's cut-off.

- Set the horizontal axis on the same pad to control the same filter's resonance.

This routing would not give you any new functionality—you could already control the filter's cut-off and resonance by tweaking the knobs on the filter—however, it would give you control over both functions simultaneously and in a very neat way.

We will look at control sources in a bit more detail later in this chapter, in the "Modulation Sources and Modulation Control Sources" section.

Modulation Elements

The modulation elements are modules that affect the audio path modules but that don't create any sound in their own right.

There is a fine distinction (and to be frank, a pretty irrelevant distinction) between modulation elements and control elements. One area where there is a significant difference is when it comes to setting parameters—particularly the parameters on a modulator. Here you will need a control element (if there isn't already one) rather than a modulation element. So for instance, you will need a control element to set the attack time on an envelope if there isn't a control element in place.

However, modulation is a technique that goes to the heart of creating sounds, so before we move on, let's look at modulation in a bit more detail.

Modulation: The Concept

The concept of modulation in a synthesizer is simple—something is changed by something else, usually in real time. Conventionally, a *source* will modulate a *destination*. So if we think about vibrato, a low-frequency oscillator would act as the source, and the pitch would be the destination.

Before we get to the detail, let's think about an acoustic instrument, such as the piano. Taking a simplistic view, the factors that have an effect on the sound are:

- Velocity
- Pitch
- Time

Effect of Velocity on a Sound

Velocity is another way to describe loudness, which in the case of a keyboard would be determined by how hard the key is hit. With MIDI we have 127 levels of loudness—this range is called *velocity*.

If you look at an acoustic piano, the velocity (the loudness) of a note has an effect in three main areas:

- The volume—there is a direct link between the volume and how hard a note is struck.
- The tone—the harder the key is hit, the brighter the tone, although the range of tones between the softest and the loudest notes may not be as dramatic as the volume differences.
- The sustain time of the note—the louder the note, the longer it sustains.

Effect of Key Pitch on a Sound

Clearly, the piano keyboard controls the pitch of the note played. However, there are other factors affected by the pitch:

- The tone—the higher the note, the brighter it sounds.
- The sustain time of the note—the higher the note, the less time it sustains.

Effect of Time on a Sound

The length of time that a note is held is also a factor in the tone of a piano. Over time:

- The sound will get duller (however bright it may have been initially).

- The volume will decay until it finally reaches zero.

Combining the Effect of Velocity, Pitch, and Time

A piano note is far more complex than may be suggested here. However, in broad terms you can see that:

- The initial volume of the note is affected by one factor only—velocity.

- Tone is affected by three factors—the initial velocity of the note, the pitch of the note, and the length of time it is held. However, you should also note that:
  - The tone *increases* in line with the increase in pitch (so the higher the note, the brighter it becomes).
  - But, the sustain time *decreases* in line with the increase in the pitch (so the higher the note, the less time that it sounds for).

- Sustain time (and also volume over time) is affected by two factors—the starting volume (which is in turn controlled by the initial velocity) and the pitch.

To mimic some of the behavior of an acoustic instrument, we need to use modulation to control a synthesizer.

Modulation Sources and Modulation Control Sources

There are many modulation sources within synthesizers—the most common are LFOs and envelopes, which we will look at in greater detail in later chapters. It is also possible for external sources to act as modulators—this is the case with velocity, the pitch bend wheel, and the modulation wheel, which are all dependent on the musician. However, as noted earlier in this chapter, controllers can be used either as modulation sources or as modulation source controllers. For instance:

- The modulation wheel could be used to control the filter cut-off—in this case, the modulation wheel would be acting as a modulation source.

- Equally, the modulation wheel could be used to control the amount of vibrato applied to a note by an LFO—in this case, the modulation wheel would be acting as the modulation source controller (in that it would be controlling the LFO depth).

Very often with modular synthesizers, when a modulation source is to be used as a modulation controller, its effect will be applied by way of a multiplier. So for instance, if you look back at SynthWiz Simple Synth, when we applied key tracking to the filter's cut-off frequency, we used a slider as the controller. This multiplied the effect of pitch, and the result was then applied to modulate the filter.

The main modulation sources are summarized in the following sections. We will be looking at the main tools in greater detail later in the book.

Velocity

Velocity is often used to control:

- The loudness of a note

- The tone of a note by modulating the filter cut-off

Velocity can be applied directly to modulate the destination, or it can be used as a modulation source controller to control another source (for instance, an envelope) that is modulating the destination. When velocity is used as a source controller, you can often achieve smoother results.

Envelopes

There are many things you can do with envelopes. If you apply the envelope to the filter negatively, it will close down the filter rather than open it up. Starting a note with the filter closed and then opening it quickly may be another useful technique if you are trying to simulate the "spit" of a brass instrument. For further simulation, you might also want to add a pitch-changing envelope at the start of a brass note.

Envelopes can act as modulation sources or can work as modulation controllers—a typical use as a modulation controller would be to slowly fade in and then fade out some LFO vibrato.

We will look at envelopes in greater detail in Chapter 6, "Modulation and Control."

Key Tracking

MIDI keyboards issue three main control messages:

- Note on—in other words, telling the synthesizer "play the note *now*" (when the key is pressed).

- Note off—in other words, telling the synthesizer "stop the note *now*" (when the key is lifted).

- Pitch. (You know what pitch is, right?)

From the pitch we can generate key tracking information. Key tracking is the process by which changes are made according to the pitch of a note.

For example, if you pluck the bottom E string of an acoustic guitar, the sound will last for more than 10 seconds. However, if you play the top E string at the highest fret, the sound will barely last for 3 seconds. With key tracking you can seamlessly control the length of an envelope to reflect the behavior of the acoustic instrument.

Key tracking can be applied in many ways—for instance, the cut-off point of a filter can be controlled by key tracking so that higher notes are brighter than lower notes.

Pitch Bend and Modulation Wheels

Most keyboards also have a pitch bend and modulation wheel (and sometimes more), which can be used both as modulation sources and as modulation controllers:

- A pitch bend wheel can generate positive and negative output. So for instance, it could open or close a filter (and it doesn't have to be permanently linked to the pitch of the sound).

- A modulation wheel only generates positive output, so it could be used either to open a filter or to close a filter, but not both at the same time.

XY Controllers

XY controllers allow you to control two destinations from one controller. As suggested earlier in this chapter, you could control a filter's cut-off frequency and the filter's resonance simultaneously. Alternatively, you could mix the output of four oscillators.

XY pads can work as a modulation source or as a modulation source controller.

Aftertouch

If your keyboard (or other MIDI controller) gives aftertouch messages, then the pressure on the keyboard while notes are sustained can be used to control your patch. You could, for instance, use aftertouch to control volume to give a swell to a held string chord.

Aftertouch can be applied directly to modulate the destination, or it can be used as a modulation source controller to control another source that is modulating the destination.

MIDI Control Change

Some MIDI keyboards also have separate knobs or sliders that output MIDI control changes. These changes can be assigned to control specific features within a synthesizer. Another common source of MIDI control messages is automation envelopes within a sequencer.

Modulation Destinations

So now we've got our range of modulators (and controllers). What can we mess with? What can we modulate when we come to building synthesizer sounds?

Here are some of the more common modulation destinations. Of course, because we're working in the modular world, we can pretty well modulate anything—the only limitation on modulation is your imagination, so regard this list as a starting point and not a boundary to your sonic experimentation.

Volume

Volume is likely to be one of the main destinations you modulate. You may want to:

- Control the volume of your whole patch—for instance, to make the patch touch sensitive or to add a tremolo effect.

- Control the volume of individual oscillators and elements so you can cross-fade between two sounds.

Filter

The two main modulation destinations in the filter block are:

- The cut-off frequency

- The resonance

Often musicians will want to control both in real time—the cut-off frequency to make a sound brighter or duller and the resonance to add some sharpness and bite to the sound. Equally, depending on your particular filter choice, there may be other features that you want to modulate—for instance, the separation of the filters (which is explained later in the book).

Pitch

The effects that can be obtained by modulating pitch include vibrato and trills as well as weird special effects. Subtle pitch modulation is also important when trying to mimic the properties of natural instruments. For instance, a slight and very short rise in pitch at the start of a note will often help re-create part of the attack of a brass instrument or a plucked string instrument.

Envelopes and LFOs are often used as modulation sources. When using an LFO to introduce vibrato, you will find that because LFO vibrato usually has a fixed frequency, the effect will quickly sound mechanical. Reducing the depth of the effect helps to stop some of the mechanical feel from becoming too prominent.

However, as I keep saying, we are in the modular world here, so we can control the modulator. Taking vibrato as an example, you could choose to control the vibrato speed and vibrato depth in real time (perhaps by hooking up an XY controller).

Pulse-Width

A fast way to change the tone of an oscillator or to fatten up a sound is to play with the pulse-width modulation. We will look at this when we look at sound sources.

Pan

The classic use for panning is auto-pan types of effects, where the sound moves regularly between the left and right channels. There are, however, more subtle uses of panning. For instance, panning can be related to the pitch of a note, with low notes panned toward the left and higher notes toward the right, as if you were sitting in front of a piano.

CPU Considerations

When creating a synthesizer or a patch, one of the key considerations is the CPU consumption. With most modern computers, it is unusual to need to worry about the CPU hit when creating a sound. However, when that sound is then used within the context of a musical performance where there will be other things happening on the host computer (such as other synthesizers running, effects being processed, audio being played, and so on), the CPU hit becomes a big issue.

Each of the featured synthesizers has been optimized to use the minimum necessary CPU, but they will still use CPU, and certain features will use more CPU than others.

The main CPU munchers are:

- The sound sources—the oscillators

- The filters

Regular oscillators and regular filters won't chew up too much of your system's resources, but when you start using specialized units (such as analog-emulating oscillators, oscillators making numerous real-time transformations to the waveform, and filters with steep cut-off slopes), then the CPU meter will rise sharply.

As a very rough rule of thumb, control elements and modulation elements will not use much CPU. Generally, control elements use close to zero CPU except where the element is being moved. Modulation elements use some CPU (as they are often dynamic). However, some modulation elements, in particular LFOs, can use nearly as much CPU as a regular oscillator. (After all, an LFO is just another oscillator.)

Very often, when you are building a synthesizer, you will be able to reduce your CPU hit by a noticeable amount by reducing the number of oscillators, using a less intensive oscillator structure, using a less steep filter, sharing filters, or using a combination of these strategies.

Synthesizer Construction Basics

The remainder of this chapter is an introduction to creating sounds by hooking up modules in the four featured synthesizers.

There is no right way and there is no wrong way to create a synthesizer/synthesizer sound. There may be more or less logical processes to follow, but in practice, it is an organic, evolving process. As you add more components and tweak the sound, you will want to add more and tweak more. Very rarely will you be able to sit down and design a synthesizer from the beginning to the end without going back and adding some elements, so please do not be misled by the fact that I know exactly what I am doing here. There are only two reasons for my design certainty:

- First, I am writing a book. That gives me the luxury of being able to go back and set out the process that I would have followed had I gotten it right first time. And of course, because this is a book, I can keep editing until I get the process right.

- Second, the synthesizers/sounds that we will be building in the remainder of this chapter are based on a synthesizer that I have already built (SynthWiz Simple Synth), and I am fully conversant with the architecture of that synthesizer.

In practice, when you come to build a sound, very often there will be a lot of playing around until suddenly you find a sound you like. You will then keep tweaking to hone in on that sound. That's fine—and you'll find that's how a lot of people program (myself included a lot of the time). However, if you want to be a bit more structured, then the process will probably be more like this:

1. Open the main audio path elements.

2. Hook up the audio path.

3. Open the modulation elements and make the modulation connections.

4. Add any controls that are needed.

5. Add visual feedback (as necessary).

6. Tweak.

7. Save.

Of course, this path will never be followed exactly, and there will be a lot of circling around, but you get the general idea.

Reconstructing SynthWiz Simple Synth

Hopefully you've got an idea of the process. Let's now take that concept and look at what it means in practice; this is the template we will follow as we replicate the synthesizer with these other tools.

Audio Path

The first step is to gather the main elements on the audio path and connect them. For the SynthWiz Simple Synth (see Figure 3.1), we need:

- A sound source

- A filter

- An amplifier

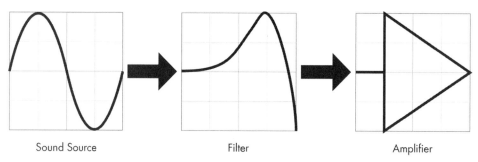

Figure 3.1 The basic audio path in SynthWiz Simple Synth.

Inputs and Outputs

Having hooked up the audio path, the next step is to add the inputs and the outputs (see Figure 3.2). In this case we will need to add:

- A MIDI input to trigger the synth

- An audio output to connect the synth to the outside world

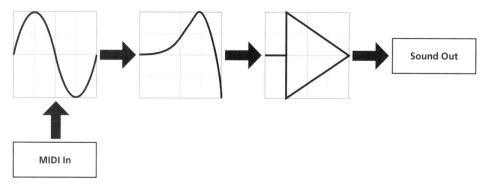

Figure 3.2 Adding the input and the output.

Basic Controls

The next step is to add in some very basic controls to the filter block (see Figure 3.3):

- The filter cut-off control

- The resonance control

Modulation Envelopes

Envelopes need to be added to control the filter and amplifier in real time (see Figure 3.4). These are often called *modulation envelopes* because they "modulate" (in other words, change) elements on the audio path.

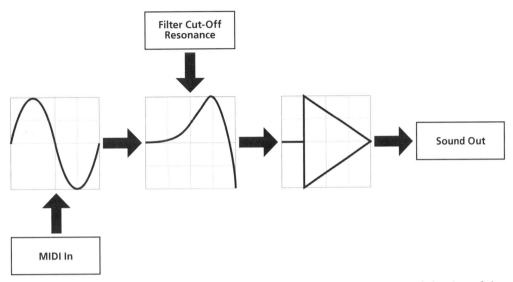

Figure 3.3   Adding the filter cut-off and resonance controls to allow some manual shaping of the tone.

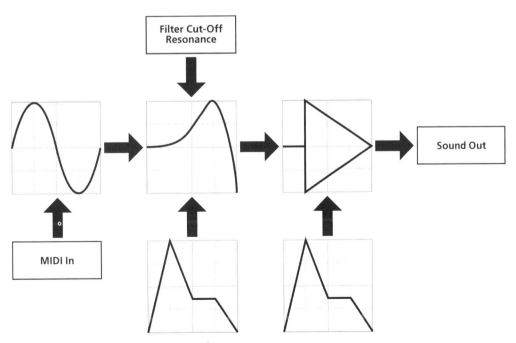

Figure 3.4   Adding the modulation envelopes.

Modulation Envelope Controls

Now that you have added the envelopes, they need to be controlled, and their use needs to be controlled (see Figure 3.5). This requires a number of sliders and some other controls:

- First, the MIDI input needs to be connected to the envelopes so that they trigger (in other words, start to play) when a note is struck (or other MIDI data is received).

- Next, the attack time, decay time, sustain level, and release time sliders need to be hooked up for each envelope.

- Lastly, the envelope depth control, which governs the extent to which the envelope has an effect on the filter, needs to be hooked up. This depth control function is performed by the Cut-Off Envelope slider in SynthWiz Simple Synth.

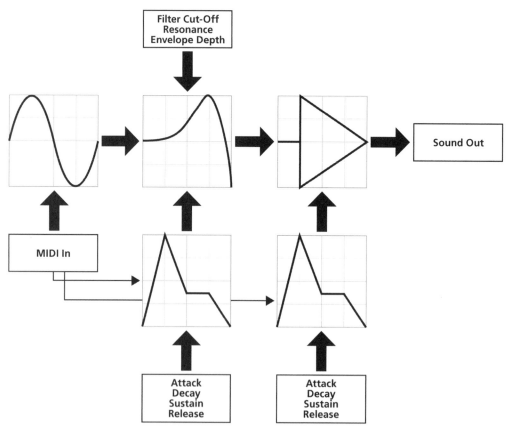

Figure 3.5 Attaching the envelope controls.

Volume

The final step (see Figure 3.6) is to attach:

- The volume control
- The output meter

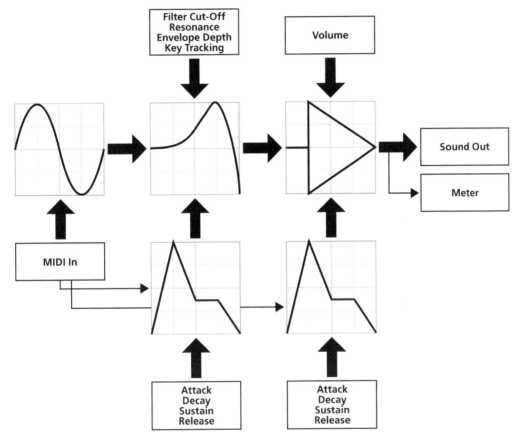

Figure 3.6   The finished synthesizer with the volume slider and output meter attached.

The Finished Synthesizer

And that's it…that's all you need to do to build a single sound.

I'm now going to move on and apply this methodology in each of the synthesizers to build a patch that replicates the functionality of SynthWiz Simple Synth. We're going to build the same sound four times, so to a certain extent there is some duplication/repetition here. However, each of the synthesizers works in a different way, and you'll find that the process is different for each of them. Equally, by undertaking the process for four synthesizers, you will get four separate perspectives on sound construction that may be applied to other synthesizers. That being said, if you get bored easily and you're only using one of the featured synthesizers, then you may want to look only at the section for that synthesizer and then move on to the next chapter.

Construction with Zebra 2

Of the featured synthesizers, in many ways Zebra 2 is the easiest to use. The reasons for this are:

- You don't need to connect the audio or MIDI inputs and output—Zebra 2 does this for you automatically.

- You don't need to connect the audio path—Zebra 2 does this for you automatically. But Zebra 2 does give you the flexibility to change (and keeping changing) things around.

- Once you've put your modules in place, attaching controls and modulators is then straightforward.

Loading Modules in Zebra 2

There's an initialization patch in Zebra 2 that is pretty close to SynthWiz Simple Synth, so I'm going to start with my own completely blank patch called –empty– (see Figure 3.7). As you can see, this has the Zebra 2 framework, but there are no modules.

In the central strip of Zebra 2, there is a matrix. In Figure 3.7, this matrix is empty. To load a module, click on the matrix, and a drop-down menu will appear (see Figure 3.8). From this drop-down menu you can select the module you want to load by clicking on it. I selected OSC1.

You can repeat the click-and-select process until all of your audio modules are selected. For this sound, the other module I selected was a filter—in this case, I selected VCF1, leaving the patch looking like Figure 3.9.

As a next step after loading the modules, I then selected the Saw Bright wave. I did this by clicking on the "default" label to the left of OSC1, which brought up the oscillator list (see Figure 3.10). From there, I selected the wave and then clicked on the close button (at the top right of the oscillator selection box).

Hooking Up the Audio Path in Zebra 2

If you look at Figure 3.9, you will see that OSC1 is in the top-left box, and VCF1 is in the next box down. These modules are located in those boxes because that is where I clicked before I made the selection from the menu. If you mis-select the location for any module, you can always click and drag the modules around.

The facility to drag modules is highly significant. There are four columns in the matrix, and the audio path passes from the top to the bottom. You can reorder the audio path—to connect, disconnect, and reorder modules—by dragging them in the matrix.

So, with the order in which I have placed the OSC1 module and the VCF1 module, I have replicated the structure in SynthWiz Simple Synth.

Figure 3.7 A completely empty patch in Zebra 2.

You will also see that there is a downward line under VCF1—this represents the audio path, which then passes to a volume control that mixes this audio flow. As there are four columns, there are four audio flows.

In the bottom row, you will see a knob marked Output. This performs the same function as the Volume control in SynthWiz Simple Synth and sets the output level for the whole synthesizer.

As a side issue, you can flow audio from one column to another; however, this operation is beyond the scope of this chapter. If you're really curious, you can check out the manual (or check out Chapter 9, "Creating Sounds").

Attaching the Modulators in Zebra 2

The process for attaching modulation sources is interesting (and intuitive) in Zebra 2. Instead of loading a module and then attaching it, you:

1. Identify the destination that should be modulated.

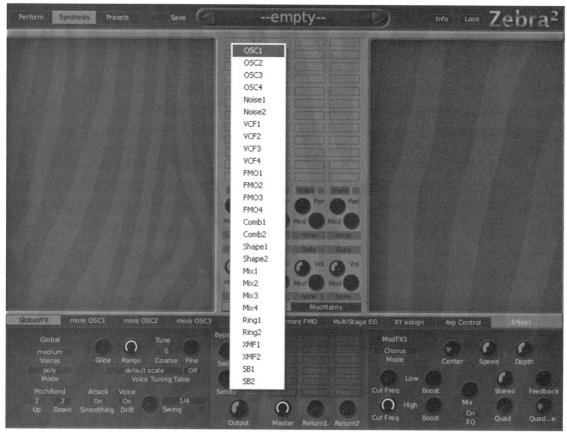

Figure 3.8 Module selection in Zebra 2.

2. Select the modulation source.

3. Dial in the depth of modulation.

So, to hook up Envelope 1 so that it can control the cut-off frequency of VCF1, thereby mimicking the Cut-Off Envelope in SynthWiz Simple Synth, the procedure is:

■ On VCF1, to the right of the Cut-Off and Resonance knobs, there are two blank controls. Click on the left of these and select Env1 from the menu (see Figure 3.11).

■ The control on which you clicked to access the menu is the knob that will now set the depth of the envelope's effect on the filter's cut-off frequency. This is equivalent to the Cut-Off Envelope slider in the Filter block on SynthWiz Simple Synth.

Figure 3.9 Zebra 2 after the audio units have been loaded. You will notice that LFO1 has been loaded on the right—this automatically happens in Zebra 2 when you load an oscillator (even though it won't be used in this patch).

By the way, if you look at the VCF1 module, to the right of the two blank assignable controls, there in a knob labeled KEYTRACK. This performs the same function undertaken by the Key Tracking slider in SynthWiz Simple Synth. This function comes as part of the module, so we don't need to load it or assign it separately.

At the bottom of the audio channel in the matrix, immediately above the Vol knob, is the label "Gate." If you click on that, a menu will appear, as Figure 3.12 shows. Select Env2, and Envelope 2 will load and operate in the same manner that the Volume Envelope operates in SynthWiz Simple Synth.

As you selected the two envelopes, these were loaded into the right-hand side of the Zebra 2 interface (see Figure 3.13). This is a useful separation: The audio chain is in the left-hand panel, and the modulation chain is in the right-hand panel.

Figure 3.10   Loading a wave in Zebra 2.

Saving in Zebra 2

We have now replicated SynthWiz Simple Synth in Zebra 2. All that remains is to save the sound (and to start messing with the controls to create sounds, of course).

To save the sound, click on the Save button (on the top bar, to the left of the Save label). This will bring up a dialog box similar to the one shown in Figure 3.14.

This dialog box allows you to:

- Name the preset

- Identify the author (the creator)

- Give a description of the preset

- Make some notes/suggestions about the usage

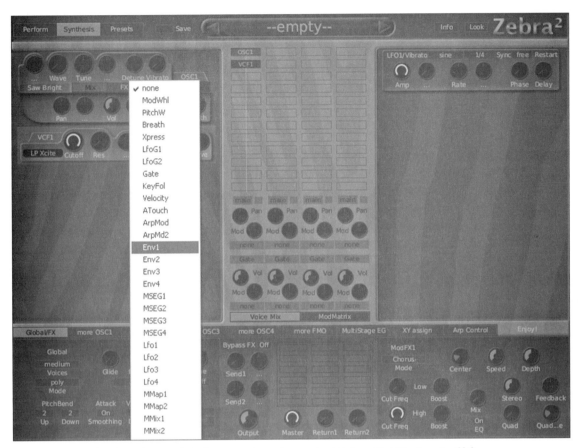

Figure 3.11 Selecting the modulation envelope to control Zebra 2's filter's cut-off frequency.

As you start to design more complicated sounds, these descriptions and usage notes will become increasingly useful (especially if you share your sounds with other people).

Construction with VAZ Modular

VAZ Modular is a classic "modules-and-wires" emulation of an analog modular synth. While there are connections between the modules, the interface does not show the wires—instead, the connections are exposed in a far easier way (which is very intuitive for the musician).

To get started with patch construction in VAZ Modular, we need a blank canvas, which can be called up by selecting File > New Bank. As Figure 3.15 shows, this will call up a mixer and an empty "synthesizer." In VAZ Modular, each bank allows you to have several synthesizers open at one time, which can then all be pushed through a single mixer.

Figure 3.12   Selecting the volume envelope in Zebra 2.

Loading Modules in VAZ Modular

For this example, I'm not worried about the mixer, so I closed it down. My focus is on the synthesizer we are going to create in the area labeled Synth 1 "New Patch" (which, incidentally, is resizable by dragging the edges).

To add a module:

1.   Right-click in the patch area.

2.   Select a module from the drop-down menu (see Figure 3.16).

Having loaded an oscillator, the next step is to load a filter and an amplifier. This is achieved by the same process of right-clicking and selecting from the menu. You will see that the menu is

Figure 3.13 The modules to replicate SynthWiz Simple Synth loaded in Zebra 2.

grouped into categories and the modules are selected from submenus. The categories are quite logical/intuitive:

- MIDI to CV
- Audio Sources
- Audio Processing
- Modulation Sources
- Mod Processing
- Routing
- Effects
- Visualization

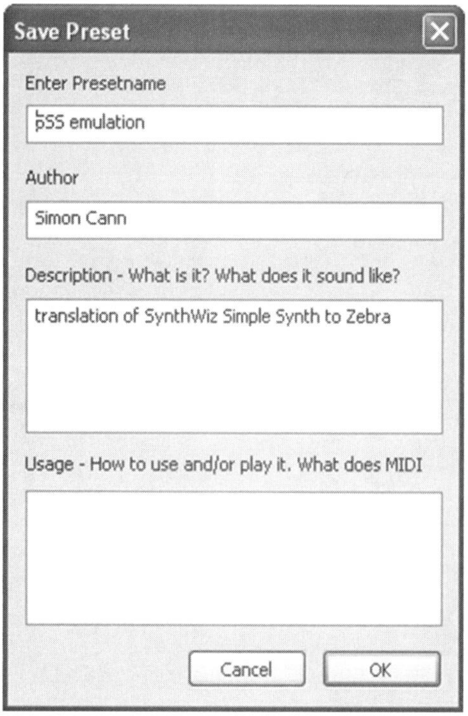

Figure 3.14 The Save Preset dialog box in Zebra 2.

Some of these categories will already be familiar, while others may not. I will explain the less familiar categories later in the book. For the moment, we will be focusing on the first four categories, and in particular, the Audio Sources category (where the oscillator module was located) and the Audio Processing category (where the amplifier and filter modules were located).

With VAZ Modular, you can move the modules around by dragging—the location of each module has no impact on the audio path. So, after a bit of dragging, I was left with four modules looking like Figure 3.17.

Hooking Up the Audio Path in VAZ Modular

At this stage, with four modules loaded, VAZ Modular does not make any noise, unlike Zebra 2. This is not altogether surprising, as we haven't hooked up the audio connections yet.

If you look at the Filter and the Amplifier modules, the first line under the heading is labeled Input, and next to that is a box showing None. This is telling us that there is no input to these units (hence sound is not passing through). The Master Controls unit does not have an input marked; instead, there are Left and Right—these are the inputs for the left and right channels.

To make the audio connection:

1.   Click on the box next to the input label—a drop-down menu will appear (see Figure 3.18).

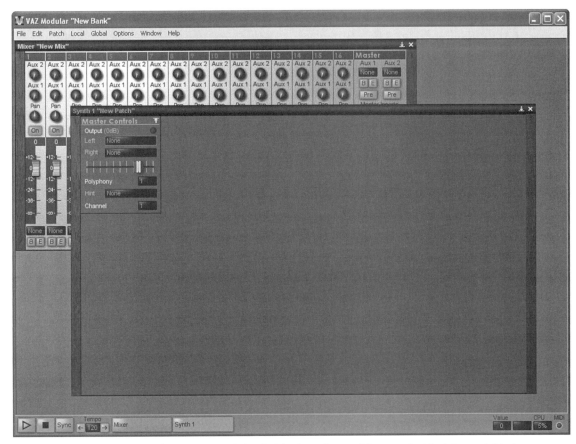

Figure 3.15 An empty patch in VAZ Modular (with the mixer poking out behind the patch). As you can see, the patch is empty apart from the Master Controls output unit. You will note that I am running the stand-alone version of VAZ Modular.

2. Select the appropriate audio source. For the filter, I selected Oscillator 1 Saw.

3. Repeat for each module that needs connecting.

The drop-down menu reflects the number of modules you have loaded, so as you load more, the list will get longer. You will note that although we have only loaded one oscillator, there were two oscillator options:

- Oscillator 1 Saw

- Oscillator 1 Pulse

This particular module only outputs two waves: a sawtooth wave and a pulse wave. These are both output simultaneously. There is no switch on the module to select between the two—instead, you need to select the appropriate wave as part of the audio routing.

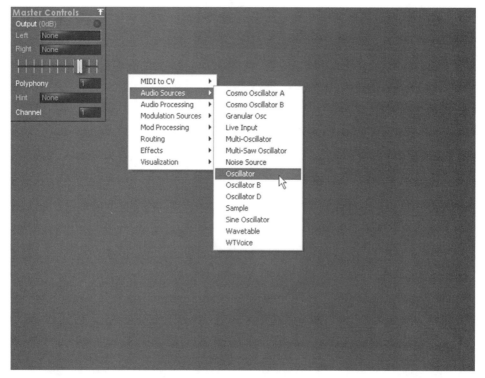

Figure 3.16 Loading a module—in this instance, one of the oscillator options—in VAZ Modular.

For this SynthWiz Simple Synth emulation, these were the audio routings I selected for the modules:

- Oscillator 1 Saw was set as the input for Filter 1.

- Filter 1 was set as the input for Amplifier 1.

- Amplifier 1 was set for both left and right in the Master Controls.

When you hook up those connections, you will see something that looks like Figure 3.19. You will also notice something else: sound.

This sound is quite annoying! I suggest you turn it down by adjusting the slider on the Master Controls module. This will give you some peace until you can do something sensible about the racket. By the way, that slider performs the equivalent function to the Volume slider in SynthWiz Simple Synth.

You might notice something else about the sound: Its pitch is fixed. It does not respond to incoming MIDI messages. Again, this is not surprising because we haven't connected the incoming MIDI messages to the synthesizer.

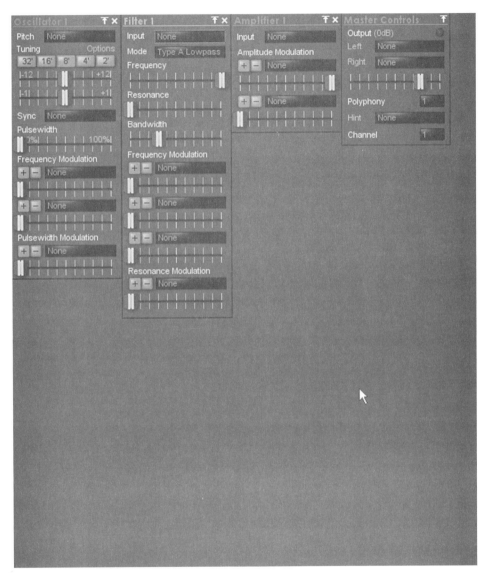

Figure 3.17 VAZ Modular with the audio path modules loaded.

In the good old days, when analog reigned supreme and there was no digital sound, synthesizers used *control voltage* to control their pitch. In other words, pitch was directly related to voltage. So, as an example, two volts may equate to the note C2, and four volts may equate to the C3 note (which is one octave higher). Don't get too hung up on the relationship between volts and pitch—not least because there were several different, largely incompatible, implementations. For our purposes, all we need to understand is that there was a connection between volts and pitch.

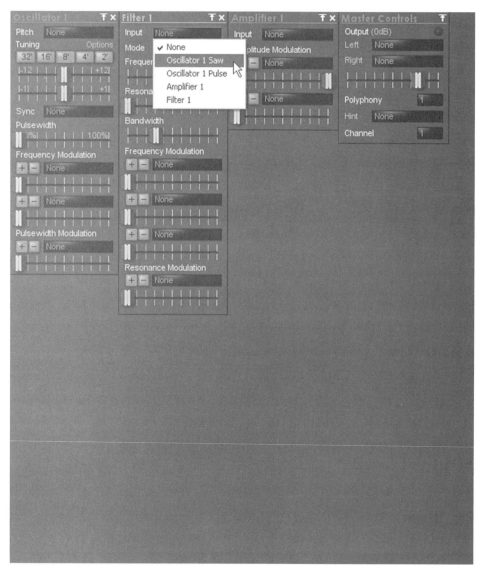

Figure 3.18 Connecting the oscillator to the filter in VAZ Modular.

To make our synthesizer react to incoming MIDI data (such as notes played on a keyboard), we need something that will:

- Respond to incoming MIDI data

- Convert the MIDI pitch information into volts (albeit digital volts within the framework of this software synthesizer)

- Pass those volts to the oscillator to control the pitch

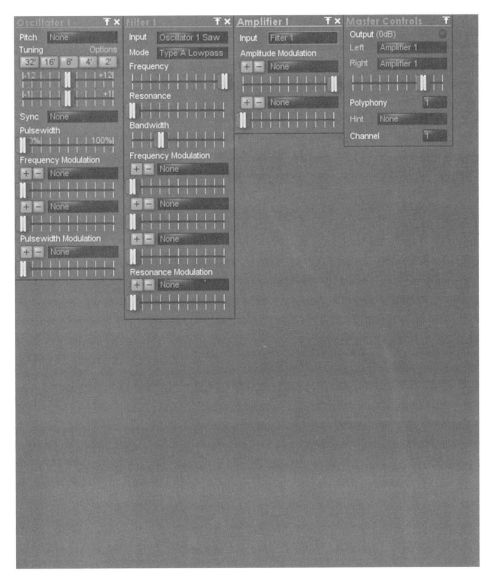

Figure 3.19   A group of audio modules connected within VAZ Modular.

Luckily, VAZ Modular supplies just such a module. It is called CV Converter, and it is accessed by right-clicking on the patch and selecting MIDI to CV > CV Converter from the pop-up menu.

To hook this up, in Oscillator 1, click in the box next to the Pitch label and select CV 1 Note Low (or CV 1 Note High). This should give you something looking like Figure 3.20.

If you slide up the volume in the Master Controls, you will still have a very annoying sound, but it will respond to incoming pitch information (and will leave the last note you played to continue to sound).

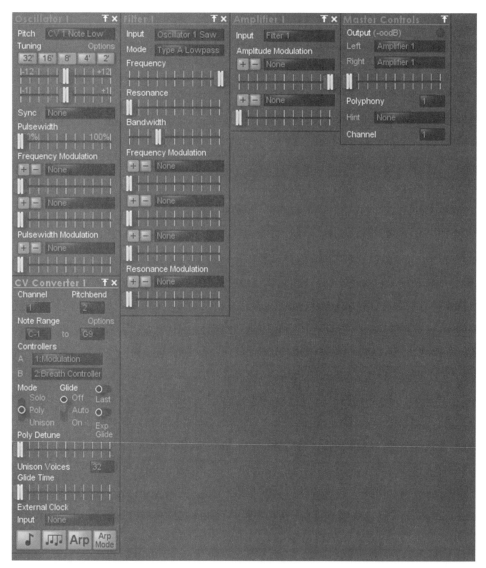

Figure 3.20 VAZ Modular with the CV Converter connected. You will see that I still have the volume in the Master Controls set to zero.

At the moment, you can play only one note at a time. That is probably not a bad thing given that we can't switch the notes off (except by using the Volume slider). When more than one note is played simultaneously, then the lower note will sound. If we had selected CV 1 Note High as the pitch source, then the higher note would've sounded. If you want to play more than one note, then in the Master Controls module, click on the Polyphony indicator. A pop-up menu will appear, from which you can select the maximum number of notes that can be played simultaneously. However, I don't recommend that you do this at present since *all* of those notes will keep sounding until you do something to stop the notes.

Attaching the Modulators in VAZ Modular

We're getting close to turning the notes off (or rather, taking control over the notes away from the machine and giving it to the musician). Before we can sort that problem, we need to add some envelopes. As you might have guessed, you can load these up by right-clicking on the patch and selecting Modulation Sources > Envelope from the pop-up menu. Do this twice to load up two envelopes.

These are ADSR (attack time, decay time, sustain level, release time) envelopes. We are going to set Envelope 1 to modulate (in other words, control) the cut-off frequency in the filter and Envelope 2 to modulate the amplitude (the level) in the amplifier. To do this:

1. In the first slot of the Frequency Modulation section of the filter, select Envelope 1 as the modulation source.

2. In the first slot of the Amplitude Modulation section of the amplifier, select Envelope 2 as the modulation source.

You will notice that under the slots where you selected the modulation source, there is a slider. (There is a separate slider for each of the slots.) These sliders are depth controls that set the extent to which the modulation source will affect the destination. For the filter, this works in the same way as the Cut-Off Envelope in SynthWiz Simple Synth's Filter block. There is no analogous control for the amplifier's depth slider, but I'm sure you get the idea about how it works.

You will notice that by default, the depth control in the filter is set to zero, and the depth control in the amplifier is set to the maximum. While there is no analogous depth slider in SynthWiz Simple Synth, that synthesizer has been designed so that the volume envelope has full control over the amplifier (which would be equivalent to setting the depth control to the maximum and then gluing the control in place).

By the way, did you notice something when you attached Envelope 2? The sound has now stopped. Even if you play a note, there is no sound (and don't forget to turn up the Volume slider just to be sure).

While this lack of sound is good—we've gotten rid of that annoying buzz—a synthesizer that doesn't make any noise is a bit pointless. So now that we've attached the envelopes, we need to do something to tell the envelopes when the note is triggered and when the note ends so that we can hear some sounds.

If you look at the envelopes, where the audio modules have their input routing, you will see that there are two options (which access drop-down menus):

- **Gate.** The gate is the instruction to the envelope to begin its cycle.

- **Trigger.** The trigger is the source that instructs the envelope to begin its cycle again while the preceding note is still held.

To hook up the gate and trigger in both envelopes, set:

- Gate to CV 1 Gate

- Trig to CV 1 Trig

Now when you hit a key, you will hear a sound.

We've now hooked up a bunch of modules. One smart thing that VAZ Modular lets us do is rename the modules. This allows us to give them helpful names, so:

- Instead of Envelope 1, I have renamed Envelope 1 as Filter Envelope.

- Instead of Envelope 2, I have renamed Envelope 2 as Amplifier Env. By the way, I'm not lazy—I would have typed Amplifier Envelope in full, but VAZ Modular limits the number of letters you can have.

When the modules are renamed, the corresponding names in the modules that are being modulated are changed, too. This is very helpful.

The process to rename the modules is straightforward:

1. Right-click on the module.

2. A pop-up menu will appear. Select the last option, Rename.

3. Rename the module and click OK.

One final tweak that is needed to replicate the functionality of SynthWiz Simple Synth is the addition of a control to replicate the Key Tracking slider. The purpose of this function is to link the pitch of the incoming note to the filter cut-off.

We already have sufficient modules loaded—all we need to do to add this functionality is wire up the modulation. In the filter, in the second modulation slot, select CV 1 Note High. And that's it—the modulation is in place, and its depth will be controlled by the slider under the slot.

Figure 3.21 shows the patch with the renamed envelopes hooked up and the key tracking put in place.

Saving in VAZ Modular

Saving sounds in VAZ Modular is simple. Select File > Save Patch As, give the patch a name, and click OK. As with Zebra 2, you can add a description about the patch and details of the patch designer (see Figure 3.22).

If you want to add a note (as is shown in Figure 3.21—however, the name of the module has been changed from Text to Notes), then right-click and select Visualization > Text.

A copy of the final patch (called SSS Emulation) is available for download.

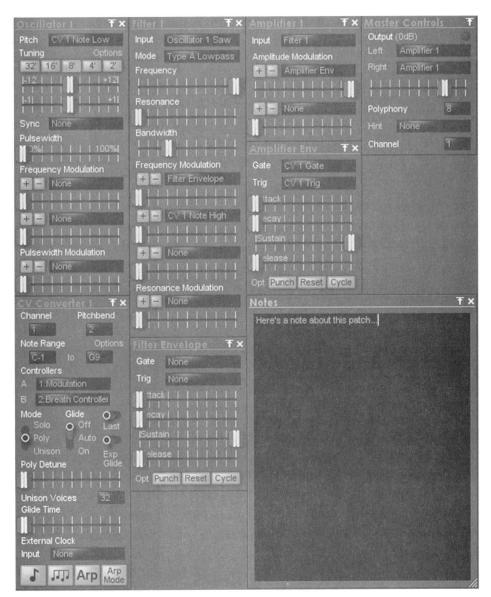

Figure 3.21 VAZ Modular set to play sounds. You can see that the Polyphony selector has been set to 8, allowing up to eight notes to be played simultaneously; a (text) note has also been added; and the interface size has been rescaled to remove the unused space.

Construction with KarmaFX Synth Modular

KarmaFX Synth Modular has many similarities to VAZ Modular. In particular, it takes a modules-and-wires approach to creating sounds. However, unlike VAZ Modular, with KarmaFX Synth Modular, you can see the wires (and the modulation paths). Not only that, but you can choose whether those wires are straight, curved, or bouncy. I've stuck with straight.

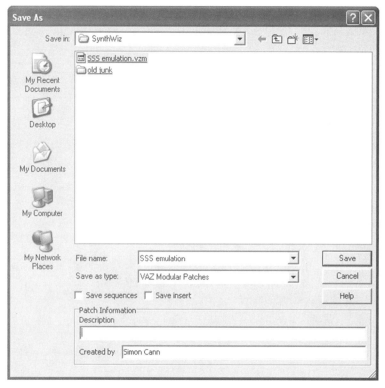

Figure 3.22   The Save As dialog in VAZ Modular.

Loading Modules in KarmaFX Synth Modular

In KarmaFX Synth Modular, most things start with a right-click, which opens a pop-up menu (see Figure 3.23).

To create a new patch, right-click and select New Patch. This will open a submenu with four options:

- **Empty Patch.** This is the patch loaded in Figure 3.23. As you can see, it is quite spartan, only having an Output module.

- **Simple Patch.** The simple patch that is created is similar to the patch we are going to create to emulate SynthWiz Simple Synth. However, just opening that patch wouldn't show you how I created the sound, so I'm going to ignore that option.

- **Simple Sampler.** The simple sampler is another simple sound, but the sound source is a sample loader (to allow for samples to be manipulated). This is a highly useful feature, but not one that we're going to use (at the moment).

- **Simple Effect.** The simple effect option allows you to create an audio effect within KarmaFX Synth Modular. This allows you to process sounds through the synthesis tools, such as the filter, and also to use the built-in effects to process sounds.

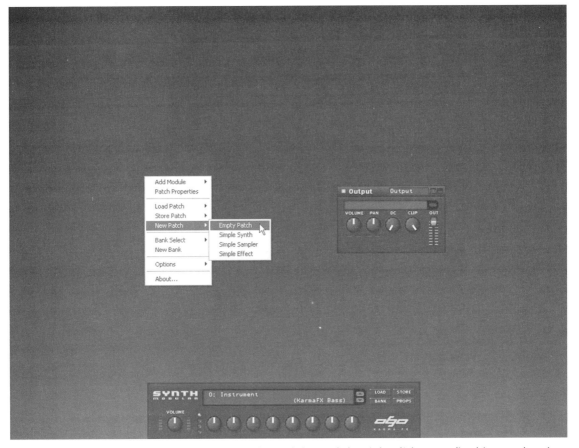

Figure 3.23 An empty patch in KarmaFX Synth Modular and the right-click menu (in this case showing how this empty patch was created).

You will also see that there is the master control unit at the bottom of the interface. To the left of this block is the Volume knob, which performs the same function as the Volume slider in SynthWiz Simple Synth (in other words, it controls the volume of the whole sound).

Now that we've got our empty patch, let's load up the modules. Right-click and select:

- Add Modules > Generator > Osc 1
- Add Modules > Filter > SVF
- Add Modules > Amplifier > Amplifier
- Add Modules > Controller > Note Pitch

You will notice that we have loaded a Controller module. Although this is not strictly part of the audio path, its use will become clear when we hook up the audio units.

Also, if you look at the filter, you will see a knob labeled Kybd. This knob controls key tracking and performs the same function as the Key Tracking slider in SynthWiz Simple Synth. Because it comes with the module, we don't need to take any further action to set up this function.

Hooking Up the Audio Path in KarmaFX Synth Modular

There are two ways to hook up the audio path (and join the other controllers/modulators) in KarmaFX Synth Modular.

Once you have hooked up two (or more) modules, the connection wires will be visible (unless the two joined modules are side by side, obscuring the wires), and there will be an arrow on the connection wire pointing from the source to the destination. It doesn't show up very well in grayscale, but you will see on the interface that:

■ Audio connections are denoted by a blue wire.

■ Modulation connections are denoted by an olive (greeny/brown, maybe orange-ish) wire.

The modules can be located anywhere within the interface; their location has no effect on the audio path. However, the wires can seem quite complicated if the modules are not arranged in a logical order.

Using Menu Selection to Hook Up the Audio Path

The first way to hook up two modules is to right-click on the top bar of the module to which you want to link. So if you want to connect the oscillator to the filter, then right-click on the top bar of the filter. This will bring up a menu, which you can see in Figure 3.24.

Figure 3.24 Using the menu to hook up modules.

The menu will indicate the modules that can be linked to the current module. As you load more modules, the menu will get longer.

You can use this method to connect more than one module. You can also use this approach to change connections. If you don't want a connection, right-click on the top bar of the module, and click on the Input submenu, where you see a check mark (tick) next to the module you do not want to be connected. This will remove the check mark and the connection.

Using Mouse Click to Hook Up the Audio Path

The other approach to hooking up modules is to use your mouse:

1.   Press and hold down the Ctrl key.

2.   Click on the top bar of the source module. Your mouse cursor will change to a large cross (see Figure 3.25).

3.   Click on the top bar of the target module. The audio or modulation wire will show the connection.

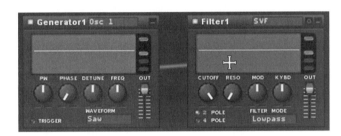

Figure 3.25   Using the mouse to connect modules in KarmaFX Synth Modular.

Audio Path for This Sound

Whichever way you choose to connect the modules, to create this sound you should connect the modules in the following order:

1.   Generator 1

2.   Filter 1

3.   Amplifier 1

4.   Controller 1

5.   Output

Note that the audio path goes through the Controller. This controls the pitch of the notes and so is rather important. Without this connection, the audio will pass, but you will probably only hear clicking from the oscillator turning over at a very low frequency.

In its current state, this patch is playable; however, we do still have some work to do. One thing you may notice is that you can only play one note at a time. To change this, on the Controller module, click on the Mode selector (at the bottom of the module). This will initially show Mono. From the pop-up menu, choose the maximum number of notes that can be played at one time. In Figure 3.26, you will see the connected modules—I have chosen Poly8, which gives a maximum of eight notes that can be played simultaneously.

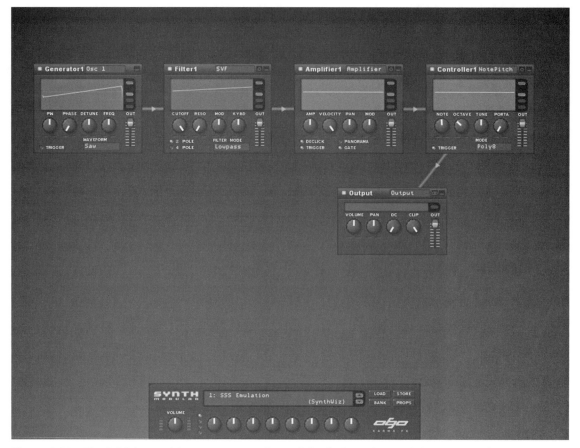

Figure 3.26 The initial sound in KarmaFX Synth Modular before the modulators are hooked up.

Attaching the Modulators in KarmaFX Synth Modular

You can probably guess how to add the envelopes: Right-click and select Add Module > Modulators > ADSR. Do that twice, and you will have two envelopes—one for the filter cut-off and one for the amplifier level.

Like when we hooked up the audio path, you can right-click and choose from a menu, or you can use your mouse. However, the modulation destination is slightly different. Unlike the audio path, we are not addressing the whole module. Instead, we are addressing a specific element of the module—the filter cut-off and the amplifier Amp level—so we need to be careful where we click. The following sections describe what you have to do.

Using Menu Selection to Hook Up the Modulation Envelopes

The first way to hook up the modulation is to right-click on the specific function to which you want to link. So if you want to modulate the filter cut-off with Envelope 1 (Modulator 1), then right-click on the Cut-Off knob in the filter. This will bring up a menu from which you can select Modulator 1.

Like when we hooked up the audio path, you can use this method to connect more than one modulation. You can also use this approach to change connections. If you don't want a connection, right-click on the knob and then click on the Input submenu, where you see a check mark (tick) next to the module you do not want to be connected. This will remove the check mark and the connection.

Using Mouse Click to Hook Up the Modulation Envelopes

The other approach to hooking up modules is to use your mouse:

1. Press and hold down the Ctrl key.

2. Click on the top bar of the source module. Your mouse cursor will change to a large cross.

3. Click on the target control in the target module. The modulation wire will show the connection.

When a knob function is modulated by another source (for instance, the cut-off is modulated by an envelope), the left LED under the modulated knob will light (in addition to the modulation wire showing up). You will notice that there is a second LED. This lights if the knob is also controlled by a MIDI source.

Controlling the Modulation Envelopes

When you have attached the modulation envelopes, you may find that your sound disappears or is replaced with a click. This is largely due to the default setting on the envelopes and their interaction with the filter and the amplifier. If this is the case, then on both the filter and the amplifier, set the Mod knob to zero. These knobs control the extent to which the respective envelopes modulate the cut-off or the amplifier. Alternatively, you could increase the sustain levels in the envelopes to their maximum.

By now, your patch should look something like Figure 3.27.

You may remember that with VAZ Modular, we had to connect trigger and gate signals. In KarmaFX Synth Modular, these functions are built into the amplifier, and a trigger is built into the envelope.

Saving in KarmaFX Synth Modular

Now that the patch is finished, it can be saved. You can give the patch a name, record the creator, and make some notes by either:

- Clicking on the Props button in the main block at the bottom

- Right-clicking and selecting Patch Properties

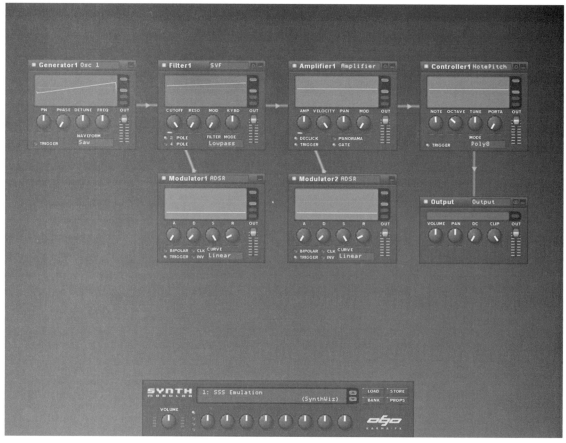

Figure 3.27 The finished SynthWiz Simple Synth emulation patch in KarmaFX Synth Modular.

In either event, you will get a dialog box similar to Figure 3.28.

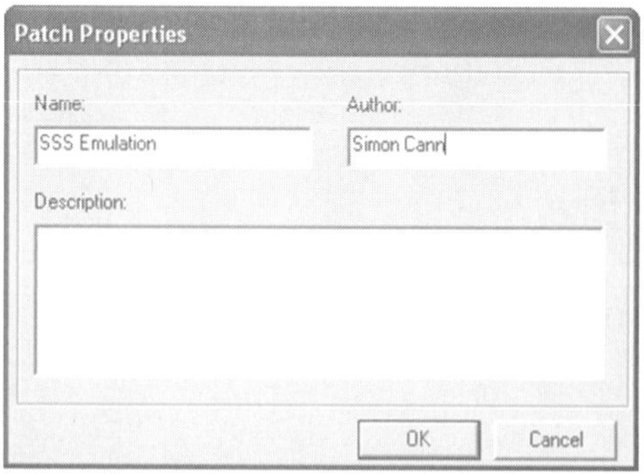

Figure 3.28 The Patch Properties box in KarmaFX Synth Modular.

To save a patch (once you have named it), click on the Store button in the main block. A list of all the patches in the current bank will appear. Click on the appropriate location where the patch should be stored, and it will be saved. If there is already a patch stored in that location, you will be asked to confirm whether you want to overwrite the existing patch.

By the way, if you want to create your own bank in KarmaFX Synth Modular, then go to the folder where your patches are stored (for me, this is C:\vsti\karma\KarmaFX\KarmaFX_ Synth\Patches, which is consistent with where I located the synthesizer's files) and look for the existing subfolders. Create your own subfolder, and the next time you open the synthesizer, the bank will be available to you (although it won't have any sounds in it until you put some there).

Construction with SynthEdit

The process for creating a synthesizer in SynthEdit is slightly different from the processes we have looked at so far. Instead of simply hooking up some wires and modules and hitting the Save button, with SynthEdit we will build freestanding synthesizers. Once finished, the synthesizers can then be used by anyone who can load Windows VSTi synthesizers. People who use the VSTi will not be able to "look under the hood" and adjust the settings—their only control over the synthesizer will be through the interface that we design.

This allows you to create hugely powerful synthesizers that do many complex things, but you can make the interface simple and intuitive for musicians, allowing them (or yourself) to focus on the music and not the mechanics.

So now the process we are going to follow will look something more like this:

1. Build the synthesizer—hook up the modules and wires.

2. Add sliders—these will be visible on the interface.

3. Label the sliders and set the ranges for the sliders and their initial settings.

4. Build the interface.

5. Export the finished synthesizer as a VSTi.

In practice, the process is not necessarily that sequential—you may go back and forth—but since the end product is a freestanding synthesizer, there is a tangible result that is not present with the purely modular synthesizers.

Saving in SynthEdit

With all of the other synthesizers, the last step after building the patch has been to then save the creation. With SynthEdit we are creating something more complex, so it is sensible to save as we go along, hence I am starting with saving. I will not make any further mention of this topic, but I do suggest you save this creation as we progress.

The process to save is as you would expect: File > Save (or File > Save As when you first go to save). These files are saved as SynthEdit files. While users cannot look under the hood and tweak a VSTi synthesizer, they can tweak to their heart's content if you share SynthEdit (.se1) files, and the .se1 file for this synthesizer is available to download from noisesculpture.com/synthwizdownloads.html (which is the same web address as the other downloads).

Loading Modules in SynthEdit

Before you start loading modules in SynthEdit, select File > New. This will create the blank canvas from which you can start to create your instrument. To load a module, right-click on the blank canvas and select the appropriate module from the Insert submenu of the pop-up menu (see Figure 3.29).

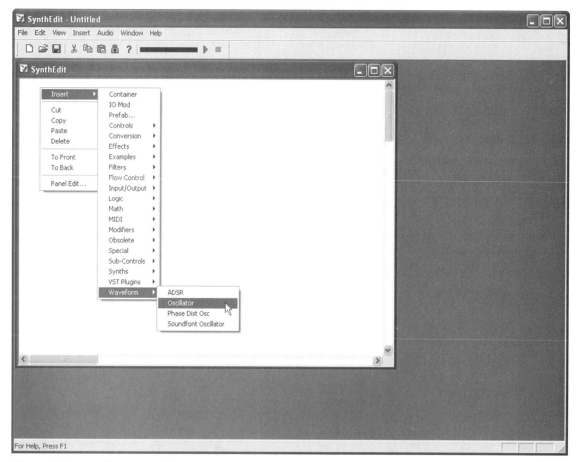

Figure 3.29   Loading a module in SynthEdit.

To create this synthesizer, we need the following modules:

- Insert > Waveform > Oscillator

- Insert > Filters > SV Filters

- Insert > Modifiers > VCA (a re-creation of a voltage controlled amplifier)

These modules will be used to create the synthesizer. However, while we are building the synthesizer, we will need some additional modules to connect up the MIDI input and audio output. These modules will not be part of the final synthesizer, but they are crucial if we are going to listen to the synthesizer as we build it. The modules we need are:

- Insert > MIDI > MIDI In

- Insert > MIDI > MIDI to CV

- Insert > Input/Output > Sound Out

The MIDI In unit is probably fairly self-evident, but the MIDI to CV module might be confusing (unless you read the earlier piece about the comparable module in VAZ Modular). In case you didn't read that piece, let me reiterate.

Analog synthesizers used to use a "control voltage" to control their pitch. With this system, pitch was directly related to voltage. As an example, two volts may equate to the note C2, and four volts may equate to the C3 note (which is one octave higher). Don't worry too much about the relationship between volts and pitch—all you need to understand is that there was a connection between volts and pitch.

To make our synthesizer react to incoming MIDI data (such as notes played on a keyboard), we need something that will:

- Respond to incoming MIDI data

- Convert the MIDI pitch information into volts (albeit digital volts within the framework of this software synthesizer)

- Pass those volts to the oscillator to control the pitch

That is the function of the MIDI to CV module.

If you read the earlier sections about re-creating this synthesizer with VAZ Modular, then you will have read about gate controls—in other words, signals that tell the synthesizer when a note starts and ends. The MIDI to CV module has a Gate output so that the appropriate messages can be passed within the synthesizer.

That's the explanation. By now, you should have something that looks like Figure 3.30.

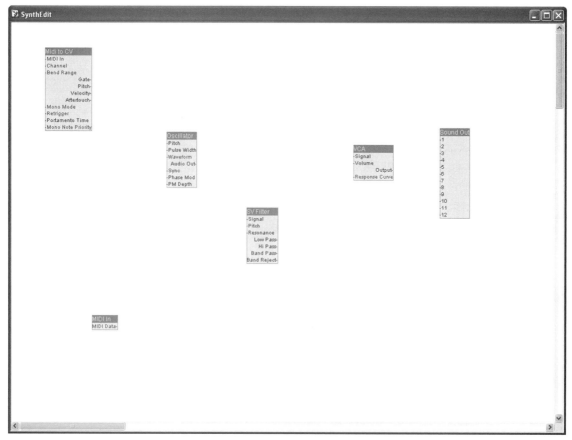

Figure 3.30 Our SynthEdit creation with the audio modules loaded. And yes, they do look rather spaced out; however, we need some room to add the other elements in this synthesizer.

Hooking Up the Audio Path in SynthEdit

There are two ways to hook up the audio path in SynthEdit:

- Using a mouse
- Choosing a menu selection

Using Menu Selection to Hook Up the Audio Path

To use menu selection to hook up the audio path in SynthEdit, the first step is to right-click on the module *from* which you wish to connect. This will open a pop-up menu, from which you should select the first item, Connect. You will then be presented with a dialog box similar to that shown in Figure 3.31.

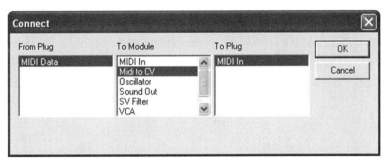

Figure 3.31   The Connect dialog box. In this case, the connection is from the MIDI In module.

The Connect dialog box presents three columns:

- **From Plug.** The From Plug column lists all of the output plugs on the selected module—you can click to select the appropriate output plug. In the case of the MIDI In module shown in Figure 3.31, there is only one output plug, the MIDI Data plug.

- **To Module.** The To Module column lists all of the available modules that you can connect to, including the source module (if it has an input). Click on the appropriate list item to select the destination module.

- **To Plug.** Once you have selected the destination module, the To Plug column will display a list of input plugs for the selected destination module to which the source module's selected plug can be connected. You can select the appropriate item by clicking on it. As you can see in Figure 3.31, the module I selected—the MIDI to CV module—only has one relevant input, the MIDI In plug.

You can review and change your selection. When you are happy with the connection, click on the OK button, and the connection will be made. You will see that a wire is added to show the connection.

Using Mouse Click to Hook Up the Audio Path
The alternate course to hook up the audio path is to:

1. Click on the appropriate output plug on the source module and hold down the mouse button.

2. Drag the "wire" to the appropriate module.

3. Hold your mouse over the chosen input plug. The plug will be highlighted (see Figure 3.32).

4. Release the mouse button.

The connection will be made, and the wire will show as a thick, dark-blue wire.

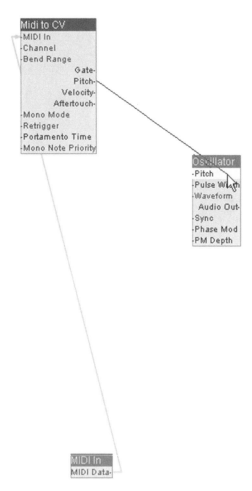

Figure 3.32 Using a mouse to hook up modules in SynthEdit.

If you have made the wrong connection, you can hit the Delete button (while the wire is thick). If you want to delete any other connection—including one created using the menu option—click on the connection. The wire will then show in thick blue. If you hit the Delete button, the thick blue wire will be deleted.

Once you have made the first connection, you can move on to the next one. When you start the next connection (or click anywhere on the interface), the thick blue wire will become a thin blue wire (and hence you will have to manually select it if you want to delete it).

Connecting Up the Audio Modules for This Synthesizer

Now that you know how to connect the modules, you can connect them in the following order, after which they should look something like Figure 3.33:

■ The MIDI Data plug on the MIDI In module should be connected to the MIDI In plug on the MIDI to CV module.

- The Pitch plug on the MIDI to CV module should be connected to the Pitch plug on the Oscillator.

- The Audio Out plug on the Oscillator should be connected to the Signal plug on the SV Filter.

- The Low Pass plug on the SV Filter should be connected to the Signal plug on the VCA module.

- The Output plug on the VCA should be connected to the 1 plug and the 2 plug on the Sound Out module. We have made the output connection twice: once for the left channel and once for the right channel. Even though this synthesizer outputs monaural audio, since it works in a stereo world, it needs to output two monaural signals to ensure maximum compatibility.

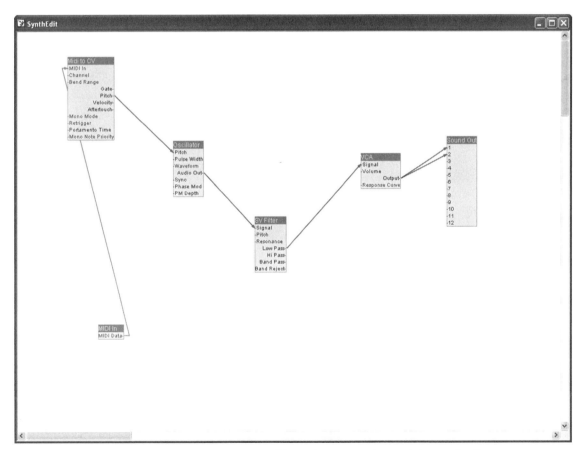

Figure 3.33 The basic audio connections to build SynthWiz Simple Synth in SynthEdit.

You will notice that there are four outputs on the SV Filter, and we have attached only one (the Low Pass plug). This particular filter offers no facility to change the filter type—instead, you have to effect the change at the audio path level.

In the top toolbar, there is a Play button (a red triangle). If you click the Play button, the synthesizer will allow the audio to pass—you can play tunes, but because there is no gate connection, the audio will continue to pass. The answer here is to click the Stop button (the red square next to the Play button).

Attaching the Modulators in SynthEdit

There are two modulators in this synthesizer, both ADSR (attack time, decay time, sustain level, release time) envelopes. You can load these by right-clicking and selecting Insert > Waveform > ADSR (twice).

The process to hook up the modulators is exactly the same as for the audio path. You can use:

- Menu selection
- Mouse clicks

So go ahead and attach:

- The Signal Out plug from the first ADSR envelope to the Pitch plug on the SV Filter
- The Signal Out plug from the second ADSR envelope to the Volume plug on the VCA

At this point you will notice that we have two modules called ADSR, and it is not immediately clear which performs which functions. This lack of clarity is particularly annoying if you are attaching modules through the menu route, because all you will see is two modules called ADSR.

Luckily, there is a way around this: We can rename modules. To do this:

1.   Right-click on the module to be renamed.

2.   Select Properties from the pop-up menu. This will expose the module's properties page, which should look something like Figure 3.34 (the properties page for an ADSR module).

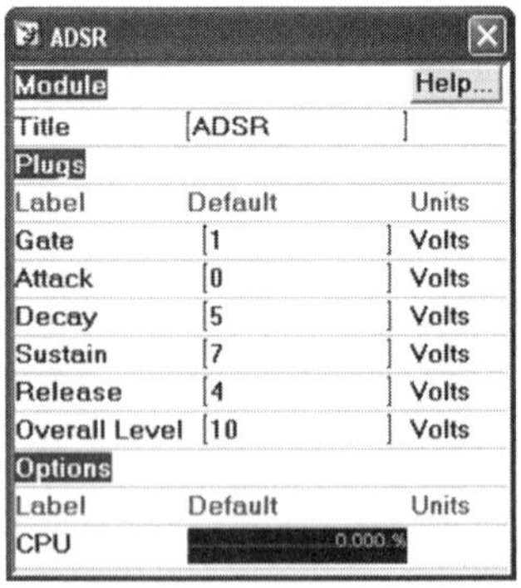

Figure 3.34 The ADSR module's properties page.

3. In the module properties shown in Figure 3.34, you will see the line "Title [ADSR]". The ADSR text can be deleted and replaced—I suggest you rename the modules as Filter Envelope and Amplifier Envelope, as appropriate.

Now that the envelopes are in place, we can hook up the gate controls. Once connected, notes will start when triggered by incoming MIDI and will stop when the key is released. If you don't connect the gate control, then played notes will continue to sound.

To connect the gate signal, click on the Gate plug on the MIDI to CV module and then click on the Gate plug on the envelope. (Do this once for each envelope.) Now if you click on the Play button and trigger sounds with your keyboard, notes will start—and if you release the keys, the notes will stop playing.

Adding the Controls in SynthEdit

You will have noticed that modules have no controls at this stage. Let's add some, starting with the oscillator. Select Insert > Controls > List Entry, which will give you a very unimpressive box with a drop-down on the front.

As a first step, attach the Choice plug to the Waveform plug on the Oscillator module (which you will see gets joined with a green "wire"). You will also notice that the name of the module has been changed—it is now called Waveform (which is useful because it controls the oscillator waveform). Next, open the properties for the Waveform/List Entry module. Under the Options, you will see a drop-down list next to the label Appearance. Select Labeled LED Stack. Close the properties page, and you will find that you have a waveform selector.

Your synthesizer should now look something like Figure 3.35.

Let's add some controls for the filter, the volume, and the envelopes:

1. Open up 13 (yes, 13) sliders (Insert > Controls > Slider).

2. Connect them as set out in the following list.

3. *After* connecting each slider, open the properties and rename them. It will become very clear why we did this renaming. You will notice that as you hook up each slider, its name changes from Slider to whatever it is attached to—it is therefore important that you only rename after attaching, not before (unless you want to rename twice).

Here are the destination connections for the sliders and the renames:

1. SV Filter Pitch (which is the second connection to that plug) and then rename the slider as Cut-Off Frequency.

2. SV Filter Resonance and then don't worry about renaming it.

3. Filter Envelope Attack and then rename the slider f Attack Time.

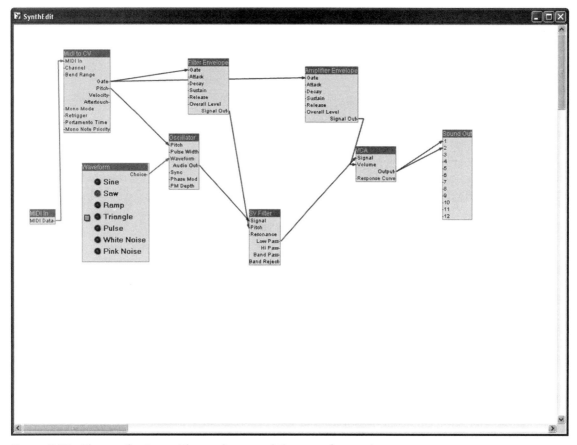

Figure 3.35   The synthesizer with envelopes and the waveform selector.

4.   Filter Envelope Decay and then rename the slider f Decay Time.

5.   Filter Envelope Sustain and then rename the slider f Sustain Level.

6.   Filter Envelope Release and then rename the slider f Release Time.

7.   Filter Envelope Overall Level and then rename the slider Cut-Off Envelope.

8.   Amplifier Envelope Attack and then rename the slider a Attack Time.

9.   Amplifier Envelope Decay and then rename the slider a Decay Time.

10.   Amplifier Envelope Sustain and then rename the slider a Sustain Level.

11.   Amplifier Envelope Release and then rename the slider a Release Time.

12.   Amplifier Envelope Overall Level and then rename the slider Volume.

And yes, I did tell you to open 13 sliders, and yes, I did only attach 12. We'll get to that last slider very soon.

Your synthesizer should now look something like Figure 3.36.

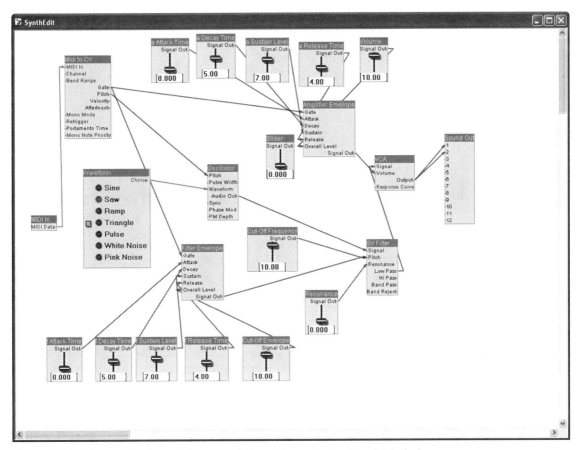

Figure 3.36 The synthesizer with most of the sliders attached and labeled.

So what have we done here?

Hopefully, some of the action is obvious. We have attached and labeled:

- The filter cut-off control
- The filter resonance control
- The attack time, decay time, sustain level, and release time sliders for both the filter and the volume envelope

The slider now labeled Cut-Off Envelope controls the output level of the filter envelope. This level determines the amount of effect that the filter envelope has on the filter cut-off frequency—in other words, it controls the depth of the filter cut-off envelope.

The Volume slider controls the output level from the amplifier envelope. Since there is no other module controlling the amplifier (VCA), this has the effect of controlling the volume of the whole synthesizer.

Adding the Finishing Touches in SynthEdit

The synthesizer is nearly finished, but there's still a fair amount of fine-tuning to be completed... and a slider to be connected.

Level Meter

The first addition is the level meter. This serves no audio purpose, but it is useful for checking whether/when the synthesizer is outputting an audio signal. To attach the level meter:

1.   Right-click and select Insert > Controls > Peak Meter.

2.   Attach the Output plug from the VCA to the Signal In plug on the Peak Meter.

That's it!! Job done. Well, not quite...I edited the properties to remove the module's name.

Key Tracking

You will remember that key tracking is where we link the filter's cut-off frequency to the pitch of the incoming note—among other things, this allows us to create "pitched" noise.

Key tracking is a bit more complicated and requires another connection to the SV Filter's Pitch plug. Before we make the connection, take a moment to think about the factors working on the filter's cut-off frequency (see Figure 3.37):

■   First, the Cut-Off Frequency slider directly controls the cut-off frequency.

■   Second, the filter envelope has an effect.

■   Third, key tracking will now also have an effect.

These three factors are separate and cumulative. However, the filter can only be 100-percent open—just because each individual factor could open the filter 100 percent, that won't make any sonic difference if they are all working together.

It takes a bit of thinking to set up the key tracking in this synthesizer:

■   The destination of the pitch tracking information will be the SV Filter Pitch plug.

■   We can take the pitch from the MIDI to CV unit.

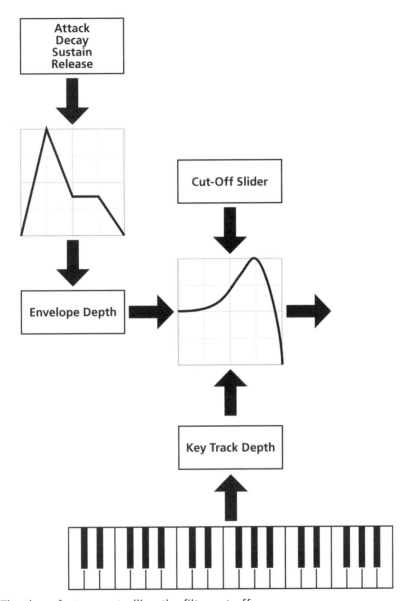

Figure 3.37   The three factors controlling the filter cut-off.

- We then need to control the amount (or the depth) of the key tracking—this is where the unused slider comes in.

- Somehow, we need to join the pitch and the slider and send the end result to the filter.

The answer here is to use a multiplier. We can load one of these units by selecting Insert > Math > Multiply. We then connect:

- The Signal Out plug on the slider to the Input 1 plug on the Multiply module and rename the slider as Key Tracking

- The Pitch plug on the MIDI to CV module to the Input 2 plug on the Multiply module

- The Output plug on the Multiply module to the Pitch plug on the SV Filter

Figure 3.38 shows the key tracking wired into place.

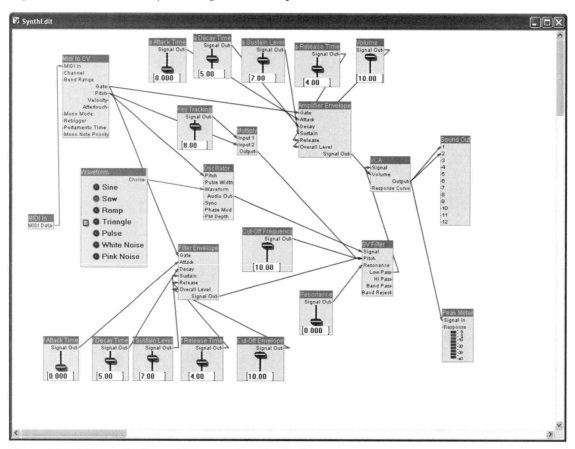

Figure 3.38   The synthesizer with key tracking hooked up.

When the Key Tracking slider is set to zero, it will multiply the pitch value by zero, giving zero. This will mean that the key tracking will have no effect at this point (as you would expect). As the Key Tracking slider is increased, an increase in the pitch of played notes will progressively open up the filter. The effect that key tracking can have on the filter is controlled by the limitation I placed on the Key Tracking slider. Let me explain....

Range Limiting

I set the maximum value for the Key Tracking slider to 1. This gives it a range between 0 and 1... which doesn't seem like much, but there is a strong logic here.

When the Key Tracking slider is set to the maximum (1), the MIDI pitch is multiplied by 1—in other words, there is no change. When this is applied to the filter, it means that there is a one-to-one correspondence between the pitch of the played note and the pitch of the filter cut-off. That is the secret behind the filtered noise sound in the previous chapter.

To set the range of a slider:

1. Right-click on the module/controller and choose Properties from the pop-up menu. (This is the same properties box in which you can change the name of a module/controller.) Figure 3.39 shows the properties box for the Key Tracking slider.

2. Set the Lo Value—in other words, the value that will be output when the slider is at its minimum setting. For the Key Tracking slider, I kept the Lo Value at its default, 0.

3. Set the Hi Value—in other words, the value that will be output when the slider is at its maximum setting. As I mentioned and as you can see in Figure 3.39, I set this at 1 for the Key Tracking slider.

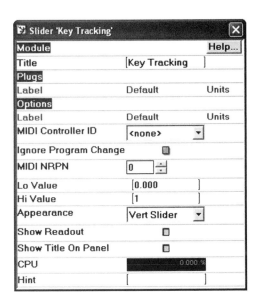

Figure 3.39 Setting the Key Tracking slider's range properties.

I left the ranges of the other sliders at their default with one exception: the Resonance slider. By default, this goes from 0 to 10. However, when the resonance in the filter is set at 10, the filter tends to self-oscillate—in other words, it starts to create its own sound (usually a high-pitched, annoying sine wave).

In the days of analog synthesizers, self-oscillation was a very useful technique because it created another oscillator. In the world of software modular synthesizers, self-oscillation of filters has few practical applications and is generally annoying, so I set the maximum resonance setting to 9 (in other words, just short of self-oscillation).

Setting the Default Values

The final step is to set the default values for all the sliders. The simplest way to achieve this is to move the sliders to the desired settings. You could also directly insert the desired values, but it's usually easier to move the sliders.

The settings that I dialed in—which are the default settings when you open SynthWiz Simple Synth—are:

- Waveform: Saw
- a Attack Time: 0
- a Decay Time: 0
- a Sustain Level: 10
- a Release Time: 0
- Cut-Off Frequency: 10
- Resonance: 0
- Key Tracking 0
- f Attack Time: 0
- f Decay Time: 0
- f Sustain Level: 10
- f Release Time: 0
- Volume: 7

If you haven't done so for a while, now would be a good time to save the patch.

We have now built the guts of SynthWiz Simple Synth—from a purely sonic perspective, there is nothing more to do. This construction will behave in exactly the same way as the VSTi, although at the moment it cannot be loaded as a VSTi, and it does look a bit messy and unstructured with all the wires going all over the place.

Interface Building in SynthEdit

Before we can make this creation into a VSTi, we need to create an interface. This is where you understand why I got rather pedantic about the naming of the controls.

SynthEdit will create an interface. It may not be desirable, but it *is* an interface, and it is better than nothing. To access the interface, right-click on the construction and select Panel Edit. If you have been following along with me, you will probably have something that looks like Figure 3.40.

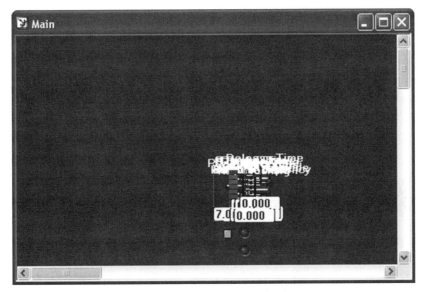

Figure 3.40   The initial synthesizer interface created by SynthEdit.

As you can see, SynthEdit has positioned all the controls in one place and given you a small window in which to work. Drag the window to enlarge it—but don't maximize it—and then drag the elements to separate them. You will probably end up with something like Figure 3.41.

If you look at Figure 3.41, you can see that it's quite difficult to see the labels for the waveforms' names. (If you can't see the labels, my point is proven.) As well as this difficulty, I wanted a background with labels to group the sliders. As a result, I created my own background. You don't have to do this—I did it because it made it easier to explain how the synthesizer worked in the previous chapter, and also, it made the screenshots for this book much clearer. As a side note, there is a grouping function in SynthEdit, but I am not using it here.

I created the background skin (see Figure 3.42) in a graphics package and saved it as a bitmap.

The default background is a textured blue square that repeats (horizontally and vertically). As you can see in Figure 3.42, my background does not repeat.

After I created the skin, this was the procedure I followed to load it (see Figure 3.42):

1. First, I closed SynthEdit (having saved the synthesizer).

2. I then located the SynthEdit skins folder. On my system, this was at D:\synth edit\skins. (Your location will depend on where you installed SynthEdit.)

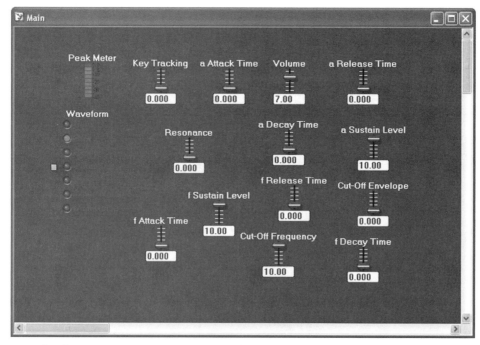

Figure 3.41   The first step to sorting out the interface controls.

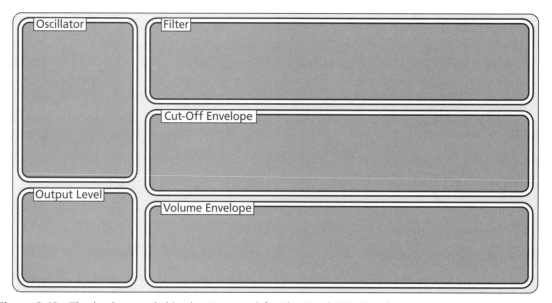

Figure 3.42   The background skin that I created for the SynthWiz Simple Synth.

3.   Within that folder, there was already one subfolder, called default.

4.   I created another folder, which I called simple.

5.   I renamed my skin bitmap as background.bmp and copied it to the simple folder.

6.   In the default folder, I located a file called background.txt. I copied this file to the simple folder.

7.   In the simple folder, I opened the copied background.txt file and changed the word true to false. I then resaved the file. This change instructs SynthEdit not to tile (in other words, not to repeat) my background image.

8.   I then opened SynthEdit and opened up the synthesizer.

9.   On the interface, I right-clicked and selected Skin > Simple.

As Figure 3.43 shows, this loaded my skin. Because I did not put any graphics for sliders or other controls into the simple folder, the defaults continue to be used, which is fine for my purposes.

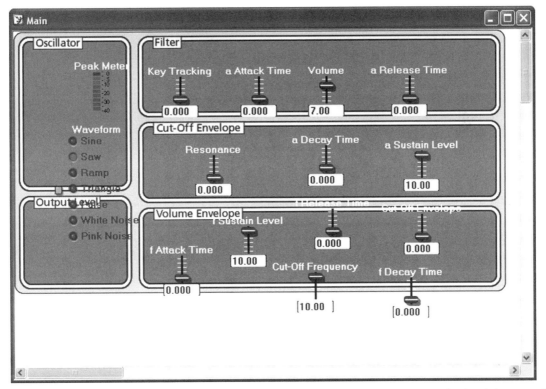

Figure 3.43 SynthWiz Simple Synth with the custom skin loaded. As you can see, the knob layout still needs some work.

Having put the background in place, there were two key actions:

- First, the controls had to be dragged to the right places. It's best to drag on the labels, not the sliders (because the sliders will…well, slide).

- Second, the window had to be resized around the background. The final VSTi size is the size of the window, so you need to drag with a degree of accuracy.

Figure 3.44 shows the final skin with the controls in place and the modules and wires in the background.

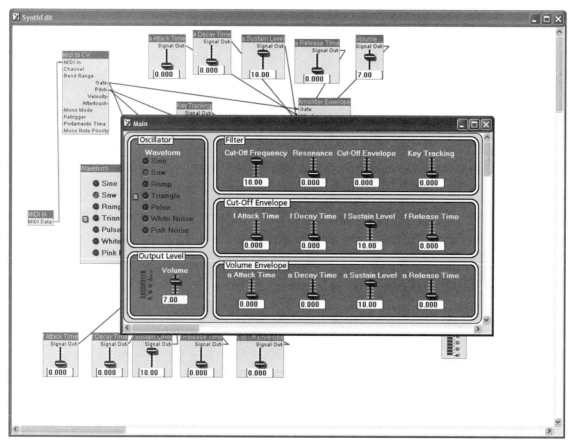

Figure 3.44   The final synthesizer.

Exporting a VSTi from SynthEdit

The synthesizer is now finished, and the interface is laid out, but there is still something missing. We now need to convert the synthesizer to a VSTi.

To create the VSTi:

1. Disconnect the MIDI In and Sound Out modules. You can do this by removing the wires, or if you're looking for the quick option, just delete the modules.

2. Select all of the modules (apart from the MIDI In and Sound Out modules).

3. Put all of the selected modules into a container. You can do this while the modules are selected by selecting Edit > Containerize Selection.

Assuming you disconnected but didn't delete the MIDI In and the Sound Out modules, you will now have something that looks like Figure 3.45. Because the MIDI In and Sound Out modules are not connected, you won't hear anything (and even if you do connect them, you will still not hear anything at this point).

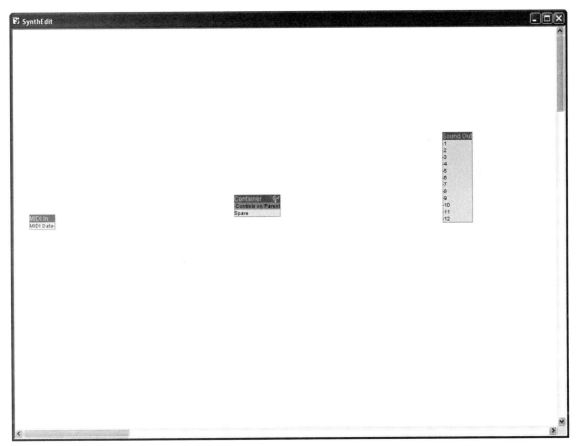

Figure 3.45 After "containerization," all of your modules will be stored in a container.

To ensure that we know which container we are dealing with—at the moment it's obvious, but when you have several, it's a bit harder—right-click on the container, select Properties, and give the container a name. I've called mine simple; see Figure 3.46.

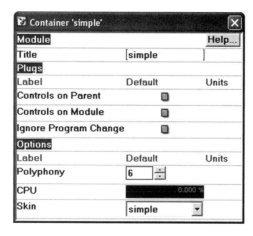

Figure 3.46 The container properties page.

As a side note, after you have containerized the modules, I suggest you check the skin. To do this, right-click on the container and choose Panel Edit. If the wrong skin is there or the interface is the wrong size, then you can sort things out at this point.

Remember how we disconnected the input and output before we containerized the modules? We now need to do some work to reinstate those connections, so double-click on the container.

When you get inside the container, you will see a new module called IO Mod, which will have one plug called Spare. This module is the connection between your synthesizer and the outside world. To connect it:

1. Click on the Spare plug and drag the wire to the MIDI In on the MIDI to CV module (or connect using the menu method). You will notice that:
    - The connecting wire shows.
    - A new Spare plug has appeared.

2. Connect the Output plug on the VCA module to the Spare plug on the IO Mod module. Do this twice to establish a left and right output so the module works in stereo.

You are now hooked up—your container should look something like Figure 3.47. If you close the container and return to the main page (with the MIDI In, Sound Out, and Container modules), you can hook up the container, and the synthesizer will play. When you go to hook up the container, you will notice that it now has input and output plugs on display. By the way, you don't need to hook up the module—I am only suggesting this for your interest.

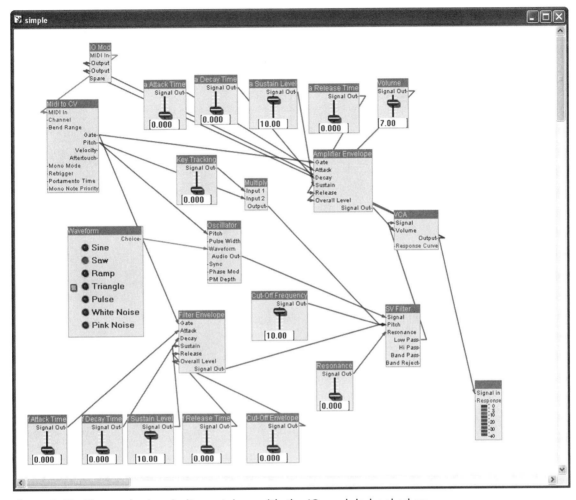

Figure 3.47 The synthesizer in its container with the IO module hooked up.

We're now ready to create the VSTi. To do this, Select File > Save as VST. This will bring up a dialog box similar to that shown in Figure 3.48.

There are a few things to pay attention to in this dialog box:

- The default Product name follows the container's name. You will see that I have renamed the Product as SynthWiz Simple Synth.

- The filename defaults to the container name with .dll added. I stuck with simple.dll.

- Every VST needs a separate four-character identifier—this is so hosts can distinguish one VST from another. This code should be entered into the 4 Char ID field. You've got somewhat over 1.6 million permutations, so I'll leave you to sort your own ID.

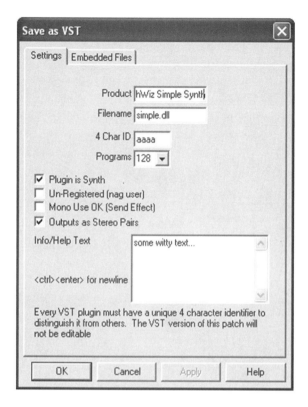

Figure 3.48 The Save as VST dialog box.

- The Programs drop-down allows you to set the number of presets associated with the synthesizer. Because this book is intending to take you "from presets," I won't dwell on this function.

- This plug-in is a synth, so that option should be checked.

- I don't feel the need to nag people, so I didn't check the Un-Registered (nag user) option.

- Because this synthesizer has no audio input, it has no use as an effect, so I did not check the Mono Use OK (Send Effect) option.

- However, I do want its Outputs as Stereo Pairs.

- The final box allows you to add some help or about text (which is accessed by right-clicking on the final VST and selecting About).

If you have not registered SynthEdit, then some of these options may not be available to you.

Once you have set the parameters, you can click on the OK button to create a VST. The first message you are likely to receive is Save File First? The answer is probably Yes, as you will probably want to save the changes made in the Save as VST dialog box, so click OK, and you should receive a message that your VST has been created.

If you receive an error, it will probably be related to the folder in which the VST is to be saved. Create the folder and resave, and you should be good to go.

Now you have created your first VSTi synthesizer. Locate the DLL file and load it up in the same manner that you would load any other VSTi. (If you're not sure about how to do that, check back to the previous chapter, where we looked at how to load a synthesizer in a host.)

About the Rest of the Book

You are now at the stage where:

- You have laid your hands on a synthesizer.

- You have twisted the knobs and, in so doing, you have changed the sounds.

- You have created your own synthesizer/sound in a modular synthesizer.

In short, you now have a grasp of all the basics and sufficient information to get up and running.

I am now going to move to the next section of the book, which is a detailed look at the first group of the various modules that are available. The chapters will all take a standard format:

- Each chapter will focus on one issue—for instance, sound sources or filters.

- The chapter will begin with an introduction to the subject—for instance, the filter chapter will talk about the various filters that are available.

- I will then look at the specific modules, paying attention to the specific functions that they can undertake, and as appropriate, looking at why you might choose to use any specific module.

This is not intended as a replacement for the user handbook—as I've said before, I have no intention of covering every module/feature of all of the featured synthesizers—but rather, it is an opportunity to look at how the features of the various modules can be applied for your own ends.

Once we have looked at the modules, in the next section of the book we will look at how to start putting the pieces together in a creative way. In particular, we will focus on:

- Architectural issues—the effect that connecting modules in a different order has on the resulting sound

- Sound design—how to build the sound that you want and need for your track

Before we move on, please take the time to make sure you have a grip on the stuff we have covered so far. If you haven't done so already, try replicating the sounds from the last chapter with the four featured synthesizers (or as many as you can run)—there are demo versions of all the synths. Try to ensure that you have an understanding of not just how the synthesizers work, but also their strengths and weaknesses in terms of sound and workflow.

Take some time to listen to them in detail—compare and contrast their sonic differences. When we start to build sounds, you are going to start making a lot of subjective value judgments about what you like and what you don't—with a wider appreciation of the tonal palette, you will be able to build better sounds.

4 An Introduction to Sound Sources

So far in this book, we have looked at subtractive synthesis, where you start with a "noisy" sound source and the tone is then shaped with a filter. With subtractive synthesis, you can easily change the characteristic of a sound by changing the sound source—in other words, by changing the source waveform.

However, subtractive synthesis is not the only way to create sounds. For instance, you could use:

- *Additive* techniques, where you bring together a number of waves to create a wholly new tone

- *Modulation* techniques (such as frequency modulation synthesis), where one waveform distorts another wave to create a radically different sound

You can then (but you don't have to) use these other synthesis methods in conjunction with subtractive synthesis in order to create an even broader palette of tones.

We are going to look at all of these techniques in this chapter, but let's start by looking at some basic waveforms.

As you listen to the different synthesizers, you will hear how waves with the same name sound different in different synthesizers. Don't get too worried about this. Instead, focus on what sounds best to you and use that sound.

Basic Wave Shapes

Let's look at some of the wave shapes that are common to virtually every synthesizer that has ever been produced. You can access versions of all of these waves in all of the featured synthesizers.

Sine Wave

The sine wave (see Figure 4.1) is perhaps the most basic element in a sound. It is the purest form of tone you can have—it consists of the fundamental note and has no overtones. If you run a sine wave through a filter, there are no overtones to filter out—therefore, the only effect that a filter

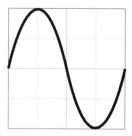

Figure 4.1 The sine wave.

would have would be to reduce the volume of the note itself. If you put any sound through a low-pass filter, as you take out the harmonics it will tend to sound like a sine wave.

On its own a sine wave can sound quite dull and is not often a first choice for programming. However, as a waveform it is often used to thicken up patches. Where a waveform sounds weak on its own—particularly if it is based on a sampled wave—adding a sine wave can give depth to a patch and add a roundness/fullness to the sound. Sine waves are also often added to bass patches to give a subsonic, foundation-shaking quality.

A final frequent use for a sine wave is in FM (frequency modulation) synthesis. It is very common (indeed, it was the only option in the original FM synthesizers) to build FM patches solely with sine waves. We will look at FM synthesis later in this chapter.

Later in this chapter we will also look at additive synthesis and see how sine waves are the components of all other waves.

Sawtooth Wave

The sawtooth wave (see Figure 4.2) tends to be the first-call wave for many sound designers.

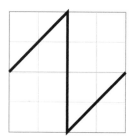

Figure 4.2 The sawtooth wave.

The sawtooth gives a bright sound that is often used as the basis for brass and string sounds, as well as general "fat" synthesizer sounds (such as stabs and basses). It is rare but not unknown to hear a raw sawtooth wave—due to the bright quality of the wave, it is usually filtered.

While a sawtooth wave is a bright wave, filtering can add warmth and depth to a sound. However, the wave also tends to dominate a broad proportion of the sound spectrum. This may not be a problem, but if your arrangement contains several patches based on sawtooth waves, you may find your mix starts to get muddy.

Some people make a distinction between the sawtooth wave and what they call the *ramp wave*. For these people, the image in Figure 4.2 is a ramp wave. In their view, a sawtooth would be the mirror image—or if you want to get technical, it has an inverted polarity—of a ramp wave (in other words, it declines over its cycle, rather than increases). From a sonic perspective the waves are identical, so I don't care for this distinction.

Square and Pulse Waves

The square waveform has a hollow quality and is often used to create "woody" or "reedy" tones, such as those found in woodwind instruments. It is also frequently used in bass sounds, either on its own or to fatten up a sound, often acting as a sub-oscillator (in other words, a note pitched below the fundamental).

A pulse wave with a value of 50% (which is when both sides of the wave are balanced) is a square wave. In between the two (as shown in Figure 4.3), you get a varying range of tones. A pulse with a 0% width is just noise. Some synthesizers separate the square and pulse, while others provide one wave and a facility for pulse-width modulation.

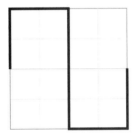
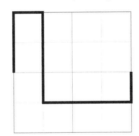

Figure 4.3   A square wave and a pulse wave.

In case there are any pedants out there, there is a school of thought that calls what I have called 50% waves 100% waves. As with the difference between sawtooth and ramp waves, this is a distinction that I don't care about. What matters to me is how any one specific wave sounds, not what it is called.

Pulse-Width Modulation

Pulse-width modulation (often called PWM) is a technique most associated with square and pulse waves. With a square wave, the positive and negative phases of the wave are balanced. When the pulse width is modulated, this balance changes to give a different-shaped wave.

The different waveforms are not simply different shapes on an oscilloscope, but they contain different spectral components, hence their different tones. These components will be discussed in greater detail when we look at additive synthesis.

PWM can either be static—for instance, a 50% wave is modulated to give a 40% wave—or it can be a continuous change (for instance, when the pulse width is modulated by an LFO). As a technique, PWM is generally used for one of two reasons. First, it changes the tone of the wave-form. Second, when two waves that have been modulated in different ways are combined, there can be a fattening effect.

Triangle Wave

A triangle wave (see Figure 4.4) gives a sound that is slightly less reedy or perhaps less sharp than a square wave. If you want to stretch a point, you could alternatively think of the triangle wave as being like a sine wave but somewhat sharper in its output (but please do not try to relate a wave's shape on an oscilloscope to its tone).

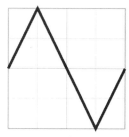

Figure 4.4 A triangle wave.

A triangle wave is often used as a low-frequency oscillator (LFO) waveform.

Noise

You might think that noise is just noise; however, you would be wrong. As we saw with SynthWiz Simple Synth, noise comes in different colors—the most common being white, pink, and brown. Each color exhibits a different composition of frequencies in the sound spectrum and hence has a darker tone. Broadly, white noise is the brightest, pink noise is slightly less bright, and brown noise is duller still.

Complex Wave Shapes: Combining Sounds

The nature of modular synthesizers is that you can use as many modules as you want (subject to your computer's CPU not exploding). This allows you to use several sound sources, and when you use more than one sound source, there is the possibility of using more than one waveform.

This is the point at which things get interesting in the world of sound design.

There are many reasons for combining sounds, which include:

- To create new tones
- To augment a weak tone
- To get a smoother sound

There are many ways that sounds are combined. For instance:

- Two similar sounds can be doubled.
- Two different sounds can be layered to create a wholly new sound.

Sounds created with multiple oscillators will generally fill a greater proportion of the sound spectrum than sounds created with a single oscillator. Accordingly, care needs to be taken to ensure that these sounds do not come to dominate a mix (unless that is the intention).

Let's now look in a bit more detail at some ways that sounds can be combined.

Doubling Oscillators

The simplest combination of oscillators is to take one oscillator, add another module, and clone its settings to the second oscillator. Simply adding a second version of the same oscillator may not do much more than increase the volume. However, the addition of a second oscillator does give many more sonic opportunities.

Oscillator Phase and Polarity

When we talk about the *phase* of an oscillator, we generally mean the position in a wave's cycle (see Figure 4.5). With one oscillator, the phase matters little; however, with two oscillators, the effect of phase can be dramatic. The other issue closely associated with phase is polarity—whether a wave starts its cycle with positive or negative movement.

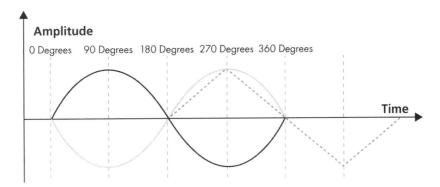

Figure 4.5 The phase of an oscillator. The gray sine wave has reversed polarity (when compared to the black sine wave), and the dotted triangle wave is 180 degrees out of phase.

If you have two waveforms that are totally in phase and are of the same polarity, then you will get reinforcement of the signal. Reinforcement is perceived as an increase in volume. If your waves are out of phase, then you will get cancellation. The effect of the cancellation depends on the individual waves: If you have two sine waves that are 180 degrees out of phase but have the same polarity, then you will get total cancellation.

Cancellation caused by putting waves out of phase/polarity is generally perceived as a change in tone, usually making the sound thinner and sharper. This may be a great result if you are after a plucked sound or a more metallic sound—it may be less impressive if you are after a really fat sound.

The range of controls over the phase and polarity of an oscillator will vary from synthesizer to synthesizer. The main controls that are likely to be important are:

- **Phase synchronization.** The phase of a note can be synchronized with the start of a note (in other words, the key strike). This means that every note from that oscillator will start from the same position in its phase.

- **Phase control.** Synchronizing the phase is half the story—once the phase of the note is locked, you need to determine where in its cycle a note begins. If you can't control the phase, then you can't consistently put one wave out of phase with regard to another (and maintain the phase relationship between the two waves).

- **Polarity reversal.** Clearly, you need to be able to reverse the polarity of a wave.

- **Free-running phase.** This may seem strange, but it is important to have the facility for the phase of a note to be free-running. This means that the oscillator could start at any point in its cycle when a note is struck and that the oscillator does not always start at a certain point in its phase. If you don't have this level of control, then you may find your sounds—especially pad-type sounds—become quite static. If you do not have free-running phase, then the phase relationship between two waves will always be the same, so each successive press of a key will give an identical note. There may be times when you want this; however, there will be times when you absolutely do not.

Hard Sync

We've talked a bit about phase. Let me introduce you to a related issue, but one that should not be confused: It is often called *hard sync*. With hard sync, one oscillator is slaved to another oscillator. The slave oscillator will restart its phase each time the master oscillator restarts its phase (see Figure 4.6).

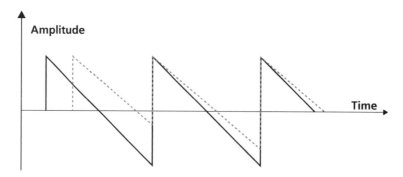

Figure 4.6 Notice how each time the black wave restarts its cycle, the dotted gray wave restarts its cycle. That is hard sync in practice. You will see that the waves do not start at the same point; however, at the first instance that the black wave restarts its phase, the gray wave is immediately brought into line.

If the two oscillators are pitched at the same level, the effect is comparatively mild (perhaps giving some cancellation). If the two oscillators are pitched differently, then one oscillator will complete its phase before the other. This means that the slave will be partway through its phase when it is retriggered. This can result in a very hard sound that is often used for creating cutting lead sounds.

Oscillator Detuning

Another common technique used with doubled oscillators is to detune one of the oscillators (or to detune each of them but in different directions). Subtle detuning can give a natural chorusing effect that is perfect for creating fullness/roundness/smoothness or for just adding fatness to the sound.

There is a balance to be struck when using this technique—if the detuning goes too far, then the resulting sound can become flabby and/or out of tune. This may be a good or a bad thing, depending on the effect you're after.

The effect of detuning an oscillator can lessen the more extreme effects of phase shifts (which may or may not be a good thing, depending on the sound you are chasing).

Multi-Oscillators

So far we have looked at doubling oscillators. However, there is no reason why you shouldn't triple or quadruple oscillators and separately detune each oscillator. Heck, you can have as many oscillators as you like—we're in the world of modular synthesizers.

Alternatively, you could use a multi-oscillator module. There are different implementations of these, but they all have the same essential characteristics. Instead of there being one wave from one module, with multi-oscillators a number of waves will be generated by a single module. These waves can be spread across the stereo spectrum, and each is slightly detuned to give a very big sound from one oscillator. Usually you will have one or more of the following controls (see Figure 4.7):

- **Voices.** The number of voices (in effect the number of oscillators within a single module) operating simultaneously.

- **Detune.** The relative detuning of each of the oscillators. The detuning will be spread across the voices, so some voices are more detuned than others, giving a rich effect.

- **Width.** The spread of the voices across the stereo spectrum. Each voice will be given its own location in the stereo spectrum.

Some oscillators also give you an element of drift or random tuning to soften/thicken (as appropriate) the effect.

At this point you may be wondering why you would use a multi-oscillator module rather than hook up a bunch of individual modules. Clearly, the individual modules route has one key

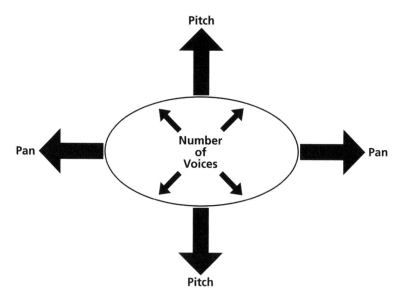

Figure 4.7 A multi-oscillator is capable of expanding the sound in many directions.

advantage in the modular environment: control. You can choose exactly how many modules you want, how they are tuned, how they are panned, and so on.

However, there are some advantages to using the multi-oscillator module approach:

- **Simplicity.** You only have to hook up one module. You don't need to be worried about hooking up each module individually and then setting a bunch of controllers and so on.

- **CPU hit.** Most of these multi-oscillator modules are highly optimized, so you might be hearing nine voices, but in practice you will only be taking a CPU hit for perhaps two voices.

Combining Oscillators

There is a fine difference between combined and doubled oscillators—I am only using different terms so that I can be clear about the different concepts. And in any event, in the world of modular synthesizers, you can combine and double.

With doubling, you take the same oscillator/waveshape and then double it (or triple it, and so on). With combined oscillators, you again take two (or more) oscillators acting together. However, the oscillators have different waveshapes; so for instance, you may combine a saw and a square wave. Alternatively, you may combine two square waves, one being an octave higher than the other.

The combinations may or may not be detuned—that is all a matter of taste—but on the whole, subtle detuning to thicken the sounds works less well in combination, but it is quite common to change the octave of a combined oscillator so that it can add some high-end bite or low-end punch or to create a wholly new sound.

For a simple practical example of combined oscillators, take a sawtooth wave and a square wave. On their own, both waves have a certain sound: Both are quite bright, and in certain circumstances this may mean that some richness and some depth of tone is lacking. You could double either of these oscillators (so, two sawtooth waves or two square waves) to get a richer tone. Alternatively, you could combine the sawtooth wave and the square wave.

Combining gives a new tone that is neither sawtooth nor square—the combined sound still has the brightness of the two components, but perhaps more weight. If you then want to thicken things up considerably, drop the square by an octave, engage the multi-mode oscillator for the sawtooth, and put the result through a filter. This is a very quick and dirty way to get a fat sound.

Take a look at Figures 4.8 through 4.11, which illustrate a few of the basic concepts. I should point out that these figures are intended to show what happens when waves are combined—these are not necessarily suggestions for what you should do. As you see, when you start combining waves, you create new tones, and more to the point, with subtle changes you can control the new tones you are creating.

Not only does this bring a much broader tone palette, but it also allows you to step away from the subtractive approach to synthesis. By combining waves—and then controlling how they are combined, particularly in terms of the relative phase, polarity of the waves, and their respective levels over time—you can create completely new sounds before you get to the filter or other audio processing tools. This is a profound change from the subtractive synthesis approach, meaning that you can create complete sounds without needing a filter.

By the way, when you start combining waves, you will find that some combinations work, and the end result is a single, coherent, new wave sound, but others don't, and you end up with two separately identifiable sounds that fight against each other. You will be able to easily hear what works and what doesn't.

Before the figures, here are a few thoughts about the illustrations to show what happens when you start combining waves:

- Figure 4.8 shows two sine waves being added: One is pitched an octave above the second. As you can see, the combination gives a wholly new wave.

- Figure 4.9 shows a sawtooth wave and a square wave being added together. The resultant wave looks something like a combination of the two (and unusually, the resulting sound sounds like a combination of the two).

- Figure 4.10 shows the results of two sawtooth waves, one of which is 180 degrees out of phase with the other. The result is a sawtooth wave, but raised by one octave. As you might imagine, this is not a particularly interesting sound—you can achieve the same sound with a single oscillator by changing its octave setting—but what is noteworthy is the sound you get when the waves are 179 degrees or 181 degrees (or other small amounts) out of phase. In these situations, you start to get a wholly new sound.

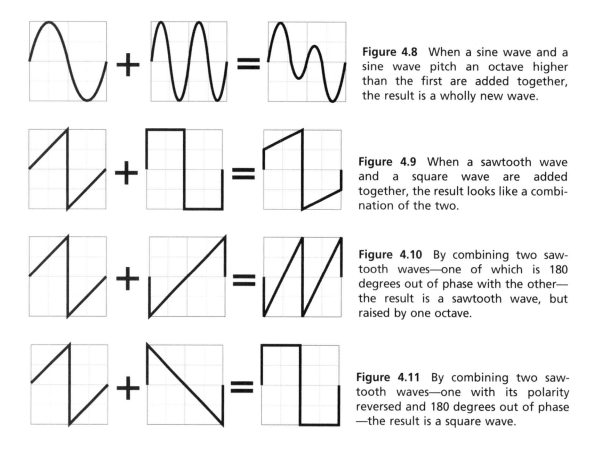

Figure 4.8 When a sine wave and a sine wave pitch an octave higher than the first are added together, the result is a wholly new wave.

Figure 4.9 When a sawtooth wave and a square wave are added together, the result looks like a combination of the two.

Figure 4.10 By combining two sawtooth waves—one of which is 180 degrees out of phase with the other—the result is a sawtooth wave, but raised by one octave.

Figure 4.11 By combining two sawtooth waves—one with its polarity reversed and 180 degrees out of phase—the result is a square wave.

- Figure 4.11 shows the effect of combining two sawtooth waves, one with its polarity reversed and 180 degrees out of phase. The result is a square wave. Again, this is not stunningly interesting, but results when they are nearly (but not exactly) 180 degrees out of phase can be interesting and will add range to your tonal palette. Figure 4.12 shows this sound being created using KarmaFX Synth Modular.

Sample-Based Synthesis

So far, the sound sources we have looked at have been oscillators—devices that output a continuous wave. However, it would be wrong to think that an oscillator is the only possible sound source. As you will see in the next sections, there are many different ways of creating the source sound. The first way I am going to look at is sample-based synthesis.

Broadly, sampling is digital recording of a sound so that the sound can be replayed giving a "perfect" re-creation of the sampled instrument. Well…that's the theory. In practice, some sample libraries give excellent results, provided you have the musical skills to play all of the parts on

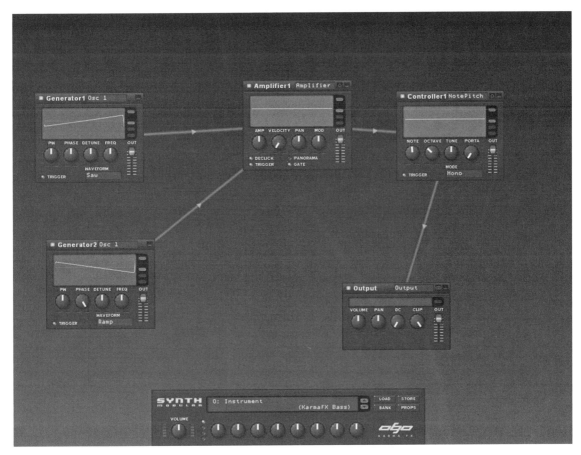

Figure 4.12   A practical example of how you would set up a patch with two sawtooth waves, one with its polarity reversed and 180 degrees out of phase. In this case the sound has been set up in KarmaFX Synth Modular. You will note that the Trigger control has been switched on for both sound generators—this synchronizes the waves to the key trigger (and therefore ensures that the Phase controls have effect).

the sampled instruments. However, more commonly (as you will read in a moment), it is impractical to take a set of samples for every eventuality, and therefore a lot of synthesis is needed.

In addition, samples are often used as the basis for creating whole new sounds, which is where we start to get interested. Before we get there, let's look at sampling in a bit more detail.

What Is Sampling?

The software tools we call samplers don't actually sample (with one or two exceptions). Instead, they play back samples that have been captured and edited with other software. None of the synthesizers featured in this book has the facility to digitally record samples—they can all play back samples. So perhaps, rather than ask what a sampler is, the more relevant question today is what is sample deployment?

To answer that question, let us look at three main approaches to sample deployment:

- Realistic representation/re-creation of a musical instrument

- Sampled waves used as the sound source in a synthesizer

- Loops

Let's consider how these approaches differ.

Realistic Representation or Re-Creation of a Musical Instrument

The most obvious and traditional approach to sample deployment is the realistic representation a musical instrument (or group of instruments)—for instance, a bass guitar or a string orchestra library. This style of sampling is behind many of the current huge sample libraries and is generally characterized by:

- Multi-samples. (Often every note in each instrument will be sampled.)

- Velocity layers included to reflect the different timbres of an instrument depending on how forcefully the instrument is played.

- Different playing techniques to reflect how musicians will create a range of timbres for the same note. These different playing techniques will often be accessed through key switching (a technique by which the player can call up or activate different sample sets) and/or "round-robin" techniques where successive samples vary (for instance, to mimic alternate up and down picking). We won't look at any sample switching techniques in this book.

The focus of this book is on synthesis, so we're not going to look at how to create a realistic representation of a musical instrument. If you want to read more, you could check out my book (written with Klaus P. Rausch) *Sample This!* (Coombe Hill Publishing, 2007).

Using Sampled Waves as the Sound Source in a Synthesizer

The second approach to sample deployment is to take a sample (or a group of samples) and use it as the sound source in a synthesizer. This means you have the option to create a sound that is a fair representation of the instrument. Or, you can mangle the sample beyond recognition—realistic replay is not necessarily the goal. Indeed, different samples are often layered to create hybrid/fusion sounds.

For the sound source, single samples (which may then be only a single wave or a whole sample) are often used. However, multi-samples can also be used in this process.

Loops

The third approach to sample deployment is loops. Originally, loops were prevalent in many dance styles, but now this approach is a mainstream technique. Again, this is an area I won't be looking at in detail.

What Is a Sample?

We have looked at the three main approaches to sample deployment, but what do we mean when we talk about a sample? If you talk to a range of people, you will find that the term *sample* is applied to many different things. Unfortunately, you're going to have to try to guess what they mean based on the context.

- **Single cycle.** A single cycle of a waveform (for instance, a sampled sawtooth wave). Many oscillators in many synthesizers are sampled single-cycle waves.

- **Single shot.** A single-shot (or one-shot) sample—for instance, the sound of an individual snare drum. This is generally what most people mean when they talk about a sample.

- **Multi-sample.** A multi-sample is composed of several individual samples (which could be single cycles, single shots, or samples with loop points), which are then organized to produce an instrument. Examples of this might be a piano or a whole drum kit with different notes sampled at a range of different velocities. A group of multi-samples is often called a *soundset*.

- **Sample with loop points.** A sample with loop points. (The loop is often called a *sustain loop*, since it sounds for the "sustain" portion of the sample.) This is where things get a bit complicated. To preserve memory and cut down on the size of a soundset, samples are often truncated (in other words, their length is reduced). To re-create the appropriate length of a note, part of the sample is then looped. With these sorts of samples—which can be laid out as part of a multi-sample—you often need some synthesis to re-create some of the characteristics that are lost through the truncate-and-loop process.

- **Phrase.** You've heard the records where you get the phrase "oh yeah" (or some other yelp from a 1960s soul singer) repeated. Phrases can be as long or a short as you want. However, in essence, a phrase is just a single-shot sample.

- **Loop.** A loop is a single-shot sample with loop points at the beginning and the end of the sample so that the whole sample is played and played…and played…and…. Loops can be anything; they don't just have to be drums. You can have a bass riff, a keyboard lick—whatever works in the context of your track.

All of these different types of samples (or groups of samples) have their place in synthesis and can be used as sound sources.

Deploying Samples

Once you've got a clean sample or a set of clean samples—and if you're not sure how to get hold of these, then let me again point you in the direction of my book, *Sample This!*—you can start to deploy your samples. As part of this process, you're going to need to make some decisions.

Single-Cycle and Longer Waves

You might want to use a wave as a sound source from which to create a synthesized sound.

When you play a wave in an oscillator, very often you are playing a sampled single-cycle wave (which might look like one of the images shown in Figures 4.1 to 4.4). In an oscillator, when the wave gets to the end of its cycle, it starts again. If it didn't, the wave would play and then there would be silence, and in any event, all you would hear would be a click. If your sample is, say, pitched at 440 Hz (which is moderately low), then one cycle would last just over 0.0022 seconds (which is why you would hear a click and not a note).

An oscillator will automatically repeat a wave (as well as re-tuning it to play the appropriate pitch) that it has loaded from its internal resources. By contrast, if you load a single-cycle wave into a sampler, then you will usually need to:

- Specify that the wave should loop.
- Determine the beginning and end points of the loop (which will often be the beginning and end of the sample). If the sample has not been cut perfectly or the loop points are not set perfectly, then there will be a click or other distortion when the wave loops.

You are not limited to single-cycle waves as a new sound source—you can use any sound. However, unless you are using very long samples, then you will probably want the sample to loop. (Without a loop, the sound will run out at some point.) By the way, if you do use longer samples, you will find that your system resources can start to get gobbled up if you use a lot of samples.

As with a single-cycle wave, it is crucial that the loop points are properly set with non-single-cycle waves. If the loops are not properly set, then there will be clicking or some other form of distortion. For setting these loop points, you can either use:

- A sampler module within the synthesizer—provided it gives you an appropriate level of control.
- A specialized audio editor. Both of these tools are outside the scope of this book.

Multi-Samples Versus Single Samples

When you play a sample, you re-tune it. In other words, you change its pitch from the original pitch at which the note was sampled to the pitch of the note that you want to play.

If you are working with a single sample that is played across the whole keyboard—as would be the case with a single-cycle oscillator wave—then that sample will be re-tuned quite drastically. In essence, the re-tuning works by playing the sample more quickly (to raise the pitch) and more slowly (to drop the pitch). With a single-cycle wave, this re-tuning is not noticeable. However, when you have a wave with inherent characteristics—for instance, a piano note—then the re-tuning becomes noticeable, especially when the re-tuning is drastic.

Typically, if you re-tune plus or minus one tone, then the re-tuning is not noticeable. Beyond that range, you may notice that the sound becomes unnatural. With extreme re-tuning, you may also encounter unwanted audio artifacts. However, the range over which a sample may be re-tuned is very much dependent on the source material and the desired audio effect. So for instance, if you are trying to maintain audio fidelity, then you could transpose an organ note over a wider range than a piano note.

To maintain audio fidelity—or simply to ensure that the re-tuning doesn't sound weird when a sample is pushed outside of its natural range—a number of samples can be used, which are spread over the keyboard. However, the transition points in multi-sample banks often give problems. Even with professionally recorded samples, it is still possible to hear where one sample range ends and the next sample range begins, although as you increase the number of samples, this problem reduces. These changes are inevitable when you are sampling real instruments.

Key Ranges

When sampling, a key consideration is which notes you are going to capture. But this is not a book about sampling—it's a book about synthesis, so I won't look at the sampling considerations, except in this one instance.

For the highest fidelity, every note should be sampled. This will also give the maximum flexibility when it comes to building soundsets. However, it takes a long time to take samples and to process those samples. Each note must be painstakingly recorded (with no buzzes, interruptions, or other extraneous noise). Then each wave must be edited by hand to trim the start and finish, add volume envelopes and loops, and set the level appropriately. This is very detailed work and takes a long time. Each additional note that is sampled increases the task to be completed. Therefore, some samplists choose not sample every note.

When you replay a sample at the pitch the note was sampled, there should be no pitch shifting, so the note will sound natural. The further you shift the note from the sampled pitch, the less natural it will sound. In this context, less natural is a relative concept—sampled real instruments will sound less natural than some sampled electronic instruments. It all depends on the particular instrument that is being sampled.

As a synthesist, when you come to load up samples, there are going to be three factors that determine how you build your soundset:

- The number of samples available. This number is finite; you can't create more samples (unless you are using your own samples and can replicate the sampling conditions).

- The sound you are after.

- The effort you are prepared to put into building your soundset.

So for instance, if you know that each of your samples is good for plus or minus one tone, then you could spread approximately three notes across the octave, as Figure 4.13 shows.

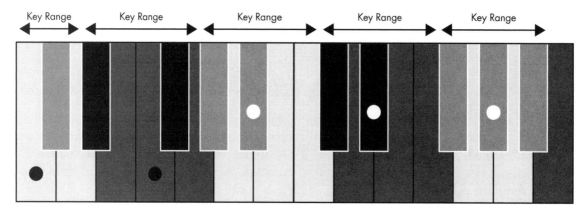

Figure 4.13 Laying out samples across a keyboard. In this example, each sample (shown by the dots) has a range of plus or minus one tone (and so is playable for the root, two keys up, and two keys down). The key ranges for each note are indicated.

You may alternatively want higher fidelity and so use a narrower range. Or perhaps you want to go wild with the synthesis, in which case you might be happy with one sample per octave. The choice is up to you.

Velocity Ranges

After the pitch of the samples to take, the second decision for a samplist is the number of volume layers to take. This decision has a direct influence on:

- The range of tones that will be available—the more nuances that are recorded, the more detailed the sample-based instrument will be.

- The amount of work—each layer of volume requires that all notes have to be re-sampled at that volume. (Otherwise, the resulting tone will be inconsistent.)

As Figure 4.14 shows, if you sample every note and take several volume layers, the number of samples adds up very quickly. (Just compare this to the number of samples used in Figure 4.13.)

As you can imagine, if you have a number of volume layers, it will take quite a while to build a soundset. Only you will know how detailed you need the soundset underlying your synthesis to be. You can then make a choice about the number of volume layers (if more than one). Alternatively, you may be happy to go with one layer and to use some clever filtering and sound manipulation to reproduce the nuances of tone.

Additive Synthesis

Much of the focus in synthesis—and indeed, much of the focus of this book—is on subtractive synthesis, where you take a sound source that is rich in harmonic content and reduce those harmonics with a filter. Additive synthesis takes the opposite approach—it takes a group of

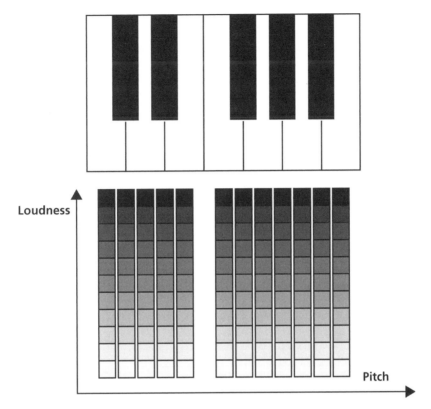

Figure 4.14 For high-fidelity reproduction of a sampled instrument that is capable of reproducing detailed nuances, you want each note to be sampled at several different volume levels.

sine waves at different frequencies and puts them together to create a new sound. The sine waves (or *partials* or *harmonics*, as they are called—the terms *partials* and *harmonics* are pretty much interchangeable) are all multiples of the fundamental frequency.

Additive synthesis requires patience to construct these new waves, but the results can be excellent. There are many advantages to this approach:

- Each partial can be individually controlled.

- The amplitude of each partial can be controlled over time, allowing for the tone of the combined wave created through the additive process to change over time.

- Individual partials can be detuned (to introduce more metallic elements into a sound), and the phase of each partial can be controlled, which gives yet more sonic possibilities.

This can be a highly detailed way of creating sounds, producing results that cannot be achieved in any other manner.

Additive Synthesis: Basic Principles

I have fleetingly mentioned that waves are made up from a combination of sine waves—different frequencies and different proportions of waves will give different results (or, as we prefer to call them, different sounds). Let's look at how the three most common waves can be constructed using additive principles.

Additive Square Wave

A square wave is made up of only odd-numbered harmonics (sine waves) with decreasing amplitudes in the ratio $1/n$ (where n is the number of that harmonic). The harmonics are therefore:

- The first harmonic (the fundamental), which has its full amplitude

- The third harmonic, which has an amplitude of one-third of the maximum

- The fifth harmonic, which has an amplitude of one-fifth, and so on

Figure 4.15 plots the amplitude of each harmonic against the harmonic's position. However, you will note that this graph only shows the first 16 harmonic positions where there should be an infinite number of harmonics.

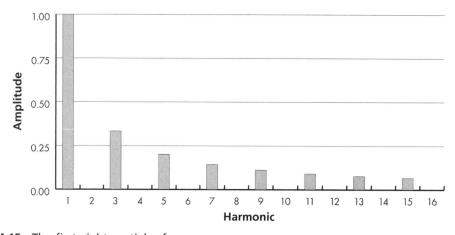

Figure 4.15 The first eight partials of a square wave.

Additive Sawtooth Wave

A sawtooth wave has both odd-numbered and even-numbered harmonics with amplitudes decreasing in the ratio $1/n$. The harmonics making up the sawtooth wave are therefore:

- The first harmonic at its full amplitude

- The second harmonic at half its amplitude

- The third harmonic at one-third of its full value

- The fourth harmonic at one-quarter of its full value, and so on

Take a look at Figure 4.16.

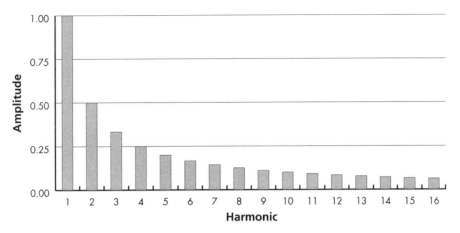

Figure 4.16   The first 16 partials of a sawtooth wave.

Additive Triangle Wave

A triangle wave has odd harmonics with decreasing amplitudes in the ratio $1/n^2$. Therefore, a triangle wave has the following harmonics:

- The first harmonic at its full amplitude

- The third harmonic at one-ninth of its full value

- The fifth harmonic at one-twenty-fifth of its full value

- The seventh harmonic at one-forty-ninth of its full value, and so on

Figure 4.17 shows this.

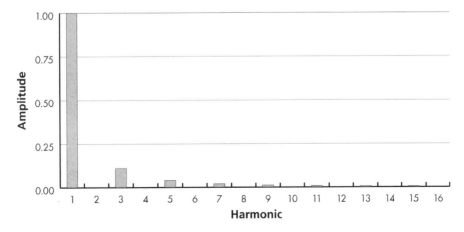

Figure 4.17   The first eight partials of a triangle wave.

Difficulties with Additive Synthesis

Additive synthesis has a reputation for being difficult. Difficult may be an understatement—additive can be hugely complex with virtually infinite permutations.

Before you can get to the complexity and the endless permutations, there is a far more straightforward challenge—creating an interesting sound. If you can't create an interesting sound, then the issues of how you control it over time and how you balance several sound sources are irrelevant.

Unfortunately, there is no magic formula for creating an interesting sound from first principles. You really need to sit down, listen, and build up some experience in creating these sounds. However, the end results will pay dividends, and this is one area where you can really create your own unique signature sounds.

Frequency Modulation (and Other Sorts of Modulation) Synthesis

For many people, frequency modulation (FM) synthesis seems both cumbersome and complicated, giving unpredictable results. However, FM is comparatively simple in concept—it just has a lot of possibilities that make it appear quite complicated. It also requires a different approach from that needed for subtractive synthesis, although it can be combined with subtractive synthesis for greater sonic control.

One of the first complications with FM is the naming. There are three names that are often applied to the concept:

- Frequency modulation synthesis

- Phase modulation synthesis

- Phase distortion synthesis

One of the key reasons for the confusion is that these terms are incorrectly applied in certain applications. Another reason is that the concepts are similar, and it is far too tedious to try to separate out the differences. For the purposes of this book, I'm going to lump all of the frequency and phase modulations under the FM heading. From a practical perspective, if you can use one type of modulation synthesis, then you can apply the principles to another type of modulation synthesis.

Operators

Instead of having oscillators, FM synthesizers have "operators," and to create an FM sound, you need two operators—a modulator and a carrier.

A modulator acts in a similar manner to a low-frequency oscillator (LFO). It modulates the frequency of the carrier—the carrier is the operator that is connected to the output and is therefore heard. However, the frequency of the modulator is much higher than would be usual for an LFO. Instead, the frequency of the modulator is in the audio spectrum so the modulator could be heard if it were to be connected to an output.

The effect of modulating a carrier with a signal in the audio spectrum is that the effect is not heard as vibrato, but instead the tone of the carrier is changed, often quite significantly.

FM sound is created by the interaction of the carrier and the modulator. This relationship does not need to be fixed—it can change over time, hence the sound created by the modulator/carrier combination can change. To my mind, FM sounds where the relationship doesn't change are quite dull and static, making them uninteresting.

Getting a Grip on FM Programming

The essential element of the FM sound is a modulator and a carrier working together. Sounds can have more than one modulator—there may be several carriers, each with their own modulator or several modulators modulating one carrier. However, there are four essential combinations of operators in FM synthesis—everything beyond these combinations is simply a variation on a theme.

Simple FM

Simple FM is where one modulator drives one carrier (see Figure 4.18).

Figure 4.18   A simple FM stack where one modulator drives one carrier.

This arrangement is the very essence of the FM sound. Most of the classic FM sounds can be built around this arrangement, although often several simple FM stacks will be layered together to achieve a thicker sound. Alternatively, some patches may be built around several simple FM stacks, providing different elements of the sound.

Often, one modulator/carrier stack alone will give a weak sound in the same way that a single oscillator in a subtractive synthesizer can give a weak sound. Modulators and carriers can be doubled to thicken up a sound in the same way that oscillators are doubled in a subtractive synthesizer.

Parallel Carriers

With parallel carriers, one modulator drives two or more carriers (see Figure 4.19).

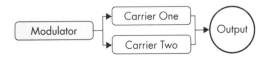

Figure 4.19   A parallel carrier arrangement where one modulator drives two carriers.

Parallel carriers allow the effect of two simple FM stacks to be achieved by using three operators rather than four. This leads to greater programming efficiency and marginally less CPU load.

The downside of parallel carriers becomes apparent if you detune one carrier (say by a couple of cents) to get a thicker sound. While the sound is thicker, there is also phase cancellation, which is primarily heard as a rise and fall in the volume.

However, if you use two simple FM stacks and detune both the modulator and the carrier in one stack, a much richer sound can be achieved without such apparent phase cancellation (but you are using more operators, so you are losing one advantage of parallel carriers).

Parallel carriers do not need to be at the same pitch. For instance, if you take one carrier at the base frequency and another one that is seven semitones higher, you have the basis for a Wurlitzer-type electric piano sound. Equally, this arrangement can yield many wooden (as in tuned percussion) type sounds.

Parallel Modulators

With parallel modulators, two or more modulators drive one carrier (see Figure 4.20).

Figure 4.20 A parallel modulator arrangement where two modulators drive one carrier.

Parallel modulators offer far more complicated and rich sounds than are available from a simple FM arrangement. However, more options give more complications—the relationship between the two modulators will have a considerable effect on the sound.

If the modulators are of the same pitch, then the effect of two modulators will be to enhance the amount of modulation. Tonally, this means that the brightening effect of the modulation will be increased.

Very simplistically, if the modulators are all set at intervals that correspond to integer multiples of the carrier's frequency, then the sound with parallel carriers will give a harmonious tone. Different intervals can give many different tones—some of which may be useful in a musical context and others of which may be considered more as sound effects.

Another simple but effective use for parallel modulators is to apply different envelope attack times. Used in conjunction with differently tuned modulators, this can give a very natural sound. Take a simple electric piano as an example:

- The first modulator could have a very fast attack and a short decay. This could be tuned to a higher pitch than the carrier to give the "bell" sound in the piano.

- The second modulator could have a slower attack and a sustain portion. This could be tuned to a pitch below the carrier to give a more bassy/wooden-type tone.

If two parallel modulators are very slightly detuned, this will lead to interference between the modulators (the same way as if two oscillators in a subtractive synth are detuned). However, the net effect is that the amount of modulation (and therefore the tone) will constantly shift as the operators cancel each other out. Depending on the particular patch, the results may or may not be desirable.

Cascade

With a cascade, one modulator drives another modulator, which itself then drives the carrier (see Figure 4.21).

Figure 4.21 A cascade where one modulator drives another modulator, which itself then drives the carrier.

With a cascade, the first modulator outputs a sine wave. However, the second and subsequent modulators are themselves being modulated. Accordingly, their output is a different waveform. Cascades can produce the richest and most complex FM timbres. A similar (but less controllable) effect can be created in a simple FM stack by modulating with waveforms other than the sine wave.

Although not illustrated in the graphic, it is possible to have more than three operators in a cascade; however, the results become less predictable, and there is a greater tendency to produce noise.

Controlling FM Sounds

The changing tone created by the combination means that sounds can be shaped without the need for a filter. However, you then need to control the interaction between the modulator(s) and the carrier(s) over time in order to give the tonal shifts that are characteristic of FM's unique sound.

In any modulator/carrier relationship, there are two key aspects that affect the sound:

- The frequency of the modulator relative to the carrier. As a general rule, the higher the frequency of the modulator relative to the carrier, the brighter (or more metallic) the sound.

- The amount of modulation. This is controlled by the output level of the modulator—the greater the output, the greater the effect of the modulator. (Again, this affects the brightness.)

To achieve the constant shifts and design the desired sound, each element must be controlled. Usually (but not always):

- The pitch relationship between each operator is fixed. So for instance, the modulator may be set to play an octave above the carrier. This relationship would then be maintained across the keyboard.

- The level of each operator is dynamic and will vary according to a range of factors, including:
  - The initial setting of the relationship to set the appropriate initial timbre.
  - Time—so as the note decays, the effect of the modulator can decay further, giving tonal shifts.
  - Velocity—in other words, the force with which the key is struck. Again, this allows a wide range of tonal shifts.

There are several tools in the armory to bring about these controls—envelopes, velocity scaling, and key scaling. We have used them all in subtractive synthesis.

Envelopes

With a subtractive synthesizer, you can control the tone over time by setting an envelope to control the frequency of the filter cut-off. With FM synthesis, you can achieve similar (or maybe better) tonal shifts by varying the amount by which the modulator affects the carrier over time. Instead of using an envelope to control the filter's cut-off, you can use an envelope to control the amount of modulation applied to the carrier.

You can use a conventional ADSR (attack time, decay time, sustain level, release time) envelope to control the amount of modulation. However, to achieve more detailed tonal results, you may find that one of the other forms of envelopes (which we will look at in Chapter 6, "Modulation and Control") gives better results.

Velocity Scaling

Velocity scaling can be used to create highly detailed sonic nuances. Velocity is often used to control the loudness of a sound. However, you can also use it to control the level by which the carrier is modulated by the modulator.

Velocity scaling does not have to have a range from zero to the maximum. For instance, if velocity scaling is controlling the tone of a sound, then you may want to set one end of the velocity range so that the sound is dull and the other so that the sound is bright. Dull and bright do not have to correspond with no modulation and maximum modulation.

Velocity scaling can give the musician immense amounts of control over an instrument, perhaps to a level where the synthesizer can come close to mimicking some of the behaviors of a real instrument.

Key Scaling

With subtractive synthesis, key scaling is usually only used to open up the filter a bit when higher notes are played. With FM synthesis, key scaling is often far more important.

It is very easy to create metallic sounds with FM synthesis. It is harder to create usable metallic sounds. One of the keys to designing FM sounds is to ensure that the overtones are appropriate.

It is quite easy to create a sound that works within a limited key range but does not work outside of that range. Often this will manifest itself as a sound that begins to sound too harsh. The harshness can be addressed in two ways:

- The modulation can be reduced. This may make the sound work outside of the first range; however, it will probably affect the original sound, perhaps making it too dull.

- The level of the operator can be reduced in certain key ranges. This is more likely to obtain the desired result. This is what we mean when we talk about key scaling (or key level scaling, as it is sometimes called).

Quick and Dirty Guide to FM Synthesis

So those are the basic elements and controls of FM synthesis. How do you use them in practice?

One of the biggest challenges in getting started with FM is the tuning. Here there are two problems:

- First, setting the pitch of the modulator can be difficult. Often, it will give a very unpleasant sound.

- Second, the pitch of the resulting sound may pose difficulties. This can arise for two reasons:
  - The pitch can be affected by the interaction of the modulator and the carrier, meaning that the resulting wave is not at the pitch you think it would be.
  - Also, the resulting waveforms can include many harmonious and inharmonious elements. If the inharmonious elements are predominant, then the resulting sound (especially if a chord is struck) may not be pleasant and may not "sound" as if it is at the right pitch.

We can't address all of those issues—some FM sound are just plain horrible and are probably best ignored (although there may be times when your aim is an unpleasant sound). What we can deal with are some of the questions about tuning ratios.

Carrier:Modulator Ratio

With a simple FM stack, the extent to which an FM sound might be perceived as being pleasing to the ear is mostly a matter of mathematics. If the carrier and the modulator have related frequencies—generally, if their frequencies are integer multiples—then the resulting sound will tend to give a far more useful and cohesive tone. Clearly, when you start getting into the world of parallel operators (especially parallel modulators) and cascades, the mathematics becomes far more complicated.

In this context, the ratio is related to the underlying frequency of the notes, so for instance, you will find that an 880-Hz modulator will work well with a 440-Hz carrier. Now, you will have noticed that we don't identify notes by their frequency, but rather by their name, so for the rest of this section, I will talk in semitones rather than frequencies. So, if we are thinking in terms of carrier:modulator ratios (or C:M ratios), where the modulator frequency is a multiple of the carrier's frequency, then:

- With a 1:2 ratio, the modulator is 12 semitones higher than the carrier. (The modulator would be twice the frequency of the carrier.)

- With a 1:3 ratio, the modulator is 19 semitones higher than the carrier (an octave plus a fifth—the modulator would be three times the frequency of the carrier).

- With a 1:4 ratio, the modulator is 24 semitones (or two octaves) higher than the carrier.

Carrier:Modulator Ratios That Work

There are innumerable permutations for the different carrier:modulator ratios that you can choose (especially when you start looking at the microtonal options—don't worry, we're not going to look at them here). These different ratios will give a range of different tones, which can then be adjusted with the level of the modulator. The range of options can be a bit daunting. To get you going, the most immediately usable ratios (in a musical context) are:

- Modulator one (and sometimes two) octave(s) below the carrier

- Modulator seven semitones below the carrier

- Modulator five semitones below the carrier

- Modulator at same pitch as the carrier

- Modulator five semitones, 17 semitones (one octave plus five), 29 semitones (two octaves plus five) above the carrier

- Modulator seven semitones, 19 semitones (one octave plus seven), 31 semitones (two octaves plus seven) above the carrier

- Modulator one, two, or three octaves above the carrier

Two octaves plus a fifth (in other words, pitching the modulator 31 semitones above the carrier) can give that classic FM bell-like tone (provided you get the envelopes—especially the modulator envelope—right).

These ratios may not work across the whole keyboard, and they are, of course, dependent on the level of the modulator. However, these are likely to be the most immediately useful ratios. With some further experimentation, you are sure to find other combinations that appeal to you. You will also find that with lower amounts of modulation, many other ratios give very appealing sounds.

Ring Modulation

Before we leave modulation as a tool to create weird sounds, let me briefly mention ring modulation, which is the effect of combining the sum and difference between two waveforms' frequencies (see Figure 4.22).

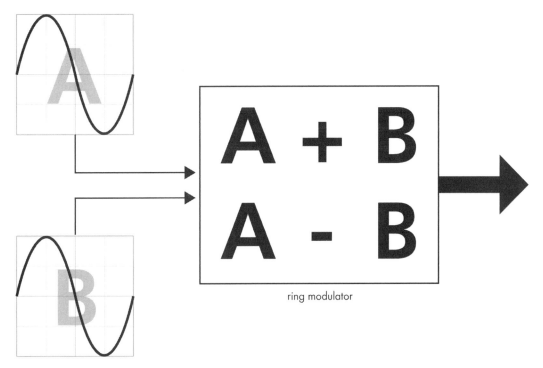

ring modulator

Figure 4.22 The principle behind ring modulation.

The results of ring modulation are often hard to predict and may not be easy to control (if you are looking for a sound that can be used in a musical context). Some synthesizers, such as KarmaFX Synth Modular (see Figure 4.23), make it easy to set up ring modulation sounds by offering a ring modulation control on the face of one of its sound-generating modules.

Figure 4.23 The KarmaFX Synth Modular Osc 2 module set up to ring modulate.

The Available Sound Sources

Before we move on to look at the specific modules and think about what they could do for you, could I add three reminders, please?

First, this is not a compare-and-contrast exercise. We are looking at a group of modules—some of which will be very similar in many ways—but the point of this is to highlight features you could use and to consider why one may be more suitable for any task. The purpose is not to definitively opine that something is "better" or "worse" than another module on some arbitrary scale.

Equally, different synthesizers achieve the same end by having options within modules where others offer more and different modules. Neither approach is better or worse.

Second, just because a particular module has a feature, that does not mean it will work:

- As described in this book
- In a similar manner to other similar or comparable modules

Third, this book is not a replacement for the operating manuals. While I will cover most modules and features in the synthesizers, I do not intend to describe every module and every feature. So for instance:

- I don't describe any of the audio input modules—I figure you can guess what they do, and this book is about synthesis, not audio processing.
- I don't see any merit in noting when every module has an output level.
- I'm not going to highlight many useful (but non-sound-generating features). For instance, some synthesizers allow fine control over certain parameters or allow you to set the range over which a control may work.
- I don't look at sample editing tools that may be included in any sampler modules.

For all of these, you will need the manual. Also, I am not here to suggest why a developer has chosen to include or not include any particular features/behaviors.

Sound-Creation Modules in Zebra 2

Like all of the synthesizers featured in this book, Zebra 2 has a range of different sound-creating modules, and within those modules there are many options. Come and have a look.

Osc: Oscillators

The basic unit of sound creation in Zebra 2 is the Osc oscillator (see Figure 4.24). When you load this module, an LFO is automatically loaded to control the vibrato. We will look at the LFO in Chapter 6.

Figure 4.24 The Osc oscillator module and its companion LFO in Zebra 2.

The basic Osc unit is quite empty. However, there are a number of tabs that open up separate functions. I'll come to the tabs in a moment, but for the moment, let's stay on the main interface. Here you will find:

- **Wave.** In Zebra 2, there is the facility to load up several waves—or variants of the same wave. You can then sweep through this collection of waves to achieve unique tonal shifts. The Wave knob controls which wave is selected to play. To the left of the Wave knob is the modulator so you can control the wave selection by a modulator (such as an envelope or an LFO).

- **Tune.** The Tune knob controls oscillator pitch adjustments over a maximum range of plus or minus four octaves. By the way, if you hold down the Shift key while making adjustments, you can make very fine changes.

- **Detune.** The Detune knob allows fine adjustments to the oscillator's pitch over the range of plus or minus one semitone.

- **Vibrato.** The Vibrato control sets the depth of the vibrato effect (which is controlled by LFO1).

Wave Selection

When you open the Osc module, by default it loads the "default" wave—a sawtooth wave. If you click on the default label, then the Oscillator Selector box will appear (see Figure 4.25), from which you can select your oscillator wave. You can audition various waves—as you click on the wave it will be loaded. Once you have made your selection, close the selector box by clicking on the Close button (at the top-right).

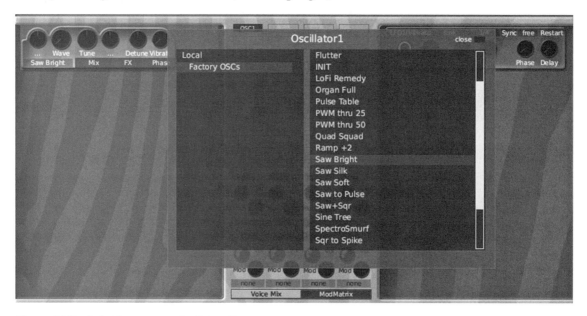

Figure 4.25 Selecting a wave in Zebra 2.

However, when you load a wave, you are doing more than that.

- With some waves (for instance, the pulse-width waves) you load up other modules (such as LFOs).

- With other waves you load a set of waves (called a *waveset*). Wavesets comprise a group of related waves that you can select by using the Wave knob. We'll look at how to modify these waves in the More Osc section (which is coming up shortly).

These two points are not mutually exclusive. In other words, you can load a multi-wave set and other modules simply by choosing certain waves.

Mix

The Mix tab (see Figure 4.26) opens up some more interesting possibilities.

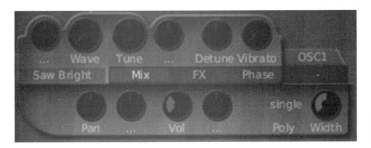

Figure 4.26 The Mix tab in Zebra 2's Osc module.

The two easy controls are:

- The Pan knob (and its associated modulator), which controls the placement of the output in the stereo spectrum.

- The Volume knob (and its associated modulator), which sets the level of the module. This volume control is useful because it allows several audio modules to be mixed before processing and before they hit the output.

To the right, there is the Single label and the Width control.

- The Single label accesses the oscillator's multi-voice setting. When set to Single, there is one voice, but by clicking on the label you can access a pop-up menu with the following options:
  - Single (one voice)
  - Dual (two voices)
  - Quad (four voices)
  - Eleven (do I need to explain?)

- The Width control sets how the voices are spread over the stereo spectrum.

When multi-voice mode is invoked, the Detune knob controls the relative detuning of the voices.

FX

The FX tab (see Figure 4.27) accesses some quite unusual settings.

This tab offers more than 20 algorithms that modify the underlying waveform. Some changes are subtle, some less so. Again, this is an area where I am not going to go into detail about all of the options.

You will see that there are two slots and that each slot has a Value (depth) control and the option to apply a modulator.

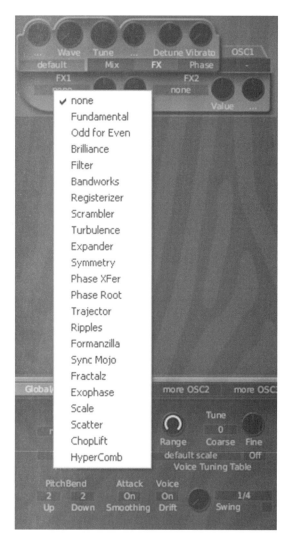

Figure 4.27 The FX options in Zebra 2's Osc module.

Phase

The last tab in the Osc module is the Phase tab (see Figure 4.28).

Figure 4.28 The Phase tab in Zebra 2's Osc module.

While the tab is labeled Phase, the key scaling settings are also accessed here. However, the main function of this tab is to add a second waveform to the signal. That second wave can then be manipulated for some interesting results.

- **Phase.** The Phase knob controls the phase of the second oscillator (relative to the first). The phase of the oscillator can be inverted by using the Inv button to the left of the Phase knob. Next to the Phase knob is a slot to select a modulator for the phase.

- **Sync.** The Sync switch hard syncs the second oscillator, which becomes the slave. The Sync knob then allows the pitch of the second oscillator to be raised over a range of three octaves. There is, of course, a dedicated modulation slot for this function, too.

- **KeyScale.** The KeyScale knob controls how the oscillator responds to incoming MIDI data—this function's operation is independent of the phase-related settings. At its default setting of 100%, there is a direct one-to-one relationship (so one semitone on the keyboard equals one semitone for the oscillator). However, that doesn't have to be the case—the oscillator can respond:

  - To a greater extent (when the KeyScale knob is set to values greater than 100%).

  - To a lesser extent (when the KeyScale knob is set to values between zero and 100%).

  - To no pitch information, so the same note is played across the keyboard (when the KeyScale knob is set to zero).

  - In reverse (when the KeyScale knob is set to negative values). In this instance, higher notes on the keyboard will result in the oscillator playing lower notes.

More Osc

Your head is probably spinning from the complexity of what is already on offer for the oscillators. I'm now going to tell you even more—this either will be highly confusing or will set your mind alight with further sound-generating possibilities. Take a look at the More Osc settings (which are shown in Figure 4.29). This is where we get into the additive and fine-detail worlds.

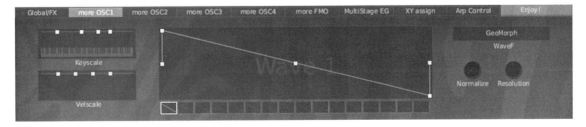

Figure 4.29   The More Osc settings for Osc 1 in Zebra 2.

To the top left of the box, you will find an image of a keyboard with a graph above it. This is another form of key scaling, so while I apologize for any confusion, please take care to ensure that you don't get mixed up with the KeyScale control mentioned a moment ago.

With this key scaling function, you can lower the volume of the oscillator in certain areas of the keyboard. The most common uses for this function would be:

- To lower (or raise) the volume of an oscillator as its pitch gets higher. If you have two oscillators set so that one gets louder and the other gets quieter as pitch increases, you could set up a nice crossfade.

- To tame any loud volume peaks. For instance, if you have a resonance peak at a certain frequency, then you could easily stamp on it by scaling back the oscillator's volume around that frequency range.

Under the Keyscale controller is a (Velscale) velocity scale controller. This works much like a velocity filter to cut out (or attenuate) certain velocities.

The main action in More Osc happens in the middle, where you see the waveform display, and this is where you can edit the waveform. Before we get there, you will notice that under the main waveform display there are 16 small waves displayed. These are the waves comprising the wave-set. When you twist the Wave knob, you will see each of these waves highlighted in turn. To select a wave, click on the icon—you can then edit that wave in the main waveform display. As you click on the wave's icon, you will note that the Wave knob turns to the appropriate position.

There are four wave-shaping options, selectable from the drop-down to the right of the wave-form display:

- **GeoMorph and SpectroMorph.** In GeoMorph and SpectroMorph modes, you can draw your waveform using up to 32 points. There are a range of tools (accessible by right-clicking) to smooth, sharpen, and so on.

- **GeoBlend and SpectroBlend.** In GeoBlend and SpectroBlend modes, a range of additive partials is spread across the spectrum. When arranged horizontally, they create a sawtooth—from that point you can cut and boost to adjust the sound.

FMO: Frequency Modulation Oscillators

Zebra 2 offers a specialized FM (frequency modulation) Oscillator (which also offers some ring modulation sounds). The beauty of this module is that it makes creating FM sounds straightforward, and a wide range of algorithms can be created with the click of a mouse. Figure 4.30 shows an FM patch using the FM Oscillators in Zebra 2.

The FM Oscillator is a sine wave oscillator that has been designed to be frequency modulated. It can be frequency modulated in one of two ways:

- It can frequency modulate itself. This is a less controllable form of FM, giving less tonal flexibility and having a greater tendency to create noise.

Figure 4.30 Making sounds with the FM Oscillators in Zebra 2.

■ It can be frequency modulated by another sound source. This is what I have done with the sound that is shown in Figure 4.30. In essence, the process to set this up is:

1. Put the first oscillator onto the audio path. This doesn't need to be an FM Oscillator, although that is what I have used in Figure 4.30. If you choose a regular oscillator, then exercise some caution over your choice of waveform, as this will have a significant effect on the sound. This oscillator will act as the modulator.

2. Next, put an FM Oscillator on the audio path, further down the audio chain (in other words, positioned below the modulator in the modules matrix). This second oscillator will act as the carrier.

3. Adjust the pitch of the modulator module.

4. Adjust the amount of FM in the carrier module until the tone is right. And that's it. (Well, in essence, that's it.)

Let's have a look at the main controls on the FM Oscillator.

Main Controls on the FM Oscillator

Many, but not all, of the controls in the FM Oscillator are very similar to those in the regular oscillator.

- **FM Mode.** The FM mode is selected from a drop-down menu. The options are discussed in the next section.

- **Tune.** The Tune knob controls the FM Oscillator pitch adjustments over a maximum range of plus or minus four octaves. The relationship between the pitch of the carrier and the modulator is one of the key elements in the FM sound. There is a modulation slot to control the pitch in real time. However, changing the carrier/modulator pitch relationship in real time does not always give pleasing results.

- **Vibrato.** The Vibrato control sets the depth of the vibrato effect (which is controlled by LFO1).

- **Detune.** The Detune knob allows fine adjustments to the FM Oscillator's pitch over the range of plus or minus one semitone.

- **KeyScale.** The KeyScale knob controls how the oscillator responds to incoming MIDI data. At its default setting of 100%, there is a direct one-to-one relationship (so one semitone on the keyboard equals one semitone for the oscillator). This offers the same options as with a regular oscillator; however, if you're creating FM sounds, unless you want something wild and crazy, keep the knob at 100% for all FM Oscillators.

- **FM.** The FM knob controls the FM depth in the carrier. In other words, it controls the extent to which the modulator is (or modulators are) modulating the carrier's oscillator's frequency. There is a modulator slot—this is one area where it will pay sonic dividends to set up a very nuanced envelope.

FM Modes

There are five FM modes that should be selected on any carrier (or on the only) FM Oscillator. The choice of FM mode will have quite an effect on the sound and the controllability of the sound.

- **FM by Input.** The FM by Input mode applies the input signals (in other words, the audio signals earlier on the same audio path) and uses them as the modulators in the FM Oscillator module.

- **FM by Self (+).** The FM by Self (+) mode uses its own output as the modulation source. A similar effect can be created by feeding back a signal into an oscillator to create an FM sound. At lower levels of FM amount, this can add some grit to the sound; however, it will quickly turn to noise.

- **RM Input.** The RM Input mode takes the incoming audio signal and the sine wave created in the FM Oscillator and ring modulates the two.

- **FM Filtered.** The FM Filtered mode is very similar to the FM by Input mode. However, there are some differences:
  - The incoming signal is passed through a low-pass filter.
  - The FM amount is set to the maximum.
  - The FM amount knob controls the cut-off frequency of the filter through which the incoming signal passes.

  This mode produces a smoother form of FM and is often a better choice when the modulation wave is not a sine wave.

- **FM Self 2 (+).** The FM Self 2 (+) mode is similar to the FM by Self (+) mode. The difference is that the signal that is fed back to become the modulation source is squared. This changes the tonal character of the sound.

More FMO

If you look back to Figure 4.30, you will see that the More FMO sub-page is displayed. This allows you to control each of the FM Oscillators in two areas.

In the top row, you will find an image of a keyboard with a graph above it. Like with the More Osc options, this is key scaling, which allows you to lower the volume of the oscillator in certain areas of the keyboard. While this may be a "nice-to-have" feature for conventional oscillators, for FM Oscillators, this control is fundamental.

Very often, you will want to rein in an FM Oscillator at a certain point for tonal reasons. For instance, often you will find that you would like to lower the FM amount at higher keyboard ranges, but you can't because that would have a detrimental effect on the sound when played at normal ranges. The answer is to use this key scaling function to pull in the modulating oscillator.

The second row of graphs, under the keyscale controller, is a velocity scale controller for each FM Oscillator. These work much like a velocity filter to cut out (or attenuate) the FM Oscillator at certain velocities.

Noise: Noise Source

The Noise module (see Figure 4.31) creates noise. However, it does slightly more than just create noise.

Figure 4.31 The Noise module in Zebra 2.

Let's have a look at the controls and see what options the module offers us.

- **Noise type.** The Noise selector gives you the choice of four noise types:
  - White noise
  - Pink noise
  - Digital noise (which is a more metallic sound)
  - Crackles (more noise...)

- **Volume.** The Volume knob controls the volume of the module.

- **Width.** The Width knob controls the stereo spread of the output if the module is working in stereo mode.

- **Filters.** There is a built-in low-pass filter and a built-in high-pass filter, allowing for considerable tonal shaping before the sound leaves the module. Neither filter offers any resonance to exaggerate the cut-off frequency and allow for pitched noise–type sounds, but both filter cut-off controls do have their own dedicated modulator slot. Clearly, the filters need to be fully open if the noise is to be heard without shaping. You should also note that the range of the cut-off frequencies of these filters does overlap, which means that it is possible to cut the signal completely. As a side note, when the digital noise source is selected, the filters change from the low-pass/high-pass combination to be far more useful for that sound source.

Sound Creation Modules in VAZ Modular

VAZ Modular has a wide and varied range of modules for creating sounds. Several of these are variations on a theme that have been customized for specific purposes.

Common Controls

Before we look at the sound generators, I want to look at the controls that are common to most (but not all) of the VAZ Modular sound-generating modules. These are located at the top of the modules:

- **Pitch.** The Pitch drop-down is where you select the controller that is sending pitch information to the module. Normally, you would choose CV 1 Note High or CV 1 Note Low.

- **Tuning.** The tuning controls affect the frequencies of the notes played by the sound module. There are three elements to this functionality:
  - The octave selectors. These are the five buttons (labeled 32′, 16′, 8′, 4′, and 2′)—the smaller the number, the higher the octave.
  - The semitone adjuster (the top slider), which adjusts the oscillator's pitch over a range of plus or minus 12 semitones.

- The cent adjuster (the bottom slider), which adjusts the oscillator's pitch over a range of plus or minus 50 cents (one semitone).

■ **Sync.** The Sync drop-down selects a source to which the waveform should be slaved. And yes, I know this isn't a pitch thing, but it is geographically close enough.

Now those are explained, so I will not mention them again.

You will also notice that each module has a range of modulation slots, many of which are very similar. There are three elements to these slots:

■ The drop-down menu from which you select the modulator

■ The orange plus and minus buttons, which affect whether the modulation is positive or negative (for instance, whether an envelope would raise pitch or lower pitch)

■ The slider (under the drop-down menu), which determines the depth of the modulation

Oscillator

The Oscillator module (see Figure 4.32) is the general-purpose sound source in VAZ Modular.

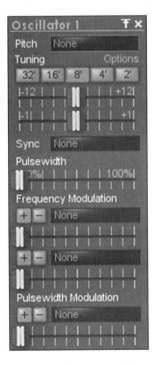

Figure 4.32 The Oscillator module in VAZ Modular.

The Oscillator module outputs two waveforms: a sawtooth wave and a pulse wave. You can select the appropriate wave in the audio routing—there is no facility to switch between the two on the interface.

- **Pulsewidth.** The Pulsewidth slider controls the width of the Oscillator's pulse wave.

- **Frequency Modulation.** The two Frequency Modulation slots allow you to select two modulators that can modulate the pitch of the Oscillator. While this can be used for "FM synthesis"–type sounds, it is best for pitch adjustments (for instance, adding some vibrato or using an envelope to get some "kick" at the start of a note).

- **Pulsewidth Modulation.** The Pulsewidth Modulation slot allows you to load a modulator to modulate the pulse width of the Oscillator's waves.

You might also want to check out Oscillator B and Oscillator D (see Figure 4.33), which offer similar functionality. (Given the similarity, I'm not going to cover them here.)

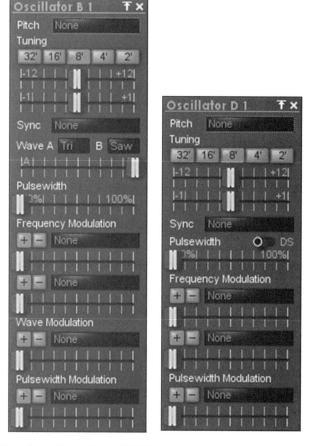

Figure 4.33 Oscillator B and Oscillator D in VAZ Modular.

MultiOscillator and Multi-Saw Osc

The MultiOscillator and Multi-Saw Oscillator (see Figure 4.34) are very similar to the regular Oscillator.

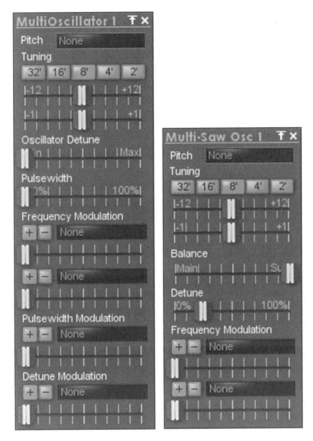

Figure 4.34 The MultiOscillator and Multi-Saw Oscillator modules in VAZ Modular.

MultiOscillator Controls

Instead of outputting one wave, the MultiOscillator outputs four waves, which can be detuned.

From the regular Oscillator, there are some additional controls on the MultiOscillator:

- **Oscillator Detune.** The Oscillator Detune slider controls the extent to which each of the separate voices within the module is detuned.

- **Detune Modulation.** The Detune Modulation slot allows you to load up a modulator to control the detuning of the separate voices in real time.

Multi-Saw Oscillator Controls

Unlike the Oscillator and MultiOscillator, which both output saw and pulse waves, the Multi-Saw Oscillator, as you will have guessed, only has the option to output saw waves. It also has a sub-oscillator, and it is the sub-oscillator where the multi-voice thing happens.

From the regular Oscillator, there are some additional controls on the Multi-Saw:

- **Balance.** The Balance slider controls the respective levels of the main oscillator and the multi-voice sub-oscillator.

- **Detune.** The Detune slider controls the extent to which each of the separate voices within the sub-oscillator is detuned.

Cosmo A Oscillator

The Cosmo A Oscillator (see Figure 4.35) is described as a phase distortion oscillator. In practice, this means it can create a wide variety of sounds. The phase distortion can be created within the module, so it has the ability to create these effects without interaction with other modules.

Let's look at the controls that are not present on the other oscillator modules.

- **Frequency Modulation.** The Frequency Modulation slot allows you to select a modulator that can modulate the pitch of the oscillator. This can be used for FM synthesis–type sounds, but as with the regular oscillator, it is best for pitch adjustments.

- **Shapers.** The Shapers control switches between two separate settings for the Hardness, Width, and Slope controls.

- **Octave Mod.** The Octave Mod controls the phase distortion modulator wave, dropping it by an octave and increasing the complexity of the wave.

- **Mode.** The Mode selector has two options: Single Cycle and Double Cycle. The Double Cycle option produces a more complex wave, which, again, can have a significant effect on the sonic output.

- **Hardness.** The Hardness control adjusts the modulator wave between a sine wave and the wave created by the combination of the Width and Slope controls.

- **Width and Slope.** The Width and Slope controls adjust the modulator wave and have a high level of interaction.

Comso B Oscillator

The Cosmo B Oscillator (see Figure 4.36) is described as producing waveforms by the masked sync of a sine wave. (In other words, a sine wave works as the modulator in a phase distortion–type module.) In practice, like the Cosmo A Oscillator, it can create a wide variety of sounds.

- **Mask.** In effect, the Mask control gives you three options (Saw, Triangle, Trapezoid) for the wave that acts as the carrier wave.

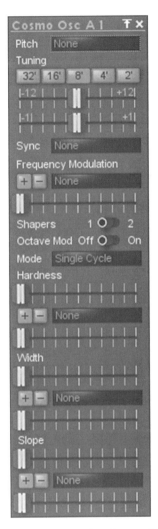

Figure 4.35 The Cosmo A Oscillator in VAZ Modular.

Figure 4.36 The Cosmo B Oscillator in VAZ Modular.

- **Waveshape.** The Waveshape slider adjusts the amount of phase distortion.

- **Frequency Modulation.** The Frequency Modulation slots allow you to select up to two modulators that can modulate the pitch of the oscillator.

- **Waveshape Modulation.** The two Waveshape Modulation slots allow the amount set by the Waveshape control to be adjusted in real time.

Noise Source

The Noise Source module (see Figure 4.37)...creates noise.

Figure 4.37   The Noise Source in VAZ Modular.

Unlike other noise sources, this has a slider that adjusts the noise on a continuum between white noise and red noise, passing pink at the midpoint. This gives a greater range of tonal possibilities.

There is also a modulation slot so you can modulate the color of the noise in real time.

Sample

The Sample module (see Figure 4.38) is a simple sample playback module.

Figure 4.38   The Sample module in VAZ Modular.

The module is intended to play back unpitched samples—in other words, the sample will play back at its recorded pitch irrespective of the key that is struck. Accordingly, you will see that there is no Pitch slot to choose the pitch control source, but instead there is a Trig control to set the trigger to start playback. Equally, there is only one tuning slider, which can adjust the sample over the range of plus or minus one octave.

You can load the sample to be replayed by clicking on the Wave selector and navigating to the appropriate sample.

Sine Oscillator

The Sine Oscillator generates sine waves. On its own this is not particularly interesting, but this module has been set up to use those sine waves to create phase modulation– (or frequency modulation–) type sounds. Figure 4.39 shows two Sine Oscillators set up to produce an FM-type sound.

As you can see in Figure 4.39, the modulation source is derived from Sine Oscillator 2. The modulation signal passes through an amplifier (which has its level controlled by an envelope and velocity) before it is fed into Sine Oscillator 1 to act as the modulator.

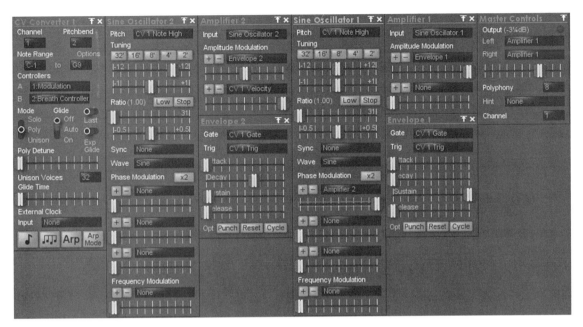

Figure 4.39   The Two Sine Oscillators in VAZ Modular set up to create an FM synthesis sound.

Let's take a look at the controls.

- **Low.** The Low button drops the pitch of the oscillator.

- **Stop.** The Stop button stops the wave, in effect switching out the oscillator.

- **Ratio.** The Ratio slider controls the pitch of the Sine Oscillator. This works to multiply the frequency, which can lead to significant pitch shifts—with each multiplication, the pitch is raised by an octave. This control can multiply the pitch by up to 31 times.

- **Phase Modulation.** The Phase Modulation slots allow you to assign a modulator. This is the modulator that will create the FM (or strictly, phase modulation) sounds. As you saw in Figure 4.39, this slot was used to attach the second oscillator (which was acting as the modulator) to the carrier oscillator. The ×2 switch doubles the effect of this modulation.

- **Frequency Modulation.** The Frequency Modulation slot allows you to select a modulator that can modulate the pitch of the Sine Oscillator. You could hook a modulator to this slot to do some FM synthesis, but the results are likely to have less tonal range than would be the case if you used the Phase Modulation process. However, this would give you a still broader tonal palette, so please do try.

Wavetable Oscillator

The Wavetable Oscillator (see Figure 4.40) is a sample playback module.

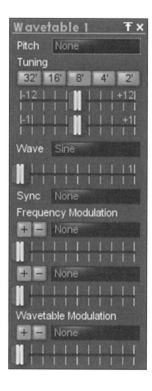

Figure 4.40   The Wavetable sample playback module in VAZ Modular.

With this module, you can load:

- Individual samples, which are then played over the whole keyboard.

- Multi-samples, which are played over specific ranges (and ideally you collect sufficient multi-samples to cover the whole keyboard range).

- Wavetables, which are collections of waves so that you can create wave-sequencing types of effects. If you have loaded a wavetable, then the Wave slider will select which wave in the sequence plays. You can also automate this by using the Wavetable Modulation slot.

You can load samples by clicking on the Wave selector. This will open the Sample Loader dialog (see Figure 4.41), where you can load and arrange your samplesets.

WTVoice

The WTVoice module (see Figure 4.42) is a simplified version of the Wavetable Oscillator, but with an envelope and an amplifier built in. The advantage of this arrangement is that you don't need to load separate amplifier and envelope modules—you can attach the Pitch control at one end and the outputs at the other, and you're good to go.

The Wave selector loads the waves (through the Sample Loader) using the same process that you would use for the Wavetable Oscillator. You can check out Chapter 6 if you're not sure how the envelope should be hooked up.

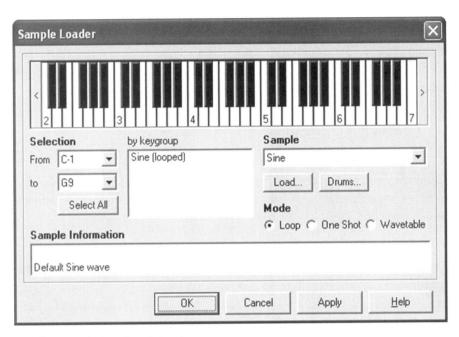

Figure 4.41   The Sample Loader dialog box.

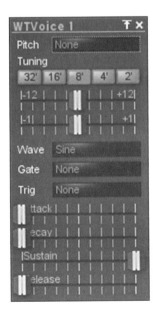

Figure 4.42   The WTVoice module in VAZ Modular.

Sound Creation Modules in KarmaFX Synth Modular

Let's look at the modules in KarmaFX Synth Modular.

Osc 1

Osc 1 (see Figure 4.43) is a fairly straightforward oscillator module.

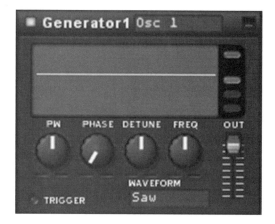

Figure 4.43 The Osc 1 module in KarmaFX Synth Modular.

There are six main controls on the module:

- **Waveform.** The waveform selector offers five wave choices:
  - Saw
  - Ramp
  - Square
  - Triangle
  - Sine

- **Pulse Width.** The PW knob controls the pulse width of the square and triangle waves.

- **Trigger and Phase.** The Phase knob controls the initial phase of a wave. However, to be really useful, this needs to be used in conjunction with the Trigger switch, which synchronizes the phase start (as determined by the Phase control) to a key press.

- **Detune.** The Detune knob allows fine pitch adjustments to the oscillator over the range plus or minus one semitone.

- **Frequency.** The Freq knob allows wide pitch adjustments to the oscillator over a maximum range of plus or minus four octaves.

Osc 2

The Osc 2 module (see Figure 4.44) is similar to the Osc 1 module in many ways. The key difference is that this module includes two oscillators. This can create a fatter sound and also a range of other sounds—however, because both oscillators are within one module, it can be much quicker and easier to set up sounds.

Figure 4.44 The Osc 2 module in KarmaFX Synth Modular.

Let's look at the main controls.

- **Waveform1 and Waveform2.** The two waveform selectors allow you to select a wave for each of the waveform slots. You can select a different wave in each slot or the same wave. Each slot offers five wave choices:
  - Saw
  - Ramp
  - Square
  - Triangle
  - Sine

- **Pulse Width.** The PW knob controls the pulse width of the square, triangle, and sine waves. The sine wave pulse-width option is not available in the Osc 1 module.

- **Trigger and Phase.** The Phase knob controls the initial phase of both waves. However, to be really useful, this needs to be used in conjunction with the Trigger switch, which synchronizes the phase start (as determined by the Phase control) to a key press. There is no option to adjust the phase of one wave in the module against the other—if you're looking for tonal shifts from putting waves out of phase, then you will need to use two separate oscillators.

- **Tune.** The Tune knob allows fine pitch adjustments to the whole oscillator unit over the range plus or minus one semitone.

- **Frequency.** The Freq knob allows wide pitch adjustments to the whole oscillator unit over a maximum range of plus or minus four octaves.

- **Mix.** The Mix control mixes the two oscillators, allowing you to shape the tone output by the oscillator. This setting can, of course, be modulated, thereby allowing the tone to change over time.

- **Ring modulation.** The Ringmod knob controls the ring modulation amount with one wave effectively ring-modulating the other.

- **Tune2.** The Tune2 knob allows fine pitch adjustments to Oscillator 2 over the range plus or minus one semitone.

- **Frequency2.** The Freq2 knob allows pitch increases to Oscillator 2 over a range of up to eight octaves.

- **Hard sync.** The Hardsync control sets Wave 2 as the slave to Wave 1.

Sampler

The Sampler (see Figure 4.45) allows individual samples or a collection of samples to be used as the sound source. As a side note, while a collection of samples can be loaded, only one sample can play at any one time in this module.

Figure 4.45   The Sampler module in KarmaFX Synth Modular.

The key controls on the Sampler module are:

- **Load, Add, Clear, and Remove.** The Load Sample button opens a file browser from which you can load samples (in WAV format). The Add button opens another slot so you can load more than one sample (by repeating the Load process). The Remove button clears the current sample, and the Clear button clears all loaded samples.

- **Import.** The Import button allows you to import multi-samples in SF2 and SFZ formats. This means you can import samples that have already been laid out over the keyboard. The SF2 format is the ubiquitous SoundFont format. SFZ is the format used in many Cakewalk synthesizers (and of course, you can read more about this format in my book, *Cakewalk Synthesizers: From Presets to Power User*).

- **Normalize and Reverse.** The Normalize and Reverse functions both work on a loaded sample. The Normalize function increases the level of the sample as far as possible without distortion, and the Reverse function flips the sample around so that it is played backwards.

- **Start.** The Start knob controls the start of the sample. This allows you to trim off the beginning of a sample, whether for artistic or technical reasons (for instance, if there is some noise or a pause before the note starts). You can, of course, also use an envelope to control the start of a note, and this may well be the best choice if you're making a change for artistic reasons. However, an envelope is not the right course if there is a technical flaw in the sample that can be remedied with the Start knob (or better still, remedied by opening up an audio editor).

- **Length.** The Length knob controls the relative length of the sample.

- **Delta.** The Delta knob adjusts the relative playing speed of the sample. This has a noticeable effect on the pitch of the note.

- **Frequency.** The Freq knob allows wide pitch adjustments to the whole oscillator unit over a maximum range of plus or minus four octaves.

- **Sample.** The Sample knob changes the current sample that is being played (if there is more than one sample loaded, and provided that Multi isn't switched on).

- **Multi.** The Multi selector switches on multi-sample mode so that different samples can be mapped to different pitch triggers and different velocity ranges.

- **Loop.** The Loop setting allows you to switch on looping and determine the loop type (forward, backward, and ping pong—in other words, backward and forward).

The Sampler unit is another example of a module that has more controls (in particular to edit the underlying samples) that I am not covering in this book.

You should also note that the Sampler stores samples as part of the patch. This has two immediate implications:

- First, patches have the potential to get quite big.

- Second, you should ensure that you are not infringing on any copyright legislation if you share any patch that includes a sample. If you are not the copyright holder for a sample, then you may be infringing on international copyright laws if you pass on any patch, including a sample where the copyright is owned by someone else.

Additive

The Additive sound module (see Figure 4.46) gives you huge amounts of control over additive waveforms.

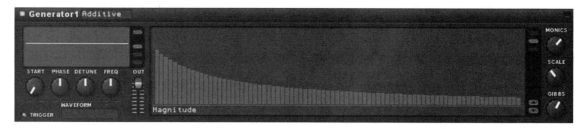

Figure 4.46 *The Additive module in KarmaFX Synth Modular.*

This module is worth taking some time to look at in detail. Before we get going, let me highlight a feature in all of the KarmaFX Synth Modular modules that is particularly relevant here. If you look to the right of the waveform display (to the left of the Monics knob), you will see three LEDs. These control the display interface, displaying different functions for each module. For the Additive module, these three display (from the top):

- **Waveform.** The waveform that is created by the sum of the sine waves (or partials). As well as displaying the waveform that is playing, in this view you can also draw the waveform to create a wholly new sound.

- **Magnitude.** The number and level of each additive partial. In this view, you can click and drag each partial to adjust its level (and thereby create or sculpt your sound).

- **Phase.** The (number and) phase of each additive partial. In the same way that the phase of a whole wave can be controlled, this setting allows you to control the phase of a single partial. Surprisingly, this can have a significant effect on a sound.

The Monics knob allows you to set how many partials are included within a waveform. You can set this over a range of 1 to 1,024 partials. With more partials, the wave can be more detailed. However, with a lower number of partials, it is much easier to adjust partials individually, and if you set the knob to 1, then you will get a single solitary sine wave.

Take a look at Figures 4.47, 4.48, and 4.49, which show a square wave created with 1,024 partials, a square wave with 8 partials, and the partials level (which you can compare to Figure 4.15). While the difference between the two square waves may not look significant, if you listen to the difference, the change is very marked.

Let's have a look at some of the other controls on the module.

- **Waveform.** The Waveform selector offers a wide range of waveforms, which are constructed through partials that can then be edited. You can also get immediate tonal variations by using the Monics control.

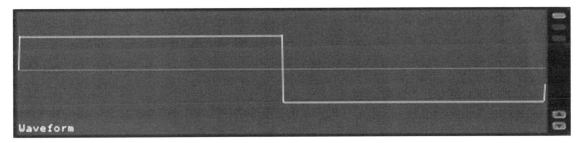

Figure 4.47   The waveform display for a square wave created in the KarmaFX Synth Modular Additive module with the Monics knob set to 1,024 (so this uses 512 partials because a square wave is constructed with odd partials).

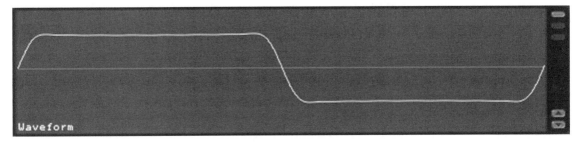

Figure 4.48   The waveform display for a square wave created in the KarmaFX Synth Modular Additive module with the Monics knob set to 16 partials.

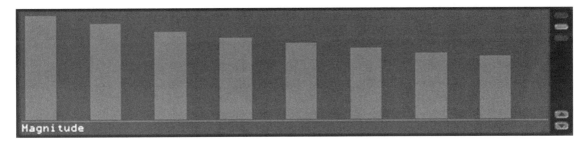

Figure 4.49   The partials display for the square wave shown in Figure 4.48.

- **Trigger.** The Trigger control synchronizes the phase of the waveform created through the additive process to a key press. The phase can then be controlled with the Start and Phase knobs.

- **Tune.** The Tune knob allows fine pitch adjustments to the whole oscillator unit over the range of plus or minus one semitone.

- **Frequency.** The Freq knob allows wide pitch adjustments to the whole oscillator unit over a maximum range of plus or minus four octaves.

- **Scale.** The Scale control scales the magnitude of the harmonics.

■ **Gibbs.** If I start focusing on mathematics and the physics of sound—rather than on what something actually sounds like—then I break out in a rash. So for the benefit of my health, let me summarize the function of this knob as saying that it allows some additive sounds to be smoothed out (or ruffled up a bit, depending on which way you twist the knob).

Pad

The Pad sound source (see Figure 4.50) is a comparatively unique module.

Figure 4.50 The Pad module in KarmaFX Synth Modular.

In some ways this module is rather like the Additive module, but where most modules—both in KarmaFX Synth Modular and in the other featured synthesizers—strive for accuracy, this module is intended to create sounds that drift, thereby making them useful for deployment in slow, evolving pad-type sounds.

As with the Additive module, in the Pad module you can:

■ Draw a waveform.

■ Set the number of partials using the Monics knob.

■ Adjust the level of each individual partial.

However, the module then applies what it calls a *harmonic profile* to soften the sound and shift it over time. There are preset harmonic profiles (one of which is shown in Figure 4.50), and you can also adjust/draw your own profile. The application of the harmonic profile is then controlled by the BW (bandwidth) control and the BWScale (bandwidth scale) control. In combination, these affect:

■ How the sound drifts

■ The range of harmonic changes

At this point, you're probably interested in the module but want some more specifics. Well... I'm not even going to begin to try to describe the sound. You're just going to have to get hold of KarmaFX Synth Modular and try it for yourself.

Noise

The Noise module (see Figure 4.51) creates noise. However, it is slightly more sophisticated than its name may suggest.

Figure 4.51 The Noise module in KarmaFX Synth Modular.

Let's have a look at the controls and see what options the module offers us.

- **Noise Type.** The most obvious initial control is the Noise Type selector. This gives us the choices of three noise types:
  - White
  - Pink
  - Brown

- **Volume.** The Amp knob gives you control over the volume.

- **Randomness.** The Seed control has an effect on the randomness of the sound. Let's just say this is pretty subtle....

- **Filters.** There are built-in 12-dB low-pass and high-pass filters, allowing for considerable tonal shaping before the sound leaves the module. However, neither filter offers any resonance to exaggerate the cut-off frequency and allow for pitched noise–type sounds. Clearly, the filters need to be fully open if the noise is to be heard without shaping. In addition, the range of the cut-off frequencies of these filters does overlap, which means that it is possible to cut the signal very easily. The Filter switch can turn off both filters so they have no effect.

- **Cycle.** When the Cycle mode is switched on, the noise takes on a pitched quality (becoming more of a buzz and less of a hiss).

Sound-Creation Modules in SynthEdit

Before we go any further, could I remind you that this book only looks at the modules that come with SynthEdit (at the time of this writing) and does not consider any of the other wonderful sonic possibilities that are available through the use of third-party modules. Equally, as I have said before, I am not intending to look at all of the modules in all of the synthesizers (and you will have seen that I did not cover all sound-generating modules in the other tools).

As a side issue, if you want to create ring modulation sounds, there is a ring modulation module in SynthEdit, which you can find under the Effects heading. I do not cover that module in this book.

Oscillator

The Oscillator module (see Figure 4.52) is the general sound source in SynthEdit.

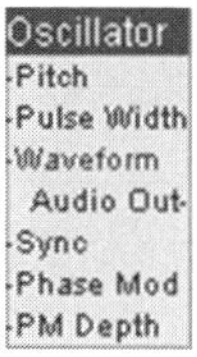

Figure 4.52   The SynthEdit Oscillator module.

There are two plugs that are common to all three sound-generating modules in SynthEdit:

- **Pitch.** The Pitch plug attaches the input pitch command (usually coming from the MIDI to CV unit) to the oscillator.

- **Audio Out.** The Audio Out plug feeds the audio signal to the next module in the chain.

The other plugs that are available on the Oscillator module are:

- **Pulse Width.** The Pulse Width plug controls the pulse width of the wave when the pulse wave is selected.

- **Waveform.** The waveform controls the waveform selection. This module comes with seven wave choices:
  - Sine
  - Saw
  - Ramp
  - Triangle
  - Pulse
  - White Noise
  - Pink Noise

- **Sync.** The Sync control hard-synchronizes the oscillator to another oscillator.

- **Phase Mod.** The Phase Modulation input is used for creating FM-like sounds. For this oscillator to be treated as a carrier, this Phase Mod plug should be attached to the Audio Out plug of the modulator oscillator(s).

■ **PM Depth.** If this oscillator is acting as a carrier for FM synthesis and another oscillator is attached to the Phase Mod plug, then this plug will control the depth of the FM effect.

The Pulse Width and PM Depth plugs can be attached to a range of controls to fix their value or modulate their values over time (or both).

Figure 4.53 shows the Oscillator properties page, from which you can set defaults and other detailed settings.

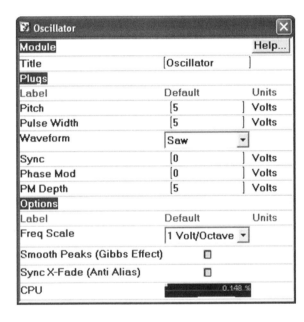

Figure 4.53   The Oscillator properties page.

Phase Distortion Oscillator

The Phase Distortion Oscillator (see Figure 4.54) is a self-contained phase distortion–generating device. It creates an FM-like sound, but with a different tone than that created by using the Phase Mod plug on the Oscillator module. Since everything is contained within a single module, it doesn't have the same flexibility that you can achieve by connecting several modules together, but it is much easier to use than a collection of modules (and, of course, because we're in the modular world, you can still hook up a more complicated arrangement if you wish).

Figure 4.54   The Phase Distortion Oscillator.

There are three pins as yet unaccounted for on the module.

- **Modulation Depth.** The Modulation Depth control adjusts the extent to which the modulator wave phase distorts the carrier wave. (Both waves are within the module.)

- **Wave.** The Wave1 and Wave2 plugs control the wave selection of the modulator and carrier wave, respectively. The wave choices are:
  - Saw
  - Square
  - Pulse
  - Double Sine
  - Reso1, Reso2, and Reso3

In addition, there is a properties page (see Figure 4.55) for the Phase Distortion Oscillator, where the defaults can be set and more detailed changes can be made.

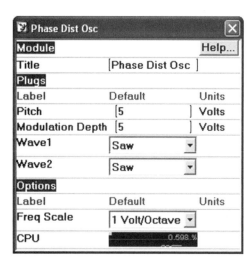

Figure 4.55 The Phase Distortion Oscillator's properties page.

SoundFont Oscillator

The SoundFont Oscillator (see Figure 4.56) allows you to use the samples underlying a SoundFont as an oscillator. This gives you access to the raw samples, so any programming information included within the SoundFont (for instance, instructions to use a filter) will be ignored.

Let's have a look at the plugs.

- **Bank.** The Bank selector chooses the SoundFont bank to load.

- **Patch.** The Patch selector chooses the SoundFont patch (within the selected bank) to load.

Figure 4.56   The SoundFont Oscillator.

- **Gate.** The Gate control triggers the sound.

- **Velocity.** The Velocity input is used to select the velocity layer when the underlying SoundFont includes more than one velocity layer. This input has no effect on the output level of the module.

- **Left (mono) and Right.** These are the audio outs, but unlike the conventional oscillators, these outputs are split across the stereo spectrum.

In addition, there is a properties page (see Figure 4.57) for the SoundFont Oscillator where the defaults can be set.

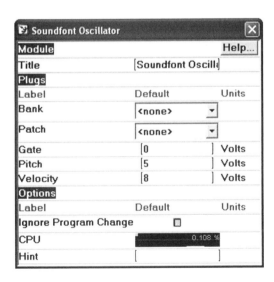

Figure 4.57   The SoundFont Oscillator's properties page.

That's enough about sound sources. Let's look at some filters.

5 Filters

A t its most basic, you can think of the filter as being a tone control. A low-pass filter is like the treble control—turn it down, and the sound gets "duller." However, a filter can do much more for you.

You will find that all of the featured synthesizers offer many filters or filter options that appear to be similar. Although they may be similar in terms of features, they are significantly different in terms of sounds, and one 24-dB low-pass filter will not sound the same as another 24-dB low-pass filter, even within the same synthesizer. This can cause confusion, but it will also give you a much broader tonal palette.

Filter Types

Let's have a look at the main types of filters that are on offer from our featured synthesizers.

Low-Pass

The low-pass filter (or if you prefer, high-cut filter) allows low frequencies to pass through it (see Figure 5.1).

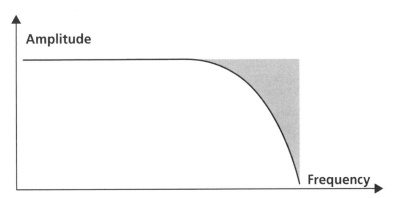

Figure 5.1 A low-pass filter allows lower frequencies to pass and cuts higher frequencies. Frequencies under the line are passed (in other words, are not affected) while frequencies above/to the right of the line are cut (the gray shaded area shows the signal that has been cut).

When a low-pass filter is fully open, all frequencies can pass through it (although some filters do cut the signal even when they are fully open).

As the filter is closed, it progressively allows less sound to pass through. You will hear this as the sound becoming duller as the higher-frequency elements of the spectrum are filtered out. (Look back to the graphs of additive waves in the previous chapter—in essence, a low-pass filter works by cutting the higher harmonics.) When the filter is almost completely closed, only the very lowest elements of the frequency spectrum can pass.

The effect that the low-pass filter will have on a sound will vary depending on the source waveform you have selected. If you choose a sine wave, then the effect of the filter will be limited. The sine wave comprises only the fundamental frequency; therefore, if the filter cuts this, it cuts the whole sound. However, if you choose a sawtooth wave, which has a lot of high-frequency information, then the low-pass filter will have a much greater perceived effect on the sound.

High-Pass

The high-pass filter (or low-cut filter) is the reverse of the low-pass filter—it allows high frequencies to pass and progressively cuts out the lower frequencies (see Figure 5.2).

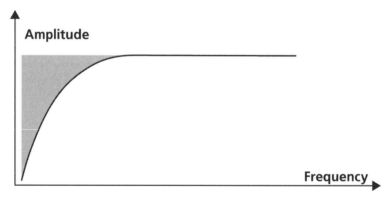

Figure 5.2   A high-pass filter. Frequencies under the line are passed (in other words, are not affected), while frequencies above/to the left of the line are cut. (The gray shaded area shows the signal that has been cut.)

As well as sound shaping, high-pass filters have another use: filtering out the junk in the lower end of the mix spectrum. How often have you listened to a track and found that it sounds muddy or dull? That could be too much bass. You only get so much dynamic range, and without filtering you may be filling your low end needlessly. This means that the key elements—your bass and kick—can't shine.

While high-pass filtering may be noticeable if you play a patch on its own, in a mix any change to the tone of a sound is unlikely to be noticeable, except with more extreme cuts. However, the net result of the low-end filtering may be to give a cleaner/fuller low end when the bass elements are allowed to come through.

Some sound designers also use high-pass filters with resonance (which is explained in a moment) to boost the fundamental tone of a patch. You can do this by tuning the resonance to the fundamental frequency of a note and engaging key tracking so that the resonance boost then follows the played note. In many ways, this is using the "filtered noise" technique we used in Chapter 2, but at the low end of the spectrum.

Band-Pass

The band-pass filter acts like a combination of a low-pass filter and a high-pass filter by cutting the frequency spectrum at both ends to only allow a narrow band of sound to pass (see Figure 5.3).

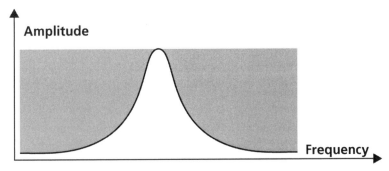

Figure 5.3 A band-pass filter. Frequencies under the line are passed (in other words, are not affected), while frequencies above the line are cut. (The gray shaded area shows the signal that has been cut.)

The frequency control determines the center frequency where the full signal is allowed to pass—from that point outward, the spectrum of sound is progressively cut. At extremes of frequency, the band-pass filter will sound similar to either a high-pass or a low-pass filter.

Band-pass filters tend to take a lot of energy out of the signal, so you may have to boost the level after the filter.

Notch (Band-Reject)

If the band-pass filter is the equivalent of burning the candle at each end, then the notch filter—sometimes called a *band-reject* filter—equates to burning it in the middle. The notch filter cuts the frequencies at its current value (see Figure 5.4).

The notch filter can be used for effect, and it can be used surgically in the mix. If you're trying to mix two sounds and they don't sit well together, it may be that they're both trying to operate in the same frequency range. In this case, you can "notch out" one of the sounds to allow the other to sit properly. You can do this in your patch design or, as many mixing engineers do, with EQ in the mix.

Peaking

A peaking (or peak) filter (see Figure 5.5) boosts the sound. The boost point and the width of the boosted band can be controlled (using the cut-off control and the resonance control, which are

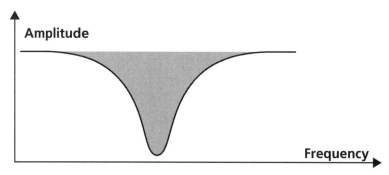

Figure 5.4 A notch filter. Frequencies under the line are passed (in other words, are not affected), while frequencies above the line are cut. (The gray shaded area shows the signal that has been cut.)

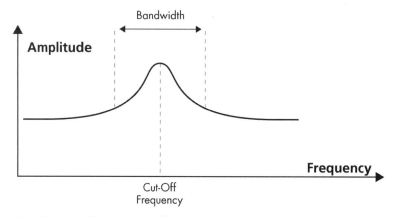

Figure 5.5 A peaking filter. Unlike the other filters, this boosts the signal—this boost is shown by the peak in the middle.

explained in greater detail shortly). You can stack several peak filters in order (whether in series or parallel) to get an effect reminiscent of a formant filter (which is discussed in a moment).

All-Pass

An all-pass filter passes all frequencies equally. This may not seem particularly useful, but as signals pass through the filter, their phase can be shifted (in a controllable manner).

Formant

Formant filters are usually used to emulate vowel sounds. Their success in this ambition is often a matter of careful choice of sound source coupled with attention to programming detail.

Comb Filters

Comb filters work by adding a slightly delayed version of a signal to itself. This causes phase cancellations and can give a slightly "chorused" or metallic type of sound. The spectrum produced by these filters looks like a comb, hence the name.

Filter Parameters

Filters have several parameters, and the controls available differ between different synthesizers and the different modules within individual synthesizers. However, there are some controls that are common to most synthesizers.

Cut-Off Frequency

The cut-off frequency is the point at which the filter starts to have effect (see Figure 5.6). So if you have a low-pass filter and set the cut-off frequency to 8 kHz, the sound spectrum above 8 kHz will be progressively reduced. However, if you are using a high-pass filter, sounds below the cut-off frequency (8 kHz) will be reduced.

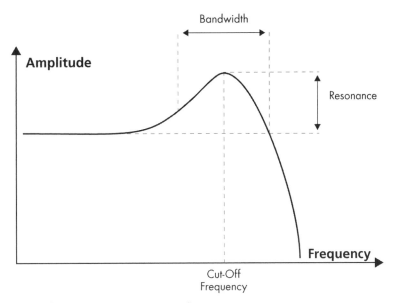

Figure 5.6   A low-pass filter with a resonant peak.

Resonance

Resonance adds some bite to a filter. It works by boosting the sound spectrum around the filter cut-off frequency, as Figure 5.6 illustrates. (Look back to Figure 5.1 to see a low-pass filter without a resonance boost.) Used in moderation, the effect is subtle and can make a sound appear brighter and/or slightly thinner (or less fat, if you prefer). When used to the extreme, the effect is noticeable—most dance records use filter sweeps with high levels of resonance.

At very high resonance settings, some filters can exhibit quite extreme behavior and will often "self–oscillate," at which point the filter will act as a sine wave oscillator. As we can easily add a sine wave oscillator, this feature is not often used.

Bandwidth

The third factor that can be adjusted is bandwidth—the width of the resonant peak (again, this is shown in Figure 5.6). This is quite a subtle adjustment, but it allows the character of the resonance to be carefully sculpted.

This feature isn't available in many modules, so if you don't see a control, then it's probably not there.

Drive

Some filters offer a drive option. This effectively works by the input signal overloading the filter, and it can give a warm/rich sound, gently moving into overdrive at higher levels.

Filter Slopes

A low-pass filter progressively reduces the volume of a sound above the cut-off point. The rate at which the sound wave is reduced above the cut-off frequency is determined by the slope of the filter.

If you have a 6-dB/octave filter (sometimes called a *1-pole* filter), it will reduce the level of the sound source by 6 dB at one octave above the cut-off point, 12 dB at two octaves above the cut-off frequency, 18 dB at three octaves above the cut-off, and so on. The effect of a 6-dB filter on a sound wave is quite subtle.

A 12-dB/octave filter (sometimes called a *2-pole* filter) will reduce the level of the sound wave's volume by 12 dB for each octave above the cut-off point.

A 24-dB/octave filter (sometimes called a *4-pole* filter) will reduce the level of the sound wave's volume by 24 dB for each octave above the cut-off point.

You will see some different filter slopes in Figure 5.7. This is an image drawn by hand and so is not to scale; however, you can see the differing results of the filter slopes.

So which is better—a 6-dB, 12-dB, 24-dB, 36-dB, or 48-dB filter? Well, that all depends…and in many ways it doesn't really matter.

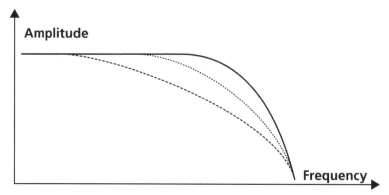

Figure 5.7   Different filter curves—the flatter curves may be more gentle, but in these cases, the filter affects a large portion of the sonic spectrum for the same amount of cut at a specific frequency.

Take a comparison between a 12-dB and a 24-dB filter—you need to think of the context in which the sound will be used. On the face of it, the 24-dB filter might get faster results. However, remember that a 12-dB filter has to work twice as hard and will affect a much greater proportion of the signal to achieve the same reduction that a 24-dB filter will make at any given frequency (that's the frequency that is cut, not the cut-off frequency), so the 12-dB filter may be more appropriate.

There are no hard-and-fast rules, but you may find that, for instance, a 24-dB filter could be a better starting point when designing bass sounds, whereas a 12-dB filter produces better results with pads or sample-based sounds. Then again, you're going to have your own considerations and will need to decide whether you're trying to shape the sound or whether you're getting surgical, so you may find another combination that works for you.

One other point to remember is that we're in the world of modulars here. That means you can stack filters together (and there are some specialized modules that do this for you in a single module). Stacking has two main effects:

- The first main effect is slope. Two filters run in series will give you a cumulative filter slope. In other words, if you have two 12-dB filters in series, they will give you the equivalent of a 24-dB filter. However, you would then need to mirror the settings between the filters in order to replicate the effect of a 24-dB filter. If you don't, then you will find that you get a different tonal result than would be achieved by a 24-dB filter, which leads us on....

- The second key result of using two filters is that you can select different settings and therefore get a broader range of sounds.

Moog, SVF, 303, Zolzer, and So On...

One thing you may notice with the filters is that in addition to describing them in terms of their function (12-dB low-pass, 4-pole, and so on), they are given other names, such as Moog, SVF (*state variable filter*), 303, Zolzer, Filter S, and the like. These names generally indicate that the filter is intended to emulate or behave in a similar manner to a piece of hardware (so a 303 filter may be expected to behave in a manner like the filter in a Roland TB-303 Bassline).

As always, these labels are only an indication of what the filter will do. You need to take the time to listen and decide which is right for you in the context of any specific sound.

Controlling Filter Parameters

To give life to a filter and change it from a simple tone control into something that helps to shape the sound in a meaningful way, we need to start modulating the filter—in other words, changing its settings in real time. Thankfully, all of the featured synthesizers offer a lot of tools to help us. The following sections describe some of the main tools you might like to consider.

Controlling Filter Cut-Off

When using a filter to shape tone, the main (but not the only) modulation controls are:

- **Envelopes.** Envelopes provide an ideal control source to shift the filter's cut-off frequency over time. The main uses for this control are:
  - To control the tone. The sound generated by natural instruments will decay over time—you can mimic this behavior with a filter controlling the cut-off frequency of a low-pass filter.
  - Squelch. It's how you get that classic synthesizer squelch....

- **Velocity.** With velocity, you can make a note brighter as it is struck harder and duller when it is struck more softly (or if you're feeling wild, you can reverse this behavior). This level of control allows a filter to mimic the properties of natural instruments.

You will find that velocity and envelopes are often used in combination when controlling filters.

The filter also acts as a volume control, so the more a filter closes, the more it attenuates the amplitude of the sound. This is particularly so when filters are being heavily used.

You can use this to your advantage by setting an envelope to completely close a filter. Take the example of a piano note—the note should have a finite length, but an ADSR envelope cannot mimic this behavior. However, a filter controlled by another ADSR envelope could cut the volume completely. Therefore, the combination of two envelopes—one controlling the volume and the other controlling the filter—could create a more accurate representation of an acoustic sound.

Key Tracking and Filters

You may want to use key tracking when setting the filter to mimic what happens naturally. If you are designing a patch to resemble the behavior of an acoustic instrument—or perhaps you are using some samples as your original sound source—then a single cut-off point may be unnatural. The high notes would be too dull, and the low notes too bright.

To remedy this, you could use key tracking, which would open the filter at higher frequencies and close it at lower frequencies, giving a more natural response. If you want, you can have an unnatural response in which the filter closes at higher pitches.

Controlling Resonance

When creating and manipulating sounds, resonance is generally used in four main ways (which are not mutually exclusive):

- To emphasize the filter cut-off, and in particular to emphasize a changing filter cut-off frequency.

- To give a brighter sound.

- To give a "thinner" sound—this is partly a result of making the sound brighter.

- To create an effect, whether that be making the filter scream or giving sounds a really squelchy character.

It is less common to control resonance in real time, but I do recommend you look for ways to do so, whether with velocity, an envelope, or through some other control. This level of detail will add valuable subtlety to your sound.

The Available Filters

Before we look at the modules that are available in the featured synthesizers, I think it is important to point out (again) that a lot of these modules look very similar—especially within the same synthesizer. Not only do they look similar, but many of the controls are exactly the same.

However, while there may be superficial visual similarities, there are sonic differences, and unfortunately, trying to describe the fine difference between two filters is quite a tough job. I can give a broad outline as to the differences that *I* perceive. However, when it comes to creating your own sounds, you're going to have to listen to hear what each module can do for you. This is hard work, but it is good—it will help you to understand just how broad your tonal palette is and how the various elements that you have at your disposal interact.

In this section, I am going to look at filters and will also mention wave-shaping devices. However, I am not going to look at EQ units (which could be considered to be filters). EQ units are covered in the FX chapter.

Most of the filters have the following controls, so I will explain them here once and won't repeat the explanation.

- **Type.** Many of the filter modules do not load specific filters. Instead, they allow you to choose a specific filter type. Some modules do not offer the choice of filter type, but instead they output a signal that has been passed through different filters—you can choose the filter type by selecting the appropriate audio stream.

- **Slope.** With some modules, the selection of the filter type and the selection of the slope are separate.

- **Cut-Off.** The cut-off control adjusts the cut-off frequency for the filter.

- **Resonance.** The resonance control adjusts the resonance boost for the filter. Some filters do not offer a resonance boost.

- **Key Tracking.** The key tracking (or key following) control links the filter's cut-off frequency to incoming pitch data (allowing the filter to respond to higher or lower notes being played).

- **Drive.** The drive control boosts the input of the filter, leading to overdrive—the drive control will control that effect (if the control is present and operative for that module).

And of course, there are modulation slots to set a modulator to control these features.

Filter Modules in Zebra 2

Zebra 2 has a number of filter modules, and within these modules there is a range of different filters available. Let's look at the main filter: VCF. You can load up to four of these filters in one instance of Zebra 2.

VCF Filter

The VCF module (see Figure 5.8) gives you the widest range of filter type choices. Each type has a different tone.

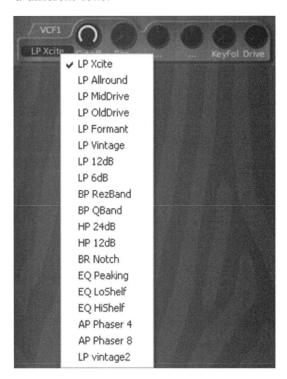

Figure 5.8 The VCF filter in Zebra 2 with the drop-down menu showing the wide range of filter choices.

I don't want to describe the nuances of all the filters (especially since you really need to hear the filters to appreciate the differences); however, let's have a look at the range of options.

Low-Pass Filters

There are eight low-pass filters available in the VCF module:

- LP Xcite, a 24-dB filter that has quite a rich sound

- LP Allround, a 24-dB filter that is claimed to have a low CPU hit

- LP MidDrive, which boosts frequencies in the middle range

- LP OldDrive, which gives a more "vintage" sound

- LP Vintage, a vintage-flavored filter

- LP 12dB, a 12-dB filter without the drive facility

- LP 6dB, a (very simple) 6-dB filter without resonance or the drive facility

- LP Vintage 2, another vintage filter

The key differences between the low-pass filters are:

- The cut-off slope—some are deeper (24 dB) and some are shallower (12 dB or 6 dB).

- Their responsiveness (or otherwise) to the Drive parameter.

- Their general behavior—some are intended to sound cleaner/crisper, while others are intended to have more of an analog feel.

Formant Filter

There is one formant filter, LP Formant. With this filter:

- The Resonance knob controls the depth of the formant effect.

- The Drive knob becomes a vowel selector that chooses the five vowel sounds.

High-Pass Filters

There are two high-pass filters:

- HP 24dB, a 24-dB high-pass filter

- HP 12dB, a 12-dB high-pass filter

Band-Pass Filters

There are two band-pass filters:

- BP RezBand, a 12-dB filter.

- BP QBand. This filter has a slightly different behavior, and at the top and bottom of its ranges it cuts virtually the whole signal. It also has no Drive parameter.

In addition, there is the Peaking filter, which acts more like an EQ boost:

- The Cut-Off knob selects the frequency to be boosted.

- The Resonance knob adjusts the bandwidth of the boosted frequency.

- The Gain knob (located where the Drive knob would usually be) controls the amount of boost.

Notch Filters

There is one notch filter, BR Notch, a 24-dB notch (band-reject) filter.

All-Pass Filters

There are two all-pass filters:

- AP Phaser 4

- AP Phaser 8

On their own, these filters don't sound as if they "do" much to the audio signal. However, if you split the signal—so you can mix a clean(ish) signal with a signal that has been through one of these all-pass filters—then you will hear the phasing effect of these filters.

XMF: Cross-Modulation Filter

The cross-modulation filter (XMF) block (see Figure 5.9) builds on the sonic possibilities offered by Zebra 2.

Figure 5.9 XMF: the cross-modulation filter in Zebra 2.

The XMF unit has quite a lot of knobs (which we'll look at in a moment), but at its most basic, it can be operated like a regular filter. In this context it offers five filter types:

- LP4, a 24-dB low-pass filter

- BP2, a 12-dB band-pass filter

- BP4, a 24-dB band-pass filter

- HP2, a 12-dB high-pass filter

- BR2, a 12-dB notch filter

Now let's get on to the clever stuff.

- **Overload.** Instead of the Drive control, you will see an Overload knob. This feels more aggressive than the Drive control in a regular VCF.

- **Offset.** The XMF filter is actually two filters—one for the left audio channel and one for the right. The offset detunes one filter by reference to the other and progressively cuts the level of the other channel.

- **FilterFM.** The FilterFM parameter allows you to frequency modulate the filter cut-off frequency. The modulation is undertaken by a side-chain (in other words, an external source, such as another oscillator). If a separate side-chain is not selected (which you do by right-clicking on the module), then the main audio source is fed to the side-chain input.

Shaper

Although the Shaper (see Figure 5.10) is not a filter, I've included it in this chapter because—as its name suggests—it can shape your sound. In this case, the primary shaping is to add distortion and roughen up the sound somewhat. Interestingly, the Shapers are available as modules (which can be loaded into the main grid) and as FX units (which can be added at the end of the audio chain). I am covering the Shapers here, so I will not duplicate this material in the FX chapter.

Figure 5.10   The Shaper unit in Zebra 2.

The Shaper includes four different shaping types, which progressively add more distortion to the signal:

- Shape

- T-Drive

- Crush

- Wedge

There are five controls on the Shaper:

- **Depth.** The Depth knob controls the amount of distortion. This control has its own modulator slot. Its effect is dependent on the Input control.

- **Edge.** The Edge control has an effect on the tone of the distortion created. This also has its own modulator slot.

- **Input.** The Input control adjusts the input signal level, which has an effect on the quality of the distortion.

- **Output.** The Output control sets the output level, allowing you to balance changes in the signal level as it is processed by the unit.

- **HiOut.** The HiOut boosts the level of the distorted signal, adding to the brightness of the output.

Comb Filter

The Comb Filter (see Figure 5.11) in Zebra 2 acts very much like a resonator: You supply a short audio impulse, and this creates a resonance, which can then be tonally shaped. As you damp this resonance, you can get very delicate staccato tones—it can also do some really crazy stuff, but we'll come on to that later....

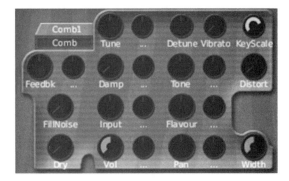

Figure 5.11 The Comb Filter in Zebra 2.

There are seven different Comb Filter options selectable from the drop-down. These are based on delay configurations and give results that range from the controlled to the wild. The first three are quite straightforward (sonically), whereas the last three are (sonically) pretty "out there":

- Comb. The Tone and Flavor knobs (described below) have no effect in this mode.
- Split Comb.
- Split Dual.
- Diff Comb.
- Dissonant.
- Cluster.
- Brown.

Let's have a look at the knobs:

- **Dry.** I'm taking this knob out of order because it might be important to look at this sooner rather than later. Unlike the other filters, the unprocessed signal passes directly through the Comb Filter, and the Dry knob controls the level of that dry signal. Therefore, if the filter is not creating any sound and the Dry control is set to zero, you will not hear anything.

- **Tune, Detune, Vibrato, and KeyScale.** The top row of controls duplicates the controls on the top of an oscillator. This very much reflects that this module is about its sound-creation capabilities as much as its filtering abilities. Like an oscillator, an LFO is loaded whenever the Comb module is loaded.

- **Feedback.** A comb filter is effectively a delay line. The Feedback setting controls the number of times the delayed signal repeats. This has an effect on the sonic quality of the effect (and does not give a series of echoes).

- **Damp.** The delayed signal that is fed back into the delay unit is passed through a low-pass filter. The Damp control adjusts the cut-off point on that feed.

- **Tone.** The Tone function performs lots of clever operations, depending on the selected comb type. On balance, the net effect is control over the tone.

- **Distort.** The Distort control dirties up the sound, giving it a brighter, dirtier sound.

- **FillNoise.** The FillNoise parameter controls white noise being fed into the filter. This can emphasize the "plucked" sounds that can be created by the filter.

- **Flavor.** Like the Tone function, the Flavor control performs many other clever operations, depending on the selected comb type. This gives further control over the tone.

- **Vol.** The Volume knob sets the output level of the filtered sound.

Filter Modules in VAZ Modular

VAZ Modular has a wide range of filter modules. Many of the designs of these filters are based on analog hardware.

In addition to the main controls that are common to all filters, there are two controls that appear on some of the VAZ Modular filter options:

- **Bandwidth.** Bandwith quite literally controls the width of the filter's resonance peak (in other words, how pointy it is, or how much of the sound spectrum it covers). Check back to Figure 5.5 for an illustration.

- **Separation.** Some filters are built by connecting several filters working together. These filters then share common controls to operate as a single unit (and are seen as a single unit with a single interface). With the separation control, the cut-off frequencies of each of the stacked filters can be addressed individually so that one will be raised in relation to the other (or others), giving differing resonant peaks and a different tone to the filter (in many ways, more like a formant filter).

Let's now look at the individual modules in VAZ Modular.

One-Pole Filter

The One-Pole Filter (see Figure 5.12) is a 6-dB filter (without resonance). It has two controls: a cut-off slider and a high-pass/low-pass switch.

Figure 5.12   The One-Pole Filter in VAZ Modular.

The Filter

The Filter (see Figure 5.13) is the general-purpose filter model in VAZ Modular. Apart from the cut-off and resonance sliders, it has a third slider that acts as a Bandwidth or a Separation control, depending on the particular filter.

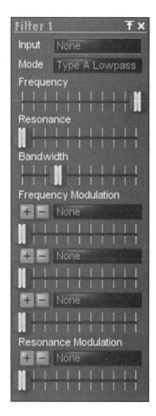

Figure 5.13   The Filter in VAZ Modular.

To select the filter type, click on the Mode selector. This will call up the Filter Mode dialog box (see Figure 5.14).

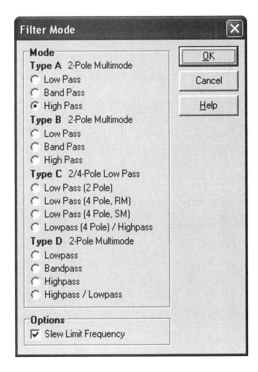

Figure 5.14   The Filter Mode dialog box.

This gives you the option of four filter types, and most of these filter types give you the option of high-pass, low-pass, and more. Let me explain a bit more.

Type A Filters

Type A are 12-dB filters where the resonance peak is *not* affected by the Bandwidth control. Three filter types are available:

■ Low-Pass

■ Band-Pass

■ High-Pass

Type B Filters

Type B are 12-dB filters where the resonance peak is controllable by the Bandwidth control. Three filter types are available:

■ Low-Pass

- Band-Pass

- High-Pass

Type C Filters

Type C filters include one 12-dB (2-pole) filter and three 24-dB (4-pole) filters.

- Low-Pass (2-pole) with no bandwidth/separation, but resonance can be modulated.

- Low-Pass (4-pole, RM) with separation control, but the final slot on the module allows the resonance to be modulated.

- Low-Pass (4-pole, SM) with separation control, and the final slot on the module allows the resonance to be modulated.

- Low-Pass (4-pole) and the third slider controls a high-pass filter. (This parameter can be modulated from the last modulation slot.)

Type D Filters

Type D are 12-dB filters where the resonance peak is controllable by the Bandwidth control. Four filter types are available:

- Low-Pass.

- Band-Pass.

- High-Pass.

- High-Pass/Low-Pass, and the separation control comes into play to create some very vocal-like tones.

Filter K

Filter K (see Figure 5.15) is a 12-dB filter.

There are only two distinguishing controls on this filter:

- A Drive control.

- A Low-Pass/High-Pass switch (and I guess you can figure what this is for).

The filter can have a pretty aggressive attitude—especially when the resonance and drive are pushed.

Filter R

Filter R (see Figure 5.16) is a four-stage filter.

Think of Filter R as being four 6-dB filters joined together, and you will get the notion as to what you can do with this filter. If you click on the Mode selector, it will give you an option of

Figure 5.15 Filter K in VAZ Modular.

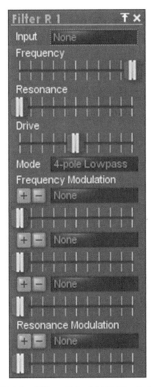

Figure 5.16 Filter R in VAZ Modular.

15 different configurations—in essence, these are 15 different algorithms for how the audio signal could be passed through the four filters. This gives you a range of different slopes and different filters joined together. The choices are:

- 24-dB low-pass
- 18-dB low-pass
- 12-dB low-pass
- 6-dB low-pass
- 24-dB band-pass
- 12-dB band-pass
- 18-dB high-pass
- 12-dB high-pass
- 6-dB high-pass

- 18-dB high-pass and 6-dB low-pass

- 12-dB high-pass and 6-dB low-pass

- 12-dB notch

- 12-dB notch and 6-dB low-pass

- 18-dB all-pass

- 18-dB all-pass and 6-dB low-pass

There's probably a combination in there that's right for you.

Filter S

Filter S (see Figure 5.17) takes a slightly different approach.

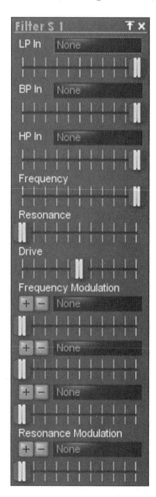

Figure 5.17 Filter S in VAZ Modular.

Filter S is three separate filters in one box:

- A low-pass filter
- A band-pass filter
- A high-pass filter

For each of the filters you can individually select:

- The audio input source (and you can have the same input for more than one source).
- The output level for that filter.

However, the cut-off, resonance, and drive controls on the module apply equally to all three filters. Therefore, if you set the cut-off frequency at (say) 10 kHz, then:

- The low-pass filter will reduce the signal above 10 kHz.
- The high-pass filter will cut the signal below 10 kHz.

SVFilter

The SVFilter (state variable filter; see Figure 5.18) is a 12-dB filter.

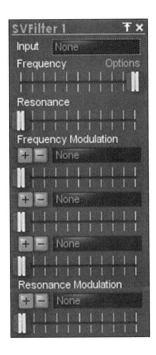

Figure 5.18 The SVFilter in VAZ Modular.

Although not obvious from the interface, this filter offers four filter types:

- Low-pass
- High-pass
- Band-pass
- Notch

These four filters operate simultaneously, with the appropriate filtered output (or outputs) then being selected in the audio routing.

Comb Filter

The Comb Filter (see Figure 5.19) is the only comb filter in VAZ Modular. Like all comb filters, it is based on a delay unit and uses short delays to create its effects.

Figure 5.19 The Comb Filter in VAZ Modular.

There are four main controls that we need to consider:

- **Frequency.** The Frequency slider controls the filter's cut-off frequency (as you probably guessed).

- **Decay/Feedback.** The Decay/Feedback switch selects how the delayed signal that is fed back into the unit is controlled by the associated slider.

- **Damping.** The damping slider adjusts the cut-off frequency of the filter through which the fed-back signal is passed.

- **Output.** The Output control balances the dry and wet signals.

Vowel Filter

The Vowel Filter (see Figure 5.20) is a formant filter that simulates (human) vocal vowel sounds.

Figure 5.20   The Vowel Filter in VAZ Modular.

The controls of the Vowel Filter are:

- **Voice.** With the Voice selector, you can choose the voice type that the vowels will emulate. The choices are:
  - Male Speech
  - Male Singing
  - Female Speech
  - Female Singing
  - Child

- **Vowels.** There are five Vowels slots—into each slot, you can load one of 10 vowel sounds.

- **Morph.** The Morph control selects—and morphs between—the five selected vowel sounds. This control also has a dedicated modulation slot.

- **Resonance.** The Resonance controls acts in the manner you would expect. Given the specialized nature of this filter, it tends to emphasize the vowel sounds.

Waveshaper

The Waveshaper (see Figure 5.21) works to (literally) reshape the audio wave as it passes through.

Figure 5.21 The Waveshaper in VAZ Modular.

This may be a rather unscientific description, but in essence, the sliders on the Waveshaper "redraw" the waveshape, giving a much wider range of sonic options. Check it out for yourself—it's quite interesting to play with but rather hard to control with any repeatable certainty.

Filter Modules in KarmaFX Synth Modular

KarmaFX Synth Modular comes with a good range of filters.

Low-Pass/High-Pass/Band-Pass/Notch Filters

There are four multimode filters that all work in a similar manner, having:

- Cut-off and resonance controls (as you would expect)

- Slope selectors to choose various slopes

- Filter mode selectors

- Cut-off modulation depth controls as hardwired knobs

- Key-scaling knobs hardwired

The filters are similar but have slightly different characteristics and some different features.

SVF Filter

The SVF filter (see Figure 5.22) is a standard analog-modeling filter.

Figure 5.22 The SVF filter in KarmaFX Synth Modular.

The filter offers:

- Low-pass filtering
- High-pass filtering
- Band-pass filtering
- Notch filtering
- 12-dB slopes
- 24-dB slopes

Zolzer Filter

The manual suggests the Zolzer filter (see Figure 5.23) can sometimes sound more analog.

The filter offers:

- Low-pass filtering
- High-pass filtering
- Band-pass filtering
- Notch filtering
- 12-dB slopes
- 24-dB slopes

Moog Filter

The Moog filter (see Figure 5.24) is intended to impart something of the characteristic of a Moog analog filter.

The filter offers:

- Low-pass filtering

Figure 5.23 The Zolzer filter in KarmaFX Synth Modular.

Figure 5.24 The Moog filter in KarmaFX Synth Modular.

- High-pass filtering
- Band-pass filtering
- 24-dB slopes
- 48-dB slopes

303-Like Filter

The 303-Like filter (see Figure 5.25) is intended to display something of the characteristic of the filter in the Roland TB-303 Bassline.

Figure 5.25 The 303-Like filter in KarmaFX Synth Modular.

The filter offers:

- Low-pass filtering (two variants)
- High-pass filtering
- 12-dB slopes
- 24-dB slopes

Comb Filter and All-Pass Filter

The Comb filter (see Figure 5.26) and the All-Pass filter (see Figure 5.27) both delay units and both share the same controls.

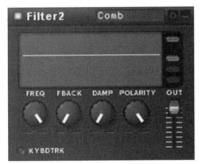

Figure 5.26 The Comb filter in KarmaFX Synth Modular.

Figure 5.27 The All-Pass filter in KarmaFX Synth Modular.

The shared controls are:

- **Frequency.** The Freq knob controls the time delay in the module for the audio signal.

- **Scale.** When keyboard tracking mode is engaged (the blue light in the bottom-left corner of the module is lit), the module frequency matches the incoming MIDI pitch. The Freq knob is then replaced by the Scale knob, which controls the scaling of the incoming pitch data.

- **Feedback.** The Fback knob controls the extent to which the delayed signal is fed back into the unit.

- **Damp.** The Damp knob adjusts the cut-off frequency of the filter through which the feedback signal is passed.

- **Polarity.** The Polarity knob controls the polarity and the level of the feedback.

Formant Filter

The Formant Filter (see Figure 5.28) mimics human vocal vowel sounds.

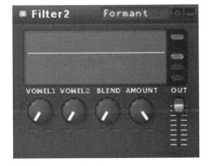

Figure 5.28 The Formant filter in KarmaFX Synth Modular.

On the interface, you will find:

- **Vowel.** There are two Vowel controls. Each allows you to select vowel sounds.

- **Blend.** The Blend control balances the two vowel sounds, allowing you to find nuances of sound between the five vowel sounds.

- **Amount.** The Amount control balances the dry and the vowel-ized sounds.

Just for kicks, try modulating the Blend control (with an envelope). This is another step on the path toward a talking synthesizer…but it's only a step—we're a long way from actually getting real speech!

Filter Modules in SynthEdit

SynthEdit offers five filter modules:

- 1 Pole HP, a 6-dB high-pass filter (see Figure 5.29)

- 1 Pole LP, a 6-dB low-pass filter (see Figure 5.30)

- All Pass, an all-pass filter (see Figure 5.31)

- Moog Filter, a 24-dB low-pass filter (see Figure 5.32)

- SV Filter, a multi-mode (in other words low-pass, high-pass, band-pass, and notch) 12-dB filter (see Figure 5.33)

Figure 5.29 The 6-dB high-pass filter in SynthEdit.

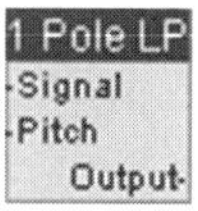

Figure 5.30 The 6-dB low-pass filter in SynthEdit.

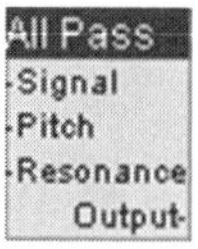

Figure 5.31 The all-pass filter in SynthEdit.

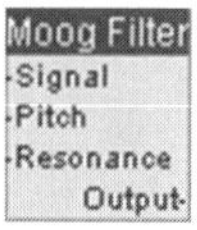

Figure 5.32 The Moog Filter in SynthEdit.

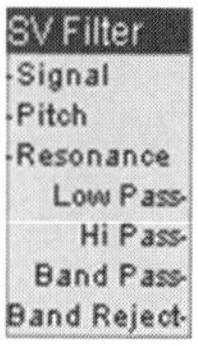

Figure 5.33 The SV Filter in SynthEdit.

Most of the SynthEdit filters are quite straightforward:

- You attach the incoming audio to the Signal plug.

- The Pitch plug controls the cut-off frequency of the filter.

- The Resonance plug (which is not present on the 6-dB filters) controls the resonance boost in the filter.

- The Output plug is where the filtered audio leaves the module.

However, the SV Filter module is slightly different. It has four filters: a low-pass, a high-pass, a band-pass, and a notch filter, which all operate simultaneously. The appropriate filtered output (or outputs) is (are) then selected in the audio routing.

In addition to the five filters, SynthEdit comes with some waveshapers. With these, connection is easy: You attach the signal in and signal out plugs, and you're set.

The Waveshaper module (see Figure 5.34) allows you to distort the shape of wave by changing control points.

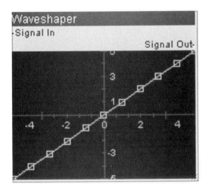

Figure 5.34 The Waveshaper module in SynthEdit.

The Waveshaper2 module (see Figure 5.35) works in a slightly different manner. It distorts the wave based on any mathematical functions that you specify—you can just input your own formula at the bottom of the module!

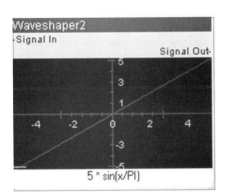

Figure 5.35 The Waveshaper2 module in SynthEdit, for mathematics fans.

Let's go wild and look at how modulation can mess with our filters.

6 Modulation and Control

We are now going to look at "automatic" modulators—in other words, modulators that you set up to behave in a certain, and consistent/repeatable, manner. To put it simply, these automatic modulators are level controls, and those levels change over time—as the level changes, the sound produced by the modulation destination changes, too.

There are three main types of modulation sources:

- Envelopes, which will we look at first.

- Low-frequency oscillators (LFOs).

- More complicated gizmos. These generally fall under the category of step generators—I'll explain more when we get to that part of the chapter.

We're also going to have a brief look at how to automate and control your synthesizer from the outside. As you will see, one of the main limitations of envelopes, LFOs, and step generators is that they can only act for a limited time—they are either "one-shot" devices, such as an envelope, or they have a short loop. With these tools, it is impractical (but not impossible) to control (say) a filter sweep over a period of 30 seconds with any real degree of precision. By using external control and automation, you can introduce this level of detail.

Introducing Envelopes

Like other modulation sources, an envelope is a level that changes over time.

Before we look at how we can use envelopes in synthesis, let's look at a real-life example: a note played on a piano. When a key is struck, the note goes from silence to the maximum volume instantaneously. From this peak—that is, from the moment of impact when the hammer comes into contact with the string—there is an immediate rapid reduction in the volume and then the note reaches a level from which it gradually fades to nothing. A picture of the volume of a piano note over time is set out in Figure 6.1.

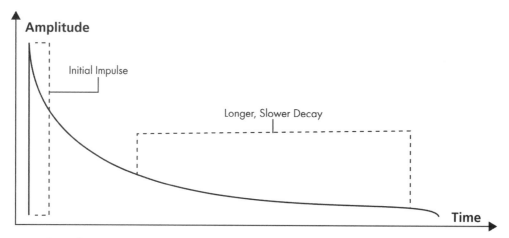

Figure 6.1 The volume envelope of a piano note.

Now, by contrast, if you think about a violin note, which slowly fades in and stays at its maximum volume until the note then gently decays, this volume pattern may look like the image in Figure 6.2.

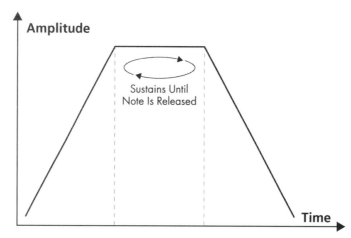

Figure 6.2 A typical sustained string envelope.

These are both examples of volume envelopes—the level that changes over time is the volume level. Applying this principle to synthesizers, to re-create the behavior of a real instrument, we can use an envelope to change a level over time. Its effect will depend on how it is applied—in other words, its effect will depend on its modulation destination. So for instance:

■ An envelope could control volume. Depending on the architecture of the particular sound, the envelope may control the level of an individual oscillator or the level of a whole patch (or anything in between or any permutations of the above ...).

■ An envelope may control a filter. If an envelope *does* control a filter, it will (generally) control the cut-off frequency (usually) to make the sound duller over time—in other words, the sound will start bright and then get duller. If an envelope modulates the filter's resonance, then it will control the amount of the resonance. For an interesting sound, you could set one envelope to close the filter over time and another envelope to increase the amount of resonance while the filter is closing.

■ An envelope can also modulate pitch. A common use for this would be to give a short (and subtle) pitch wobble at the start of a note to give the sound more emphasis.

Let's look at some of the envelopes that are available in the featured synthesizers.

ADSR Envelopes

The ADSR envelope is the "classic" envelope (see Figure 6.3) and is available in all of our featured synthesizers (see Figure 6.4).

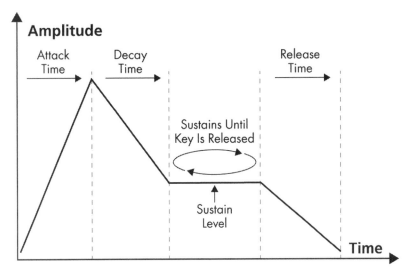

Figure 6.3   The ADSR envelope.

There are four main controls for the ADSR envelope:

■ **A: Attack Time.** The Attack Time is the time it takes for the sound to reach its maximum level after the note is triggered. It is a feature of ADSR envelopes that the maximum level— and nothing less than the maximum level—will be reached at the end of the attack phase. Using the example of a piano, the attack time would be zero—in other words, it would take no time for the sound to go from nothing to the maximum volume. For a string-type sound, the attack may be slower.

   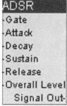

Figure 6.4   The ADSR envelope modules in the four featured synthesizers.

- **D: Decay Time.** The Decay Time controls how quickly the sound drops (to the sustain level) after it has reached its maximum volume. Again, using the example of the piano, the decay time would be fast, but it would be longer than the attack time.

- **S: Sustain Level.** The Sustain Level is the level of an envelope while a key is held. This level stays constant until the key is released. This may be perceived as a weakness if you are using this type of envelope to mimic the behavior of a real instrument, where the volume will continue to gently decay over time.

- **R: Release Time.** The Release Time is the time it takes the sound to decay to zero after a key is released.

You will notice that with the ADSR envelope:

- Once the sustain part of the envelope has been reached, the note does not decay until the key is released.

- There is no function in the envelope to determine how long the note sustains. (The only control over this is by releasing the key.)

So, assuming you can get the attack and the decay right for a piano-type patch, you would not be able to accurately replicate the piano because the envelope does not decay to zero over time. Figure 6.5 illustrates the differences in crude terms (although it doesn't show that the ADSR envelope could sustain indefinitely).

The next weakness with this type of envelope (and this applies to all envelopes) is that real sounds do not necessarily increase or decrease in a linear manner. Take the example of a slow-swelling violin—in practice, the attack of the note is likely to have two phases:

- First the note will go from nothing to a very quiet level very quickly.

- Then, the note volume may increase exponentially.

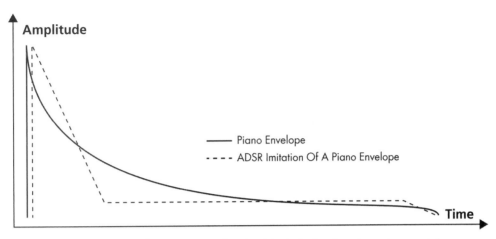

Figure 6.5 The ADSR-type envelope may not be the ideal choice for piano-type patches.

You could almost see the attack as having three phases—a fast phase, followed by a slow phase, followed by another fast phase. Figure 6.6 illustrates this point. It also shows why it may be difficult to use a synthesizer to accurately replicate natural instruments.

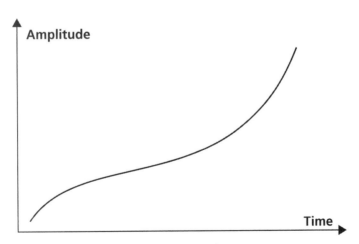

Figure 6.6 The attack phase of a "swelling" string sound.

So if the ADSR envelope has limitations, what other choices are there? Lots, but let me just stop you there. I don't want you to think of the ADSR envelope as being limiting. Many synthesizers have this style of envelope for good reasons: It works and it is easy to use.

I should also point out at this stage that if you want a piano sound, the optimal solution would be to hire a studio with a piano and a good recording room and get an experienced piano player to record the part. Failing that, there are some excellent sample libraries with highly detailed and playable pianos available, but again, I suggest you find a skilled piano player.

DAHDSR Envelopes

A step up from the ADSR envelope is the DAHDSR envelope. This structure is featured in a number of synthesizers, but in our featured synths, only VAZ Modular has this unit (which is called the Super Envelope); see Figure 6.7.

Figure 6.7 The Super Envelope in VAZ Modular. This is a DAHDSR envelope.

The controls on the DAHDSR envelope are:

- **D: Delay Time.** The Delay Time is the period before the envelope begins. Generally this isn't used, but it is useful, especially if you want different elements of a sound to come in after the initial attack.

- **A: Attack Time.** The Attack Time sets the time it takes the note to reach its maximum level once the envelope cycle has begun (in other words, after the delay period has ended).

- **H: Hold Time.** After the completion of the attack phase, the envelope remains at its maximum level for the Hold Time.

- **D: Decay Time.** The Decay Time is the time it takes (after the Hold phase is complete) for the note to change from the maximum level to the sustain level.

- **S: Sustain Level.** The Sustain Level is the level at which the envelope will remain until the key is released.

- **R: Release Time.** The Release Time is the time it takes the envelope's level to reach zero after the key is released.

If you set the Delay and Hold controls to zero, the envelope will work as a conventional ADSR envelope.

Figure 6.8 shows the DAHDSR envelope in practice.

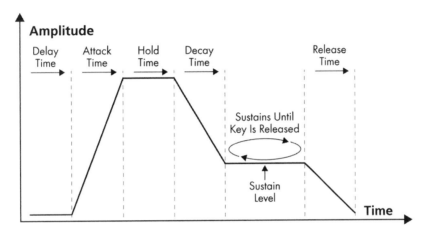

Figure 6.8   The DAHDSR envelope.

One use for this envelope is to increase the time that the sound stays at the level reached after the attack phase has been completed. This can make the sound behave as if the signal is being constrained by a compressor or a limiter. Using this hold stage in moderation can give a sound more subjective punch.

Multi-Stage Envelopes
We've looked ADSR and DAHDSR envelopes. The natural progression is multi-stage envelopes— envelopes that can have as many stages as are needed (or if not limitless stages, then at least lots).

With a multi-stage envelope, you can:

- Set an envelope node—you can add (or remove) as many node points as are needed.

- Set the level of that node.

- Set the time of that node (in other words, the time between the previous node and the current node). With some envelopes you can link the node to a division of the beat.

- Set the curve of the transition between the node and the previous node, so the change could be linear or sudden.

- Set a node as the beginning of a loop section.

- Set a node as the end of a loop section (thereby designating the remaining nodes as the decay section of the envelope).

As you can see, this gives huge flexibility, and it also allows you to create rhythmic patterns with envelopes (which can be especially effective when the nodes are linked to the tempo of an underlying track).

There are multi-stage envelopes in:

- VAZ Modular (see Figure 6.9).

- Zebra 2 (see Figure 6.10).

- KarmaFX Synth Modular. (This envelope is shown later in this chapter.)

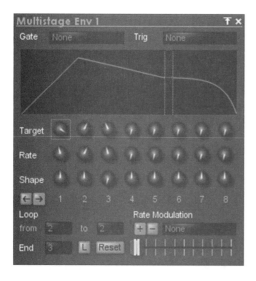

Figure 6.9 The Multistage Envelope in VAZ Modular.

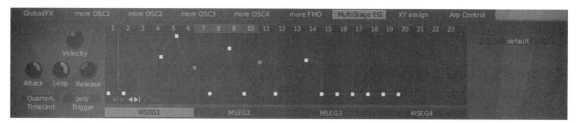

Figure 6.10 One of the four MSEG (multi-stage envelope generator) modules in Zebra 2.

If you look at Figure 6.10, you will notice that there are three knobs to the left of the multi-stage envelope controller:

- Attack
- Loop
- Release

These act (respectively) to scale the speed of:

- The attack portion of the multi-stage envelope—in other words, the nodes from the start until the beginning of the loop section
- The loop section
- The release section—the nodes from the loop end marker until the end of the multi-stage envelope

Other Envelope Controls

We've had a good look at the main envelope modules and the main envelope controls. Let's move on and look at some of the more specialized features.

Envelope Curves

As well as giving control over the envelope, many of the envelopes also give control over the curves—in other words, how the level changes from one point to the next. This can be most clearly seen in the multi-stage envelope curves (see Figure 6.9 as one example); however, other units, such as the ADSR envelope in KarmaFX Synth Modular and the envelope in Zebra 2, allow curve control, too.

Changing a curve can have a significant effect on the perceived effect of the transition. For instance:

- A linear curve will give a smooth and uniform transition.
- A slow curve will mean the level initially changes slowly but gets more dramatic over time.
- A fast curve will mean the level initially changes quickly but gets slower over time.

These curves are illustrated in Figure 6.11.

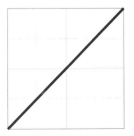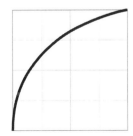

Figure 6.11 Linear, slow, and fast envelope curves.

Bipolar Envelopes

No, we're not talking about envelopes that have issues....

Most envelopes are unipolar—in other words, they output only positive values. Clearly, the polarity of these envelopes can be flipped so that they output only negative values.

However, there are envelopes that are bipolar—in other words, they can output positive *and* negative values during the same cycle. One particular use for this is with envelopes that control pitch—you can raise *and* lower a note (where a regular envelope could raise *or* lower a note). One envelope that includes bipolar functionality is the Envelope module in KarmaFX Synth Modular (see Figure 6.12). This is also another example of a multi-stage envelope.

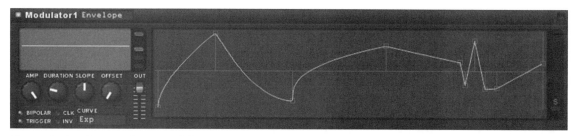

Figure 6.12   The Envelope module in KarmaFX Synth Modular in a multi-stage envelope with bipolar capability.

Envelopes and Samples

When you load up samples, the samples will have their own volume envelope. In this case you should think about the interaction between samples and the envelopes. If the wave has a slow attack time, you cannot make it faster simply by choosing a fast attack with your envelope. If you want to get more attack in this situation, you are going to have to change the place from which the sample starts to play. This will have a secondary effect (which may or may not be desirable) of changing the sound and feel of the sample.

Conversely, you can take a sample with a fast attack time and apply a slower envelope. Again, this will change the sound of the sample (which is rather the point of this book ...). However, you may then lose some of the initial tone of the sample.

Key Tracking and Envelopes

We have mentioned key tracking elsewhere in the book—this is the process by which pitch information can control another element within the sound.

Key tracking can be used within some envelopes. For instance:

- All of the controls in the basic Zebra 2 envelope can be modulated. (See the addition foldout row of modulators illustrated in Figure 6.13.)

- The Super Envelope in VAZ Modular can have each of its controls modulated.

- All of the functions in the KarmaFX Synth Modular ADSR module can be modulated.

Figure 6.13   In the Zebra 2 Envelope module, you can use pitch and velocity information to modulate each and every one of the envelope's parameters.

This technique can be very useful for replicating the behavior of natural instruments. For instance, if we think about the volume envelope of a piano, as the notes get higher they sustain for a shorter period and conversely, as the notes get lower they sustain for longer. Modulation of an envelope's parameters allows us that level of control.

Of course—as you can see in Figure 6.13—you can also use velocity tracking in a similar manner to increase the real-time control over an envelope that a player may have.

Envelope Followers

An envelope follower module extracts the volume envelope shape from an incoming audio signal and converts this to a level that can be used as a modulation source. Hopefully it goes without saying that you will also need to connect an audio source in order to control an envelope follower.

The envelope followers all follow a fairly standard format, having similar controls that often are similar to those on a conventional envelope (such as attack time, decay time, and release time). In essence, these controls adjust how quickly the envelope follower will respond to an incoming audio signal.

You can find an envelope follower in three of our featured synthesizers.

- In KarmaFX Synth Modular, you can find the EnvFollow (see Figure 6.14).

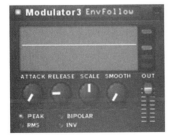

Figure 6.14   The EnvFollow module in KarmaFX Synth Modular.

- In VAZ Modular, you will find the Env Follower module (see Figure 6.15).

- In SynthEdit, you can find the Peak Follower module (see Figure 6.16)

Figure 6.15   The Env Follower module in VAZ Modular.

Figure 6.16   The Peak Follower module in SynthEdit.

Low-Frequency Oscillators (LFOs)

A low-frequency oscillator oscillates at a low frequency—for our purposes, it oscillates below the audio threshold. (In other words, if you connect an LFO output to an audio output, you would not be able to hear any sound, although your speaker would be moved.)

The prime uses for an LFO as a modulation source are:

- To modulate pitch, giving vibrato effects

- To modulate volume to give tremolo effects

- To modulate filter cut-off to give wah-wah or gating/stuttering effects (which we'll look at later in this chapter)

There are two key differences between a regular envelope and an LFO:

- A regular envelope is a single-shot modulator—in other words, it begins, it modulates, it sustains at the sustain level (if there is a sustain phase in the envelope—there will be if it's an ADSR envelope), and then it ends. By contrast, an LFO is generally a single-cycle wave that repeats.

- A regular envelope is unipolar—in other words, it will output only positive values or only negative values. By contrast, an LFO is bipolar—it will output positive and negative values within a single cycle.

I am stressing the term *regular envelopes* here since, as you have already seen, a number of envelopes have a loop function and hence can behave like LFOs under certain circumstances. There is no right or wrong time to use an LFO or an envelope with a loop—choose whatever is right for you and whichever will help you get the best sound.

Main LFO Controls
Let's look at the main LFO controls in the following sections.

Wave Shape
The most common LFO shapes are:

- **Sine.** The sine wave produces an even and rounded modulation source.

- **Triangle.** The triangle wave has virtually the same effect as the sine wave, but the changes are constant. This may give a crisper sound when compared to the sine wave. Both the sine and triangle are ideal waves for vibrato, tremolo, or wah-wah effects.

- **Sawtooth.** Depending on whether the wave is applied positively or negatively (and equally, depending on whether the module differentiates between saw and ramp waves), the sawtooth provides either:
  - A rising modulation source that drops abruptly after reaching the maximum value
  - A falling modulation source, rising to a peak and then gently falling

- **Square.** The square wave is either at its maximum or at its minimum. This wave tends to be used as an LFO to give rhythmic effects. It can also be used to modulate the pitch to give trill-type effects.

- **Random.** The random wave gives an output value from the LFO that is a random value. Again, this wave is often used for creating rhythmic effects.

However, while these may be the most common shapes:

- Many LFO units offer a whole range of other waveforms and the possibility of morphing between waves.

- We're in the modular world, so we can do a lot to mess around with LFOs.

Frequency
The LFO frequency or speed control affects the frequency of the LFO. If an LFO is used as a vibrato source, then the speed control will affect the frequency of the vibrato. Most LFOs (while acting as a low-frequency oscillator) have a range of around 0.1 cycles per second to about 20 cycles per second.

LFOs can also have their frequency synchronized with the tempo of a track so that the time it takes the LFO to complete a whole cycle is a subdivision of the track's tempo. This option is often used in conjunction with rhythmic effects.

Depth/Amount

The depth or amount control of an LFO determines the extent to which it modulates the destination. In practice, an amount setting will often control the size of the LFO wave, but the net impact is on the depth of modulation.

Allied to an LFO's depth, you may sometimes find delay and fade controls:

- Delay sets the time between the note being struck and the LFO starting its cycle.

- Fade sets the time (after the delay phase has been completed) over which the LFO fades in—the LFO reaches its full value at the end of the fade phase.

However, while these two controls are only present on some LFOs (for instance, the KarmaFX Synth Modular has a Fade control on its LFO module), they are not necessary in the modular environment. Then again, the amount control isn't necessary in a modular environment either. Through the modular routing, you can set up an arrangement to control the depth of the LFO modulator without needing to touch the LFO unit.

Take a look at Figure 6.17. This is a patch set up in VAZ Modular, where an envelope is used to control the modulation depth of the LFO.

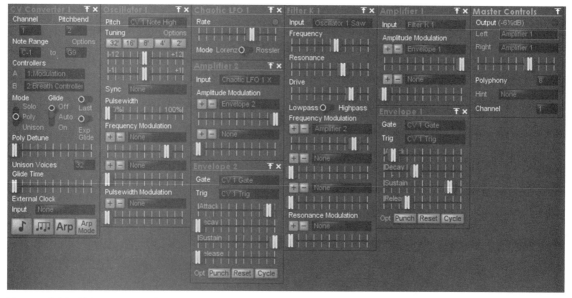

Figure 6.17   Using an envelope to control LFO modulation depth in VAZ Modular.

With this setup:

- The oscillator feeds into the filter.

- The LFO source is Chaotic LFO.

- The output of the LFO is fed into Amplifier 2.

- The level of Amplifier 2 is controlled by Envelope 2.

- Amplifier 2—in other words, the output from the LFO that is controlled by Envelope 2—is set as the modulation source for the filter's cut-off.

This allows a very detailed level of control over the amount of modulation of the filter by the LFO over time.

I chose to use an ADSR envelope because it allowed me to increase and decrease the level of the LFO. I could have used the delay envelope (not shown) if I just wanted to delay the effect of the LFO.

Phase

In the same manner that a conventional oscillator will have a phase, so will an LFO oscillator, but if the effect of an LFO is to be heard immediately, then in many ways the initial phase of an LFO can be more significant. Because LFOs are bipolar, their output will be positive and negative. If you are expecting a positive modulation and you get a negative modulation, then you will not get the sonic result when you press a key.

However, if you are going to control the phase, then you also need to synchronize the phase to a key press. Many LFOs allow you to synchronize the phase to a key press and to then control the phase.

That being said, you will also want to use free-running LFOs (where the LFO may be anywhere through its cycle when the note is triggered) because free-running LFOs do not have the consistent effect on a sound that key-synchronized LFOs do.

Monophonic/Polyphonic LFOs

Linked to the issue of free-running LFOs is the issue of monophonic and polyphonic LFOs. Let me explain:

- With monophonic LFOs, a single oscillator is used whenever that LFO is invoked. So if you are using an LFO to add some vibrato to a pad, when you play a chord, all of the notes will be governed by the same LFO and will have the rise and fall of their pitch synchronized. The effect may not be particularly natural in this instance (in fact, in practice it can sound quite horrid).

- With a polyphonic LFO, each separate note has its own LFO, which will start its cycle at a different time from any other LFO. Using our pad example again, this could mean that if you are using a polyphonic LFO to modulate a chord, some notes could have their pitch raised while others could simultaneously have their pitch flattened. This may give a more desirable result for a pad, but it is less useful for rhythmic sounds.

LFO Modules

Let's have a quick look at some (but not all) of the LFO modules that are available in the featured synthesizers. These all perform the same basic functions, so I don't want to explain in detail what each does. However, I will point out one or two interesting features that you may find useful.

KarmaFX Synth Modular LFO

The KarmaFX Synth Modular has one LFO unit (see Figure 6.18). This is a very general-purpose LFO unit intended for a wide range of duties, so it has a number of waveforms, has trigger-synching, and has control over polarity, among its many functions.

Figure 6.18   The LFO module in KarmaFX Synth Modular.

LFOs in VAZ Modular

VAZ Modular has a range of LFOs. Some are simpler than others—for instance, the Sine LFO and the Triangle LFO (see Figure 6.19) are simply a sine wave and a triangle wave LFO and nothing more. The Chaotic LFO (also shown in Figure 6.19) is similar but has a choice of three (chaotic) waves that are selectable in the audio routing.

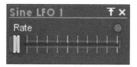 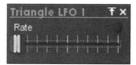 

Figure 6.19   The Sine LFO, Triangle LFO, and Chaotic LFO in VAZ Modular.

VAZ Modular also has three more fully featured LFOs that, among other things, allow you to morph between waveshapes. This can give variation in the effect of the LFO, and if you morph in real time, can give some shifting sonic results. There are two "conventional" LFOs (LFO and LFO B) and a third module, Tempo LFO, which is a tempo-synched LFO. These are all shown in Figure 6.20.

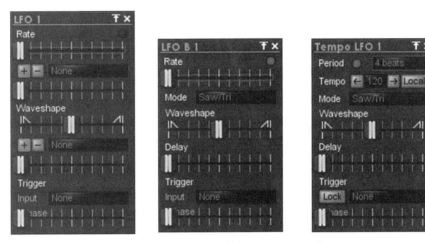

Figure 6.20   The LFO, LFO B, and Tempo LFO modules in VAZ Modular.

LFOs in Zebra 2

Zebra 2 offers LFOs in two flavors:

- The regular LFO (which is called a voice LFO).

- Global LFOs, which have a reduced feature offering (in particular, they cannot be modulated in the same way). However, these global LFOs do have the option to be retriggered every measure or on multiples of a measure.

Figure 6.21 shows the LFOs.

Figure 6.21   The Zebra 2 LFOs—the voice LFO is on top, and the global LFO is below.

Both LFOs come with a wide range of waveforms, including user-defined waves, which we will look at in the "Step Generators" section later in this chapter.

One other difference is that voice LFOs have the option to switch between:

- Gate mode, where the LFO is retriggered whenever a key is hit

- Free mode—in other words, free-running mode, so the LFO may be at any point in its cycle when it is called into use

Creating an LFO in SynthEdit

SynthEdit takes an interesting approach to LFOs: It doesn't offer one. Instead, you can use a regular oscillator pitched below the audio frequency. Take a look at Figure 6.22, which shows an oscillator acting as an LFO hooked into the SynthWiz Simple Synth structure.

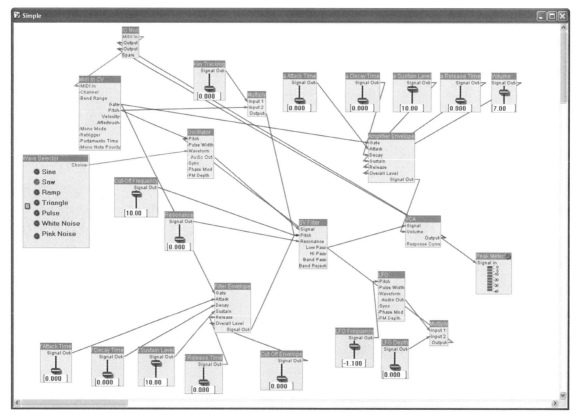

Figure 6.22   An oscillator acting as an LFO added into SynthWiz Simple Synth. The LFO is in the bottom-right corner.

Here's what I did to add the LFO:

1. Loaded up a regular oscillator, renamed it as LFO, and set the wave to the sine wave.

2. Loaded a slider, which I connected to the Pitch plug. I then renamed the slider as LFO Frequency and set its Lo Value and Hi Value to −5 and 0, respectively.

3. Loaded a Multiply module and attached the LFO (oscillator) Audio Out to the Input 1 plug of the multiplier. The Output plug was then attached to the Pitch plug in the existing sound-creating oscillator.

4. Loaded another slider, which I attached to the Input 2 plug on the Multiply module. I renamed the slider as LFO depth and set its Lo Value and Hi Value to 0 and 1, respectively.

As with the example earlier on, this LFO could easily be controlled by an envelope. To do this I could either:

- Replace the LFO depth slider with the LFO envelope, or ...

- Attach both the LFO depth slider and the LFO envelope to the second plug on the Multiply module. Both would then have an effect on the LFO depth, so there could be some permanent vibrato and some vibrato that changes over time.

Step Generators

Step generators are conceptually quite straightforward, but they are very powerful, too.

With a step generator, you can specify:

- The number of steps.

- The time base of those steps. So for instance, you could specify that 16 steps is equivalent to a measure (a bar), in which case each step would last for one sixteenth note (see Figure 6.23).

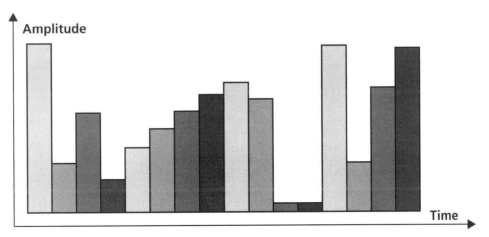

Figure 6.23   Sixteen steps in a step generator.

- The level of each step.

- The length of time that each step sounds. So for instance, instead of each step lasting for the whole value, it could last for half of its value—in our example of 16 steps, each step would last for one thirty-second note, but would still sound on every sixteenth note (see Figure 6.24).

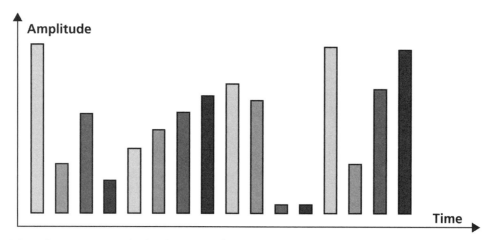

Figure 6.24   Sixteen steps with the duration of each step reduced to give a more staccato sound with greater emphasis on the beat.

Like LFOs, step-generator patterns can be looped. Unlike (most) LFOs, the musician can precisely determine the pattern to be played. Spend a few minutes with a step generator, and you will quickly get lost in the rhythmic patterns. You will find that you can modulate:

- Volume to give rhythmic patterns

- Filter cut-off to give rhythmic patterns, too, and to shift the tone with each step

- Filter resonance to shift the color of tone changes with each step

And that is just for starters....

There are a number of different step generators in the featured synthesizers, and each goes about its business in a slightly different way.

The Step module in KarmaFX Synth Modular (see Figure 6.25) is perhaps the most easily accessible of the step generators.

As well as letting you set the level of each step, on a global basis, you can set:

- The length of each step

- The decay rate of each step

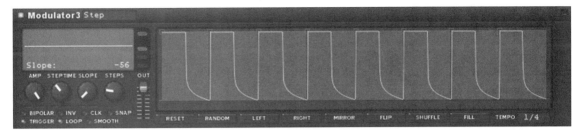

Figure 6.25 The Step module in KarmaFX Synth Modular.

The combination of these two allows you detailed control over how each step sounds. There are a few other slightly less usual functions that give you even more options:

- The module can be set up to output unipolar (positive or negative value) or bipolar (positive and negative values). This means the module can work more like an LFO than an envelope, if you want.

- There is a smooth control so that the level smoothly transitions from one step to the next. This means the module can work more like an envelope than an LFO, if you want.

- There is also a snap function so that if you are modulating (for instance, pitch), then the step level will snap to the nearest meaningful value. Using the pitch example, this means that you can create melodic sequences with the Step module.

The Sequencer Row in VAZ Modular (see Figure 6.26) gives you a lot less control than the Step module in KarmaFX Synth Modular. However, this does make it easier to operate.

With the Sequencer Row, each step has a value selected by the corresponding slider. However, the stepping is not controlled by the module—instead, you need to add a modulator to control which step is triggered. So for instance, you could use an ascending sawtooth LFO to move through each step.

The LFO unit in Zebra 2 will also behave like a step generator when the user wave is selected. As you can see in Figure 6.27, when the user wave is selected, a foldout appears at the bottom of the LFO, and you can literally draw the wave, or rather, you can set the level for each step.

As well as being able to select the number of steps and the level of each step, you can choose between:

- Wave mode, in which the level transitions smoothly between each point

- Step mode, in which the level jumps from one point to the next

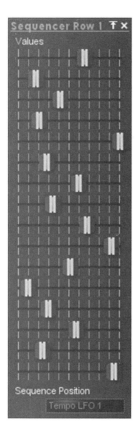

Figure 6.26   The Sequencer Row in VAZ Modular.

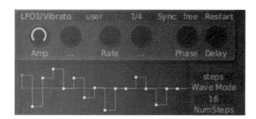

Figure 6.27   The LFO in Zebra 2 with the user wave selected operates as a step generator.

Lastly, please do remember that while the user-drawn LFO may not have complete flexibility, if you do need to get more detailed, you can always use a multi-stage envelope in Zebra 2, which will allow you to do many other things (such as draw the curve between node points).

Synthesizers in Real Time: Control and Automation

So far, all of the tools we have looked at—envelopes, LFOs, and step generators—have given a wide range of control over the sounds created by a synthesizer. However, these all have two limitations:

- First, these controls are not operated in real time (nor are they recordings of real-time changes).

- Second, the time over which these controls work is limited. An LFO or step generator has a certain number of steps, and at a certain point it becomes impractical to add yet another node to an envelope.

These issues can both be addressed in a very straightforward way by looking outside of the synthesizers to the controls that can be applied. In this context, there are three main controls that can be applied:

- The most obvious form of control is to move knobs in real time with your mouse. This can be a bit clunky, so thankfully, there are some tools to help us. One of the most useful tools is the XY pad, which I will look at in a moment.

- Another way to control a synthesizer's parameters is through external hardware. Many keyboards also include some knobs and sliders that can be applied to control specific functions within a synthesizer.

- Lastly, MIDI and audio hosts that can run synthesizers can help us. All hosts have automation controls—you just need to hook them up. By using a host's automation, you can:
  - Record parameter changes in real time
  - Program in parameter changes that are not practical within a synthesizer (for instance, a filter sweep that lasts 30 seconds and that has to coincide with other events in the track)

Let's have a look at all of these options in a bit more detail.

XY Pads

Zebra 2 and VAZ Modular both offer XY pads. We're going to have a quick look at some of the things you can do with the XY pads in Zebra 2 (see Figure 6.28).

XY pads allow you to connect two modulation sources to one controller, so for instance, you could connect the horizontal axis of an XY pad to control a filter's cut-off and the vertical axis to control the same filter's resonance. This would allow you to control both functions with one mouse click, which is far more intuitive and a much quicker way of working than clicking on the individual knobs. It's also often much easier to make fine adjustments to an XY pad.

In addition, while an XY pad can control two parameters, it is not limited to only two. (This is especially the case with VAZ Modular because you can make unlimited connections.) For instance, on one single axis you could set the controller to open up one filter while closing another. Alternatively, you could raise the level of one oscillator while cutting the level of another. Then again, you might want to step through the available waveforms while detuning

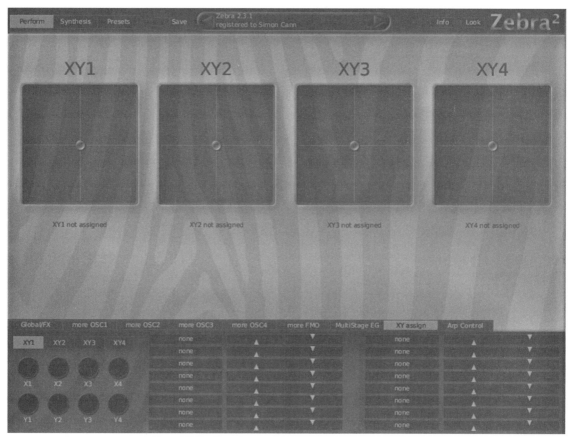

Figure 6.28 The Performance page in Zebra 2 showing the XY pads (which are currently unassigned). The XY assign controls are shown at the bottom of the page (although you could quite easily access any of the other tables while showing the XY pads).

the oscillator.... The options can give the musician very real levels of control that can add to a performance.

Before we look at how to attach and use XY pads, there is one point I must stress. These are real-time controllers—they do not change the original programming of a sound.

Assigning the XY Pad in Zebra 2

If you look back to Figure 6.28, you will see there are three blocks.

■   In the left block, you can select the XY pad to which your destinations are being assigned. You will also see X and Y knobs—these allow you to see the current XY settings and to adjust them (which you might want to do if the XY pads are hidden because you are looking at the Synthesis page and not the Performance page).

- The center column controls the X assignments (in other words, the destinations controlled by moving the XY controller horizontally).

- The right column controls the Y functions (in other words, the destinations controlled by moving the XY controller vertically).

To assign a destination:

1. Click in one of the unassigned boxes for either an X controller (center column) or a Y controller (right column)—unassigned boxes are labeled "none."

2. Find the appropriate destination on the pop-up menu (see Figure 6.29). Note that you can only assign to loaded modules.

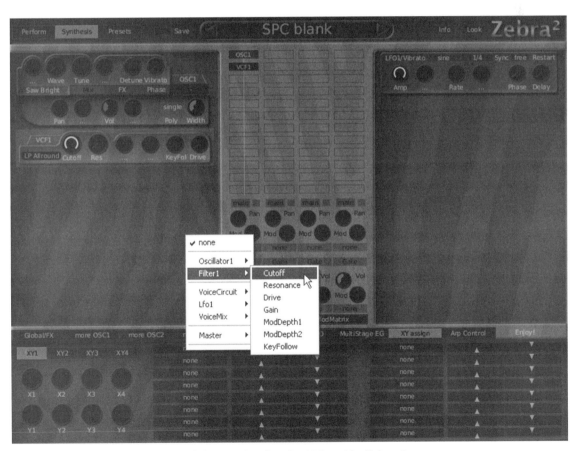

Figure 6.29 Selecting the control destination for the XY pad in Zebra 2.

3.   Select the appropriate destination from the menu.

4.   Repeat until all destinations have been selected. You can, of course, assign further controllers or remove any existing controllers at any point.

Once the assignments are completed, you can rename the pad and add some notes to remind yourself what it does. To do this:

■ Double-click on the pad's name (XY1, XY2, XY3, or XY4) over the top of the pad to rename the pad.

■ Double-click under the pad (XY1 not assigned, and so on) to add some notes.

Another way to assign a destination is to go to the knob you want to control:

1.   Right-click on it.

2.   Select the appropriate XY controller from the Assign To submenu.

Setting XY Pad Ranges

When you assign a destination, you will see a red to yellow fade bar is added between the arrow-heads to the right of the assignment name.

■ The red to yellow fade bar shows the current setting on the assigned destination. You can drag this bar to adjust the setting. (As you do, the corresponding knob on the controlled module will be adjusted.)

■ The top arrow (pointing down) indicates the maximum extent of the control of the pad. So if you are controlling the filter cut-off, then the top arrow will indicate the maximum extent to which the XY pad will open the filter. You should note that there is not necessarily any correlation between the red to yellow fade bar, the bar's location, and the effect of the top (or bottom) arrow.

■ The bottom arrow (pointing up) indicates the minimum extent of the control of the pad. So if you are controlling a filter cut-off, then the bottom arrow will indicate the minimum setting for the filter when the XY pad is moved. Again, there is no correlation with the red to yellow fade bar.

■ When the top arrow is to the left of the right arrow, then the effect of the XY pad is reversed. (In other words, movement to the left/downward will increase values.)

■ If you set a range where the minimum and the maximum controls are *both* above or are *both* below the setting for the destination, then:

   • When the XY pad is at its default (middle) position, the value set by the knob (in other words, the red to yellow fade bar) will apply.

   • When the XY pad value is increased, then the destination will be controlled over the range from the destination knob to the maximum value set by the top arrow.

- When the XY pad value is decreased, then the destination will be controlled over the range from the destination knob to the minimum value set by the bottom arrow (even if that minimum is higher than the minimum set by the destination knob).

- As the XY pad passes from its maximum value to its minimum value, at the middle point it will pass through the default setting. If you are (for instance) controlling a filter, then it could be fully open at the maximum, partially open at the minimum, and closed by default. Therefore, as you travelled from maximum to minimum, the filter would be fully open, then fully closed, and then partially open—there would not be a direct transition from maximum to minimum without passing through the default position.

More Complex Applications of XY Pads

VAZ Modular offers the perfect complement to the XY pad: the Vector Mixer (see Figure 6.30).

In essence, the Vector Mixer is a four-into-one audio mixer. However, it does have a twist on

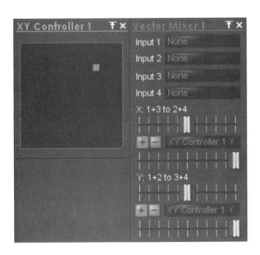

Figure 6.30 The XY Pad in VAZ Modular hooked up to a Vector Mixer.

that concept—instead of simply mixing the four levels, it balances their combination, and that combination is controlled by two sliders, which can be attached to the XY pad.

If you attach the XY pad to the Vector Mixer and set the modulation sliders to the maximum amount (as I have done in Figure 6.30), then the XY pad will fully control the mix of the four sound sources. This will mean that in each of the four corners, each sound will be isolated, and in between those extremes you can mix the four elements to taste. Among other applications, you could use this to create a perfectly blended sound source that could then be controlled and adjusted in real time.

MIDI Learn

It's easy to control your synthesizer with your MIDI hardware. For instance, you may have a bank of knobs on your MIDI keyboard that you want to use to control your synthesizer.

The easiest way to attach your hardware is by using MIDI Learn. This functionality is available in KarmaFX Synth Modular, VAZ Modular, and Zebra 2. The principles are virtually the same for each synthesizer, so I'm going to illustrate the setup with Zebra 2.

To assign your hardware controller, open up Zebra 2 and have your hardware at hand, then:

1. Right-click on the control that you want to attach to your hardware. A pop-up menu will appear (see Figure 6.31).

2. Click on MidiLearn.

3. Waggle your hardware control that you want to assign.

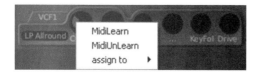

Figure 6.31 MidiLearn and MidiUnLearn in Zebra 2. You will also notice the Assign To submenu, which can be used to assign the knob's function to the XY pad.

And that's it...you're done. The hardware will now control that parameter.

To unassign the parameter (in other words, to tell Zebra 2 to forget the assignment):

1. Right-click on the parameter.

2. Select MIDI UnLearn.

And the assignment is forgotten.

Automation

To automate a control from outside the synthesizer, you will need some audio production software, such as SONAR or Project5 from Cakewalk, Logic from Apple, Live from Ableton, or Nuendo or Cubase from Steinberg. These are just a few examples—there are many other software suites out there from which you could choose.

As I've already mentioned, these suites perform a number of functions:

■ Routing MIDI inputs from MIDI hardware attached to the computer to the plug-in

■ Recording MIDI data (and subsequently transmitting that recorded data to the relevant plug-in on playback)

- Editing (and accepting manual input) of MIDI data (whether in the form of notes or controller information)

- Managing the audio output of the synthesizer and connecting it to the computer's hardware

- Displaying the plug-in's interface

In other words, in the context of synthesizer automation, these suites do exactly what we need. When we want to automate data, the suites give us two options:

- Record the data (in the same way that other MIDI information will be recorded).

- Draw (in other words, manually input) the necessary data.

The procedure for both of these will vary depending on the software you are using. I will illustrate the basic principles using Project5 from Cakewalk. If you want to know more about Project5, I suggest you also check out *Project5 Power!* (Course Technology PTR, 2008).

Project5 allows for MIDI data to be created in two forms:

- As clips—in other words, as short segments of information that can be moved around and repeated. Since this doesn't offer much more than we already have with the tools in the synthesizer, I'm not going to look at that option.

- As track data—in other words, as information that is related to a track. The advantage of track data is that it can be applied from the start of a song to the end of a song without needing to be repeated, looped, or otherwise messed with.

In conjunction with Project5, I'm going to use KarmaFX Synth Modular for this illustration. As you will see, KarmaFX Synth Modular may not be the most straightforward synthesizer to automate, but I think it is useful to see some of the messing around that is necessary to get various pieces to work together.

Preparing to Automate

The difficulty with controlling a modular synthesizer is the extensibility of each sound (in other words, the number of modules that could be controlled is limitless) and the permutations of how that limitless number of modules could be hooked up. With any one synthesizer instance, most hosts can control up to 128 destinations—however, choosing the right ones to control may not always be easy.

Therefore, while there's nothing intrinsically difficult about automating a modular synthesizer, there are sometimes a few extra steps to be taken. With KarmaFX Synth Modular, the most important step is to identify the knobs to be controlled. We need to do this for three reasons:

- First, so that KarmaFX Synth Modular knows which knobs to output data with respect to.

- Second, so the synthesizer knows where to route the incoming data.

- Third, so there is no confusion about what is being automated and what is not.

So to get going, the first step is to load KarmaFX Synth Modular into Project5 and to load up your patch. I presume you have an idea of how to load your synth of choice into your audio software of choice, so I won't repeat the steps here.

Let's say, just for argument's sake, that we want to automate the Amp knob on the Amplifier module. To designate this knob as the one to control:

1. Right-click on it, which will bring up a pop-up menu (see Figure 6.32).

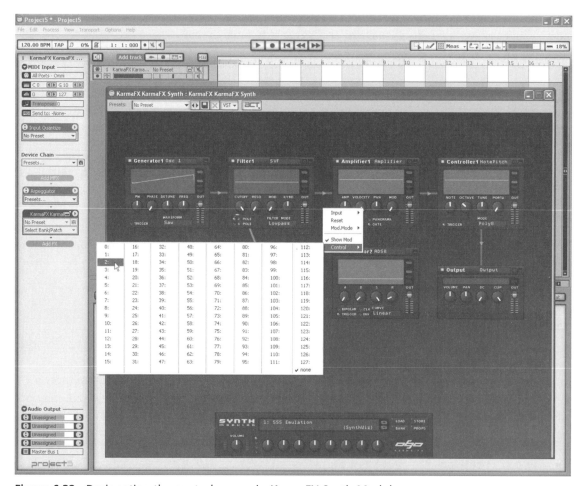

Figure 6.32 Designating the control source in KarmaFX Synth Modular.

2. In the pop-up menu, select Control, which will open up a submenu. This submenu gives you 128 options—these are the 128 destinations that any host will be able to control with respect to a single instance of a synthesizer.

3. I selected the third slot (labeled 2—counting starts from 0 around here...). Having made this selection, when the submenu is next accessed, the label Amp shows against slot 2 to show that the slot is assigned.

4. You can repeat these steps to make other knobs controllable.

And that's it—you're now set up to record and draw automation.

Recording

The process to record automation is straightforward, but it only works for assigned knobs. Some synthesizers (mostly fixed-architecture synthesizers, but also Zebra 2) automatically do this assignment. Often modulars do not, hence the process we went through with KarmaFX Synth Modular in the previous chapter.

In Project5, to record automation of an assigned control:

1. Arm the track in which the synthesizer has been loaded (see Figure 6.33).

2. Hit the Record button so the song begins to record.

3. Move the knob to be automated—in this case, the Amp button on the Amplifier.

4. Once the part has finished, hit the Stop button and disarm the track.

Your automation will now be recorded (even if you can't see it—and I'll explain how to display automation in the next section). If the automation isn't quite right, then you can either re-record it or manually edit it (using the drawing process set out in the next section).

Drawing

As with recording automation, you can only draw (or edit) automation for knobs that have been assigned. If you draw automation for a knob that hasn't been assigned, then the automation will not have any effect because there is nothing to connect the source to the destination.

The first step to drawing automation—or to displaying automation that has been recorded using the process in the previous section—is to select the automation control. Some audio software can display several control lanes simultaneously, but Project5 can only display one lane at a time. (However, you can record more than one lane of modulation.)

To select the automation lane in Project5 (see Figure 6.34):

Track Arm Button   Record Button   Parameter to Record

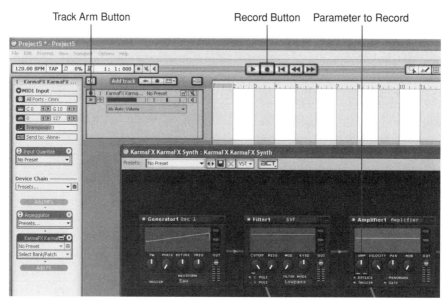

Figure 6.33 The process to record automation in Project5.

1. Engage the Show Automation function (by clicking on the Show/Hide Automation button).

2. Select the Automation destination from the Assign the Automation Lane drop-down menu. In Project5, this drop-down gives several options. We'll select DXi > DX Automation and then the third slot. The DX bit probably won't make much sense to you—it's a Cakewalk thing—but the third slot is important. You remember that when we prepared the automation, we selected the Amp knob and assigned it to the third slot. Here we're selecting the same third slot—the unfortunate effect of the interaction between Project5 and KarmaFX Synth Modular is that the Amp label does not translate through.

Drawn Automation   Show/Hide Automation

Draw Automation Tool   Automation Tool

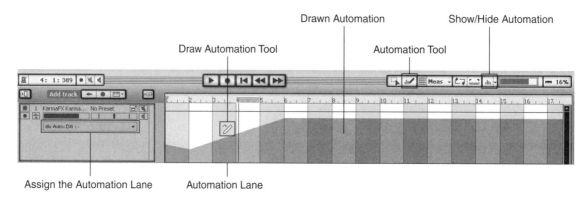

Assign the Automation Lane   Automation Lane

Figure 6.34 Assigning the control lane and drawing track automation in Project5.

Once the lane has been assigned, click on the Automation Tool button, and when you hold the mouse cursor over the automation lane, the Draw Automation tool will show. (The mouse cursor will look like a pencil.) You can go ahead and draw the automation (or edit existing automation).

If that's all clear, then we'll move on and look at some of the global controls.

7 Global Controls and Other Modules

As you will have realized by now, there are many ways to achieve the same result, even within a single synthesizer. Equally, when comparing one synthesizer to another, there is a multitude of different options to achieve a broadly similar sonic end result.

You will also have seen that different modules have different features and that the setup of the different synthesizers varies. As a result of this, there are some modules that exist in one synthesizer but for which there is no comparable module in another. For instance, there is an amplifier module in SynthEdit, KarmaFX Synth Modular, and VAZ Modular, but not in Zebra 2. This is not a fault on the part of Zebra 2—due to its design, an amplifier is not needed. Equally, as another example, there are some mathematical units in SynthEdit that do not exist in KarmaFX Synth Modular. Again, this is not a fault but a reflection on how the modules in KarmaFX Synth Modular can address all of the issues addressed by the mathematical modules without recourse to other modules.

Anyway, this chapter is intended to bring together the last few modules that haven't been featured, whether because they don't appear in all synthesizers, their use is limited, or they simply don't fit elsewhere. In addition, I will cover some of the more global synthesizer controls that you may want to consider when building your sounds.

Global Controls

There are a few features that fall under the heading of global controls—in other words, controls that apply to the whole synthesizer, not just a module (even if the knob to control the function may reside on a specific module). Many of these features appear on virtually all synthesizers, not just the ones featured in this book, so I want to quickly look at the general principles without covering any specific synthesizers.

I may repeat some of these points in a specific context when I look at some of the individual modules later in this chapter.

Polyphony

Polyphony is the number of notes that a synthesizer can play. Usually this will be set to one or a bigger number. Okay, that sounds daft...let me explain.

Sometimes, you will want to set your synthesizer to play only one note at a time—this is called *monophonic*. You may do this in order to achieve a certain sound or to replicate the behavior of a certain instrument (for instance, a flute). Often, you will use monophonic mode in conjunction with portamento, which I will explain in a moment.

If you don't want monophonic mode, then you will usually set the maximum number of notes that can be played simultaneously (in other words, the polyphony) to a number greater than one. Your natural inclination will probably be to set the number to the largest available number; however, there are two reasons why you may not choose the largest number.

- **CPU hit.** Each note you play is likely to have a direct hit on your CPU. Therefore, by restricting the number of notes that can be played, you will limit the hit on your CPU.

- **Clarity.** Particularly when you are playing sounds with long release times, it is possible to get an inharmonious racket when several notes are decaying (or old notes are decaying and new notes are struggling to be heard). By limiting the number of notes that can be played simultaneously, you will ensure that the old notes don't hang around for too long.

Usually, a polyphony setting of around eight notes is sufficient. However, for fast and intricate pieces, you may sometimes want a higher setting.

When you set polyphony, you also get into the world of voice stealing—in other words, the decisions about which of your existing notes needs to die if you are going to make way for a new note.

Most synthesizers have clever algorithms; generally they will seek to kill notes in the following order:

- Notes in their release stage—in other words, where the key has been released but the note is still sounding, starting with the earliest played note

- Notes where the key is still held, starting with the earliest played (in other words, the longest held)

Now clearly, you may be holding a note (and it may be the longest held) for a good reason—for instance, it may be a root bass note. In this case you will find that some (but not all) synthesizers allow you specify whether the lowest (or highest) note should avoid the cull.

Portamento

Portamento is a very useful effect. It is more commonly called *pitch glide*, and it happens when you play a first note and then a second. With portamento, the second note will not sound at its correct pitch immediately, but instead, the pitch will glide from the first note to the second. This effect is often used if you want to mimic the sound of the fretless bass (and also for some lead sounds).

That's the principle—and it all sounds quite straightforward—but there are several options around portamento. As you will read in a moment, many of these options are available in the featured synthesizers.

As a side note, portamento does work with chords, but—to my ear, at least—it always sounds bad. So for the sake of your hearing, I suggest you engage monophonic mode before trying portamento—and if there's the option, select last note priority (so that the last played note will sound). That warning made, let's get on and look at some of the usual controls in portamento.

Legato Mode

In legato mode, the portamento glide will occur only if the first note is still held when the second note is struck. In other words, if you release the first key and then strike the second key, there will be no legato effect, and the second note will immediately sound at its correct pitch. The clear advantage of legato mode is that it allows you to control the portamento effect by your playing.

In regular (or non-legato) mode, the glide will always occur. This can give slightly surprising results if you don't remember which note was played last.

Retrigger Envelopes

Often allied with legato mode is the non-retriggering of envelopes.

Usually, when you strike a note, you want the envelopes to have effect. In other words, you want the volume to be increased, you want the filter to be moved, and so on. However, when you are playing legato (in other words, there is no break between the notes), you often don't want the second note to trigger the envelopes—instead, you want it to sound as if it is a continuation of the first note. Think of a fretless bass, where the note slides from one pitch to another—in this case, there is no retriggering of the envelopes (in other words, the player does not pick the note again).

Glide Time

The glide time is the time it takes to glide from one note to another. There is usually a glide control to set the time and sometimes another switch to select how the time is calculated.

- **Fixed time.** With a fixed time setting, the glide will take the same time irrespective of the range of the glide, so the glide for one semitone will last as long as the glide for five octaves. With this setting, short glides (maybe up to five semitones) are sonically more effective.

- **Variable time (or per-note time).** With a per-note glide time, the time of the glide varies by the length of the range, so long glides take longer than short glides, but on balance, the length of the glide divided by the number of notes covered is fairly constant.

Pitch Bend Range

I'm sure you can get your head around pitch bend ranges without too much explanation. These are the settings that control the maximum extent to which a note will be bent when the pitch wheel on a keyboard is pushed. Commonly, a range of plus or minus two semitones is set, although anything up to plus or minus one octave is not out of this world.

That being said, you can bend over a much greater range depending on any particular setup. Also, depending on how your synthesizer lets you route things, you may be able to set up different oscillators to respond differently to bend data. For example, you could use this so that when you push the bend wheel, a single note transforms to become a chord.

Amplifiers

I've already mentioned that amplifiers don't exist in all synthesizers. Beyond that, their implementation and application is different between the synthesizers that do have an amplifier module. For instance:

- In VAZ Modular, the effect of an LFO on a modulation destination can be controlled (perhaps by an envelope) by routing it through an amplifier where the envelope modulates the amplitude of the envelope.

- In KarmaFX Synth Modular, a similar effect can be achieved by modulating an LFO module's Amount control with an envelope.

Neither approach is better or worse—they are simply the result of different design decisions by the developers. Each decision is perfectly reasonable, and the implementations are flawless in their execution.

So against that background, let's have a look at the amplifier modules. In many ways, these are very dull units—they make a signal louder or softer without adding color.

The Amplifier module in KarmaFX Synth Modular (see Figure 7.1) features, among other things, the following controls:

- **Amp.** The Amp knob controls the level of the incoming signal—this is the knob to modulate with an envelope or LFO for volume-related effects.

- **Velocity.** The Velocity knob controls the extent to which incoming MIDI velocity information will modulate the Amp level. Since there is a dedicated knob, you don't need to add another modulator.

- **Pan.** The Pan knob allows you to place your signal in the stereo panorama. Again, this control means that you don't have to place the audio in the stereo field later in the audio routing.

- **Mod.** The Mod knob controls the amount by which the Amp control is modulated (assuming you set a modulation source). Again, this makes the routing much easier to set up because you don't need to add additional modulation controllers.

Figure 7.1 The Amplifier module in KarmaFX Synth Modular.

The VCA module in SynthEdit (see Figure 7.2) is a much simpler module:

- **Signal.** The Signal plug connects the incoming signal.

- **Volume.** The Volume plug controls the level of the amplifier (in other words, the amount of amplification or attenuation). This is where an envelope, LFO, or level control can be connected.

- **Response Curve.** The Response Curve plug gives the user access to various response curves to tailor how the input signal is amplified.

- **Output.** The Output plug is where the signal exits the module.

Figure 7.2 The VCA amplifier module in SynthEdit.

VAZ has some interesting amplifiers: the Amplifier and the Amplifier B modules (see Figure 7.3).

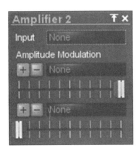

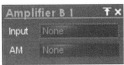

Figure 7.3 The Amplifier and Amplifier B modules in VAZ Modular.

The Amplifier module allows you to select the input, and there are two amplitude modulation slots, each of which allows:

- The amount of modulation to be controlled by an associated slider

- The polarity of the modulation to be set to positive or negative

Clearly, this approach gives a certain level of control. The Amplifier B module takes a more straightforward approach:

- Like the first amplifier, you can attach an audio source. (If you couldn't, it wouldn't be much of an amplifier.)

- You can also attach one (and only one) modulator.

- However, there are no controls for the modulator—the modulation source modulates to the maximum extent, and that is it.

There will be times when the more straightforward approach works and other times when you want a more detailed level of control.

Switches, Mixers, and Splitters

Okay, I'll come clean. That's probably a bit of a misleading heading.

I figure you know what a switch is, right? You select one audio flow out of several options and route that elsewhere. Alternatively, you route a single audio flow to one of a number of options—for instance, by using the Chaser 8-Way module in VAZ Modular (see Figure 7.4). And you understand the notion of splitting—you can send a signal to more than one destination. So that leaves mixers.

Figure 7.4 The Chaser 8-Way module in VAZ Modular.

A lot of mixing happens automatically. For instance, in KarmaFX Synth Modular, you can connect several sources to one module, and those sources will be mixed. In SynthEdit, you can connect two (or more) input signals to one plug, and they will be mixed. However, you may want a slightly higher level of control, and that is where the specialized mixing modules come in.

In KarmaFX Synth Modular, there is a Mixer module (see Figure 7.5).

This module mixes two signals (and only two signals). The main control is the Mix knob, which balances the two signals.

SynthEdit has the X-Mix module (see Figure 7.6).

Figure 7.5 The Mixer module in KarmaFX Synth Modular.

Figure 7.6 The X-Mix module in SynthEdit.

This module is intended to balance two incoming signals (Input A and Input B). The mixed signal is then sent to the output (Signal Out). The Mix plug allows you to balance the respective proportion of each signal.

VAZ Modular offers a cross-mixing functionality with the Mixer 2-Input module (see Figure 7.7).

Figure 7.7 The Mixer 2-Input module in VAZ Modular.

The Mixer 2-Input module allows you to balance two incoming signals and gives control over the cross-fading. In addition, the module offers a modulation slot. VAZ also offers a range of other mixers: the Mixer 3-Input and the Mixer 4-Input (see Figure 7.8).

The Mixer 3-Input allows you to set the level of each input and then gives you a modulation slot for further control. The Mixer 4-Input allows you to mix the four inputs with no modulation options.

In many ways Zebra 2 does not need a mixer—the mixing happens without human intervention, and you can always direct one module's audio output into another audio channel. However, Zebra 2 does offer a channel mixer (ChannelMix) module (see Figure 7.9).

The ChannelMix module gives you several mixing options and the facility to flip the left and right channels. In addition, it allows you both to balance the respective levels of the left and right channels and to convert the signal to mono and then place that mono signal within the stereo panorama.

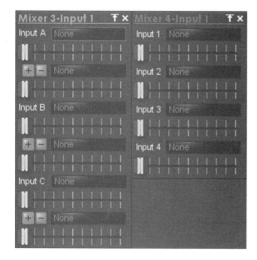

Figure 7.8   The Mixer 3-Input and the Mixer 4-Input in VAZ Modular.

Figure 7.9   The ChannelMix module in Zebra 2.

In addition to the Channel Mixer, Zebra 2 also offers a Modulation Mixer (see Figure 7.10).

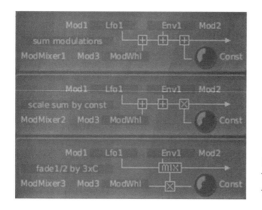

Figure 7.10   The Modulation Mixer module in Zebra 2. The three modules are the same; the difference is in their control configurations.

The purpose of the Modulation Mixer is to:

- Add several modulation sources together.

- Allow several modulation sources to be connected to one modulation destination.

- Give greater control over the modulation sources' effect on their destinations.

The Modulation Mixer allows three modulation sources to be combined and also includes a Constant parameter so that more modulation can be added or the resulting output can be scaled. The three modulation sources can be combined in three ways.

- **Sum Modulation.** In Sum Modulation mode, the three modulation sources and the constant are added together to create a single modulation source.

- **Scale Sum by Const.** In Scale Sum by Const mode, the three modulation sources are added together. The resulting signal is then scaled by the Constant knob.

- **Fade 1/2 by 3xC.** With Fade 1/2 by 3xC mode, the first two modulations are added, and the constant is scaled by Modulation 3, which is then also added.

VAZ Modular has a simpler version of this unit: the ModExpander (see Figure 7.11), which routes three modulation sources into one. It also has an Offset control, which adds a fixed value to the output signal (much like the Constant knob in Zebra 2).

Figure 7.11 The ModExpander module in VAZ Modular.

Inputs and Outputs

One thing you don't need to address within Zebra 2—since it's dealt with as part of the framework—is MIDI inputs. And unless you want to get clever, you don't need to deal with outputs, because the signal will flow there automatically. KarmaFX Synth Modular also releases you from having to hook up MIDI inputs. It does offer an Input module (to connect audio in for processing) and an Output module (to which all of the sounds destined for the outside world can be connected). The modules are shown in Figure 7.12.

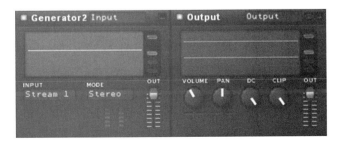

Figure 7.12 The (audio) Input and Output modules in KarmaFX Synth Modular.

As I said, with KarmaFX there is no need to connect up any MIDI inputs—the routing happens automatically. However, you can use the MIDITrig and the MIDIData modules (both shown in Figure 7.13) to control and assign MIDI data.

Figure 7.13 MIDITrig and MIDIData modules in KarmaFX Synth Modular.

By contrast, SynthEdit requires that you make all the connections yourself. Clearly this means you have to do more work, but it does also mean that you can manage—and control—each individual connection. Take a look at Figure 7.14, which shows the main hookup modules and the MIDI to CV unit. As you can see, there are separate audio in and audio out modules (Sound In and Sound Out, respectively), there is a MIDI In module (to route incoming MIDI data), and the MIDI to CV unit is a separate unit.

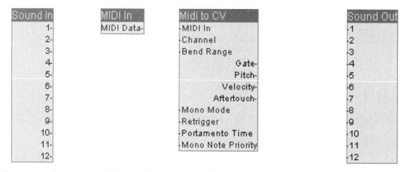

Figure 7.14 The Sound In, Sound Out, MIDI In, and MIDI to CV modules in SynthEdit.

The MIDI to CV module is one of those modules that doesn't make any sound, but it does a lot of things and is vital to a synthesizer. Analog synthesizers sent their internal message by the use of voltages (*control voltages*, as they were known). These voltages would control pitch (whether oscillator pitch or the cut-off frequency of a filter), loudness, and so on. While SynthEdit (like all of the synthesizers in this book) is a digital animal, it uses a voltage paradigm to hook up and control all of the modules. Hence, although we are not creating real voltages, within the SynthEdit framework we need incoming MIDI data to be converted to volts, and that is what the MIDI to CV module does.

Let's take a look at the plugs:

- **MIDI In.** The MIDI In plug connects from the MIDI Data plug on the MIDI In module. It is the plug through which all incoming MIDI data flows into the MIDI to CV unit in order to be reprocessed for onward distribution.

- **Channel.** The Channel plug determines to which incoming MIDI channels the MIDI to CV module will respond. By default, it will respond to all incoming MIDI data.

- **Bend Range.** The Bend Range plug determines the maximum pitch bend range output by the MIDI to CV module when incoming MIDI data includes pitch bend data.

- **Mono Mode.** When Mono Mode is engaged, only one note at a time can be played. This feature is often used in conjunction with Retrigger and Portamento.

- **Retrigger.** When Retrigger mode is engaged (which also requires Mono Mode to be engaged), if a note is held and a new note is played (before the first is released), then the envelopes for the new note will be triggered. If the envelopes are not retriggered, then the existing note will continue to sustain at the new pitch. As mentioned earlier, this non-retrigger feature can be useful for fretless bass and note-bending types of sounds.

- **Portamento Time.** Portamento works so that when one note is held, the next note slides to its pitch (and usually this works best if there is no retriggering). The Portamento Time control sets the time over which the slide completes.

- **Mono Note Priority.** If you are in Mono Mode (so you can only play one note), then you need to ensure you are playing the right note. Mono Note Priority allows you to specify which note should be played. There are three choices:
  - **Highest.** The highest held key will sound.
  - **Lowest.** The lowest held key will sound.
  - **Last.** The last played key will sound.

- **Gate.** The Gate control attaches to an envelope to pass the instruction when a note has been triggered and the envelope cycle should begin.

- **Pitch.** The Pitch plug passes pitch-related information—for instance to an oscillator, to the filter cut-off control, or in connection with other pitch-related modulation.

- **Velocity.** The Velocity plug passes MIDI velocity (key-strike force) information to the appropriate module—as an example, this information could be used to control or modify the filter cut-off frequency.

- **Aftertouch.** The Aftertouch plug passes MIDI aftertouch information.

VAZ Modular includes a CV Converter module to translate incoming MIDI data into a form that can be understood by the other modules and a Master Controls module (both are shown in Figure 7.15) to attach the audio output to the outside world.

Figure 7.15 The CV Converter and Master Controls modules in VAZ Modular.

Unlike SynthEdit, many of the controls of the CV Converter are accessible on its interface. Also unlike SynthEdit, the various outputs from the CV Converter are not displayed on the interface (but they are accessible by the other modules).

Although this might be doing things back-to-front and it is hidden from view, the CV Converter outputs the following data:

- **Note Low and Note High.** The CV Converter outputs the highest and the lowest note (except when Last is set on the interface). This allows you to select through the audio routing whether you want pitch data to be based on the highest or the lowest played note.

- **Gate.** The Gate output sends note-on and note-off information.

- **Trig.** The Trig output is used to retrigger the envelopes when the envelope is already open.

- **Velocity.** The Velocity output sends MIDI velocity data to the selected destination.

- **Pressure.** The Pressure output transmits MIDI aftertouch messages.

- **Control A and Control B.** The Control A and Control B outputs pass the MIDI data from the controllers attached to two controller slots on the interface (which is described in a moment). Usually the modulation wheel would be one of the connections.

Now let's look at the CV Converter interface:

- **Channel.** The Channel setting determines to which incoming MIDI channels the CV Converter module will respond.

- **Pitchbend.** The Pitchbend setting determines the maximum pitch bend range (in semitones) output by the CV Converter module when incoming MIDI data includes pitch bend data.

- **Note Range.** The Note Range sets the lowest and the highest incoming MIDI note to which the CV Converter will respond.

- **Controllers.** The Controllers slots allow you to assign incoming MIDI data controllers. This data is then made available as an output from the CV Converter (see earlier).

- **Mode.** The Mode switch sets how the CV Converter responds when more than one note is played.
  - **Solo.** When Solo is selected, only one voice is played. That will be the Note Low or Note High, mentioned earlier.
  - **Poly.** When Poly is selected, many voices will sound.
  - **Unison.** When Unison is selected, multiple voices (as set by the Unison Voices setting, which is explained in greater detail in a moment) will play a single note.

- **Glide.** The Glide controls how a note pitch glides from one note to another. This effect is best when single notes are played, but it does work for chords (although it sounds fairly yucky). There are three settings:
  - **Off.** When set to Off, there is no gliding.
  - **Auto.** This is legato mode. When a key is held and a second note is played, the next note slides to its pitch.
  - **On.** This is effectively "non-legato" mode. When a note is triggered, it slides to its pitch from the previously played note, even if that note is no longer playing.

- **Exp Glide and Glide Time.** When Glide mode is engaged, the Glide Time slider controls how long it takes to slide from one note to the other.
  - When Exp Glide is not engaged, the time it takes to glide from one note to the next will be set by the Glide Time slider, irrespective of how large the glide range may be.
  - When Exp Glide is engaged, the Glide Time is calculated on a per-note-of-jump basis—in other words, each note in the glide has a set time, so it will take longer to make long glides than it does to make short glides.

- **Last.** When Solo is selected, the Note Low or Note High outputs will output the lowest or the highest played note, as appropriate. If Last is engaged, the CV Converter will instead output the last note played.

- **Poly Detune.** Unison mode works rather like a multi-voice oscillator, but with a subtle difference. With a multi-voice oscillator, one oscillator outputs several voices (which can be detuned). These voices then pass through the audio chain. With Unison mode, the whole patch is effectively duplicated, so if there are eight voices, then the number of oscillators will be multiplied by eight, the number of filters will be multiplied by eight, and so on. In short, there will be eight separate audio channels, each of which can be detuned by using the Poly Detune control. The effect can give a huge sound (and can melt your CPU).

- **Unison Voices.** The Unison Voices setting controls the number of voices that will be played for each note in Unison mode. If this is greater than Polyphony (set in the Master Controls section), then the number of voices will equal that Polyphony setting. If the Unison Voices number is small enough that there are sufficient voices of Polyphony for multiple groups, then polyphonic playing (in other words, chords) will be allowed.

Inverters, Multipliers, Mathematics, and Logic...

Now I'm going to consider some of the more complicated (or, if you prefer, obscure) modules. These modules don't appear in every synthesizer—some achieve the same end by different means, and others don't provide the functionality. I'm not going to look at every obscure module, but there are some that can be quite useful, so I will briefly highlight those.

Clever Stuff in VAZ Modular

Let's have a look at one or two modules in VAZ Modular.

Gate Logic

The Gate Logic module (see Figure 7.16) creates a gate signal—in other words, it sends a note-on or a note-off message to another module. With the Gate Logic module, if certain conditions are met, then the gate signal is transmitted.

Figure 7.16   The Gate Logic module in VAZ Modular.

There are two inputs in the Gate Logic module—the interaction of these two creates the logical conditions. Any input can give a positive or a negative value. Some inputs, such as envelopes, give unipolar values (in other words, positive or negative—these can be switched with an inverter), and some inputs, such as LFOs, give bipolar values (positive and negative).

- **And.** In And mode, if both inputs are positive, then a gate signal is generated.

- **Or.** In Or mode, if either input is positive, then a gate signal is generated.

- **Xor.** In Xor mode, when the inputs are different, a gate signal is generated.

The Not switch reverses the behavior of each operation, so when it is engaged:

- **And.** In And mode, if both inputs are negative, then a gate signal is generated.

- **Or.** In Or mode, if either input is negative, then a gate signal is generated.

- **Xor.** In Xor mode, when the inputs are the same, a gate signal is generated.

Inverter

The Inverter (see Figure 7.17) is a simple module that inverts the polarity of a signal (making positive negative and vice versa).

Figure 7.17 The Inverter module in VAZ Modular.

MinMax

The MinMax modules (see Figure 7.18) have two outputs:

- One outputs the loudest signal.

- The other outputs the quietest signal.

Figure 7.18 The MinMax 2-Input and MinMax 8-Input modules in VAZ Modular.

The difference between the two modules is the number of inputs—one has two, so both inputs will always be output, and the other has eight, so you will only hear two outputs (even if these change).

Scaler

The Scaler (see Figure 7.19) is a highly utilitarian module that limits the range of a signal by setting its minimum value and its maximum.

Figure 7.19   The Scaler module in VAZ Modular. Not designed for fish...

Clever Stuff in SynthEdit

Let's have a look at a few modules in SynthEdit.

(Simulated) Logic Gates

SynthEdit includes a number of modules that perform similar tasks to the Gate Logic module in VAZ Modular. However, unlike VAZ Modular, SynthEdit does not present one module, but instead gives you a range of modules so that you can choose the one that's right for the specific purpose.

All of the logic gate modules appear (at first glance—as you can see in Figure 7.20) to have only one input; however, as you connect the first input, you will find that a second input is created, and so on, meaning that you can have several input sources.

Figure 7.20   The logic gates in SynthEdit. From left to right: the AND Gate, the NAND Gate, the NOR Gate, the OR Gate, and the XOR Gate.

The five modules will all create a gate signal—in other words, a note-on message—if certain conditions are met:

- **AND Gate.** The AND Gate will generate a gate signal if all input levels are high.

- **NAND Gate.** The NAND Gate will generate a gate signal if all input levels are low.

- **NOR Gate.** The NOR Gate will generate a gate signal if the input level is high.

- **OR Gate.** The OR Gate will generate a gate signal if any input level is high.

- **XOR Gate.** The XOR Gate will generate a gate signal if only one input level is high.

Mathematical Functions

Remember that SynthEdit uses a voltage-based model to route its signals internally. Against this background, there are a number of modules that allow mathematical functions (see Figure 7.21). These mathematical functions work directly on the voltages.

Figure 7.21 The mathematical function units in SynthEdit. From left to right: Ceiling, Divide, Floor, Multiply, and Subtract.

The mathematical units are:

- **Ceil.** The Ceiling module rounds up the output voltage to the next integer amount.

- **Divide.** The Divide module divides the value of Input 1 by the value of Input 2.

- **Floor.** The Floor module rounds down the output voltage to the next integer amount.

- **Multiply.** The Multiply module multiplies Input 1 by Input 2.

- **Subtract.** The Subtract module subtracts Input 2 from Input 1. There is no corresponding addition module since two sources connected to the same plug will automatically be summed.

The Level Adjuster module (see Figure 7.22) performs a similar function to the Multiply module (in that it will multiply the two inputs together), but the output is then normalized.

Figure 7.22 The Level Adjuster module.

You remember that when we built SynthWiz Simple Synth, we added a Key Tracking slider that multiplied the pitch output from the MIDI to CV unit to create the modulation source, which was what we used to control the key tracking. When we did that, we set the range of the Key Tracking slider from 0 to 1—in other words, the range was set so that the pitch output would always be reduced. With normalization, the full range would be allowable and would be rescaled so you could achieve the same sonic result without needing to mess with the range settings.

Inverter
The Inverter (see Figure 7.23) is a simple module that inverts the polarity of a signal (making positive negative and vice versa).

Figure 7.23 The Inverter module in SynthEdit.

Visualization Modules

Although this book is intended to be all about the sound—and I do encourage you to keep using your ears as I have advocated throughout this book—the visualization modules that come with the synthesizers do play an important part in sound creation. They are there to show you:

- First, that something is going on. Particularly when you are hooking up modules, it can often be useful to receive some visual feedback to show that a signal has reached a certain point in the signal chain.

- They also show you some of *what* is going on. For instance, they may show a level or give you an indication of a waveform. Although this data may not be 100-percent scientifically perfect, it is often very good and will give you an indication about where problems may be or what is happening in your sound.

I'm going to look again at VAZ Modular and SynthEdit. The reason for this is simple: With KarmaFX Synth Modular, the displays are already built into the modules, and with Zebra 2, there are no visualization modules. Therefore, by default, we have two synthesizers to look at.

Volt Meters

A volt meter will display the voltage that is output from a module. This can be particularly useful if you are troubleshooting.

The Volt Meter in SynthEdit (see Figure 7.24) displays the input voltage as a figure. However, you need to exercise caution if you play more than one note, because this may confuse the meter.

Figure 7.24 The Volt Meter in SynthEdit.

The CV Meter in VAZ Modular is slightly more sophisticated, showing the first input voice. However, instead of displaying the voltage as a decimal amount, it displays the data as a meter (see Figure 7.25).

Figure 7.25 The CV Meter module in VAZ Modular.

Level Meters

There are two level meters in SynthEdit. The first is a simple LED Indicator (see Figure 7.26) that shows when a threshold level (which you can set and adjust) has been reached.

Figure 7.26   The LED Indicator in SynthEdit.

The second level meter in SynthEdit is the Peak Meter (see Figure 7.27), which, despite the name, is actually a bar graph–style meter.

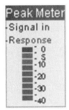

Figure 7.27   The Peak Meter in SynthEdit.

You can switch the response of the meter between linear and decibels (its default).

The Meter unit in VAZ Modular (see Figure 7.28) is a stereo meter.

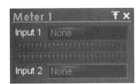

Figure 7.28   The Meter unit in VAZ Modular.

Frequency Analyzer

The Frequency Analyzer in SynthEdit (see Figure 7.29) shows the signal's harmonic spectrum—in other words, it shows you how much energy (how much loudness) the signal has at any point

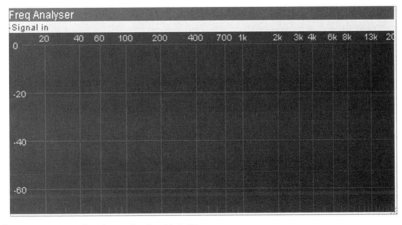

Figure 7.29   The Frequency Analyzer in SynthEdit.

in the spectrum. If you check back to Chapter 5, this analyzer gives a real-time display of the effect of a filter (and the other elements) on a sound—in certain circumstances, you will see that those graphs do actually reflect what happens in practice.

Oscilloscope

An oscilloscope will display control voltages and audio voltages as a graph. Typically, you can use these tools to display waveform shapes (similar to the waveforms that were graphically represented in Chapter 4).

The Scope module in SynthEdit (see Figure 7.30) has two plugs, allowing you to attach two input sources. The Scope can then display the two signals simultaneously.

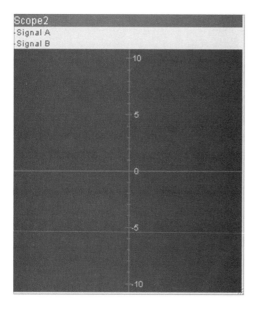

Figure 7.30 The Scope module in SynthEdit.

Like the SynthEdit Scope module, the Oscilloscope in VAZ Modular (see Figure 7.31) can accept two inputs, which it can display separately.

The module then has a few other controls.

- **Amp.** The Amp knob controls the vertical scaling of the displayed wave, allowing you to display it more clearly.

- **Time.** The Time knob controls the horizontal scaling of the displayed wave, again allowing you to display it more clearly.

- **Link.** The Link setting locks together the waveforms from the two inputs on the same time axis.

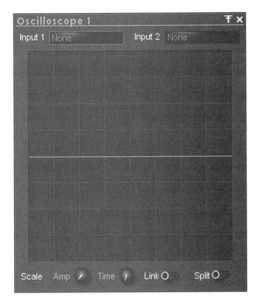

Figure 7.31   The Oscilloscape in VAZ Modular.

- **Split.** When the Split switch is engaged, Input 1 is displayed on the top half of the oscilloscope and Input 2 on the bottom half.

One of the difficulties with an oscilloscope—any oscilloscope—is that you rarely get one voice. Even if you play one note, that may actually result in many voices from several oscillators. VAZ Modular has a module to address this issue: the VoiceSelect module (see Figure 7.32).

Figure 7.32   The VoiceSelect module in VAZ Modular.

With the VoiceSelect module, only the selected voice is passed. There is only one slider on the module, which can be used to select which voice is passed.

I think we're ready for some effects now, don't you?

8 FX Units

There are many aspects to consider when looking at FX in the context of sound design. There are several good reasons for using FX that come with a synthesizer, and there are equally some good reasons not to use these units.

The FX units in most synthesizers are not of the same quality as commercially available plug-ins (although the quality is improving, and there are some great units in the featured synthesizers). By comparison, the FX units that come with synthesizers are usually designed for a specific purpose and therefore don't have unnecessary features, so they have a modest CPU consumption. However—depending on the effect you are after—if you want CPU efficiency, it may be preferable to have a number of synthesizers all feeding into one high-quality/high-CPU external FX unit rather than have those same synthesizers all running their own lower-quality FX unit.

There are some FX sounds that are integral to a patch's design—for instance, distortion. Integral FX units allow a sound and the effect to be stored as one patch, making the sound more transportable. If external FX are used, then each element would have to be separately stored if the sound is to be reproduced on a different system.

You can also do some really slick things with built-in FX units that you cannot achieve with external units. For instance, you can:

- Control an FX send with velocity

- Vary the depth on an effect with aftertouch

- "Duck" an effect so that it is not heard while the note that will be effected is heard or while the key is held

Of course, with VAZ Modular being able to load external effects units and store them as an integral part of the sound, you can have the best of both worlds.

Deployment of FX

FX units are deployed in one of two ways: as insert FX units or as send FX units. In the world of modular synthesizers, these are not mutually exclusive. However, let me explain the practical differences, as they do have implications for your architectural considerations.

255

Another point to remember is that because we are working in a modular environment, several units can be hooked together at different points in the audio chain for wider sonic possibilities. However, this is not possible with Zebra 2, as the FX units are located in a separate section at the end of the audio path.

Insert FX

With insert FX, the whole of the audio signal passes through the FX unit (see Figure 8.1). So if you want to add a distortion effect, then you will want the whole signal to be distorted by the fuzz box. It would be rare (but not impossible) to mix a clean and distorted signal together when you have full control over the amount of the distortion. EQ and compression are other typical examples of insert FX.

Figure 8.1   The signal flow through an insert FX unit.

Send FX

With send FX, you send part of your signal to the FX unit and then add a purely effected signal back to the dry sound (see Figure 8.2). Examples of FX units that are grouped under the send FX heading are modulation effects (chorus and so on), delays, and reverbs.

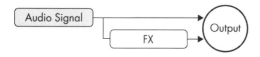

Figure 8.2   The signal flow through a send FX unit.

Using FX in Practice

All of the featured synthesizers offer a range of FX units. Rather than summarize the key features of the units and then look at the specific FX units that are available for each of the synths (as I have done in earlier chapters), I will group everything together for each category since most of the features on the units are similar. So for instance, with distortion units, I will look at the general and the specific together. I will not point out any features that are unique to one unit (unless it really is a standout feature).

Throughout the rest of the book I have stressed that I am not covering every module offered by every synthesizer. That principle particularly applies here, where there are enough FX modules on offer to write a whole book. I will be covering the main modules with more of a focus toward those that have sound-shaping properties.

Distortion and Overdrive Units

Most people are used to hearing distortion used in an extreme way. However, depending on the amount of control you are given over the distortion, it can be used in a much more subtle manner. Typically, you should be able to squeeze the following spectrum of tone color from most distortion units:

- At very low levels, you are unlikely to hear much effect, but the distortion can have the effect of warming up a sound.

- With a touch more effect, you will often find that a sound can feel more "vintage," as the distortion effect takes out some of the top end of the signal.

- As the effect increases, the signal will start to break up. This might be a useful setting for sound effects.

- The next step is to move into proper overdrive. (Start thinking of rock guitars, and you will get the picture.) This overdrive-type effect can be quite controllable and quite musical.

- Finally, you will get out-and-out distortion, which may be hard to control or use with any subtlety.

When you use a distortion unit, it is usually very easy to get a piercing sound that dominates the track, rather than a warm, overdriven sound that may fit in context. If you are trying to re-create the sound of overdriven guitars, remember that all the rockers play their guitars through speakers—inefficient speakers that cut off most of the signal above 4 kHz. To re-create this effect, you may need to add a filter and perhaps some EQ after the distortion unit.

Also, if you are looking for realism, then the distortion needs to be very controlled. Even heavily overdriven guitars can still sound clean(ish) if they are played very lightly. Ideally, you should be able to control the amount of distortion by the velocity of the notes. To get more control and more "gearing" in the distortion (in other words, a much greater range of overload), modulate the distortion depth with velocity as well as controlling the volume of the signal with velocity.

One other thing you can do if you are trying to create a screaming lead guitar–type sound is to add a high-pitched sine wave to simulate feedback. Give this sine wave a very slow attack (perhaps five seconds) or make it separately controllable (for instance, assign its level to the modulation wheel), and you will have another level of control.

"Analog" Distortion

Distortion comes in two flavors: analog and digital. Analog distortion is an emulation of the hardware world, where distortion is created by overloading an input. This distortion can often be characterized as being "warm" (although it can be cold, clinical, and harsh).

Most analog-style distortion units offer several controls:

- A mode selector, so you can select the style of distortion (from soft and tube-like to burn-your-ears-off)

- A drive level (or input control) to set how much distortion is created

Two examples of this style of distortion unit are:

- The Overdrive unit in VAZ Modular (see Figure 8.3)

- The Clipper unit in SynthEdit (see Figure 8.4)

Figure 8.3   The Overdrive unit in VAZ Modular.   **Figure 8.4**   The Clipper unit in SynthEdit.

"Digital" Distortion

In contrast to analog distortion, digital distortion can be nasty and harsh (which is great if you're into that sort of thing). However, that's not to say you can't make digital distortion softer.

You will remember that in Chapter 1 we talked about audio fidelity in the digital realm. In essence, there are two factors that determine the quality of digital audio:

- Bit depth—the number of levels of loudness a digital waveform can have

- Sample rate—the number of slices into which a waveform is cut

In essence, digital distortion units work by reducing the bit depth and/or the sample rate, thereby degrading the resolution of the wave, as Figure 8.5 shows. This (literally) changes the wave shape, leading to digital distortion. When you use this type of effect, please use it with care, as the results can be truly horrid at extremes.

These units usually have two controls:

- Bit Reduction, to reduce the bit depth of the wave (in other words, to reduce the number of levels of loudness)

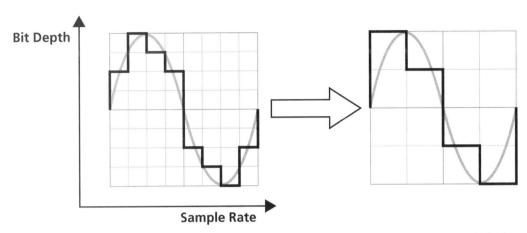

Figure 8.5 Digital distortion units work by reducing the bit depth and/or the sample rate, which degrades the resolution of the wave, leading to digital distortion. As the bit depth and sample rate are reduced, the amount of distortion is increased, and the character of the distortion also becomes harsher.

- Sample Rate, to reduce the number of samples, which requires that some samples are discarded, so this can quickly lose fidelity

Examples of this sort of unit include:

- The Decimator unit in VAZ Modular (see Figure 8.6).

- The Distortion unit in KarmaFX Synth Modular (see Figure 8.7). However, this unit includes elements of analog and digital distortion in the same unit, giving a broader range of tones.

- The BitShuffle module in KarmaFX Synth Modular (see Figure 8.8).

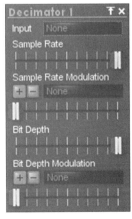

Figure 8.6 The Decimator in VAZ Modular.

Figure 8.7 The Distortion unit in KarmaFX Synth Modular.

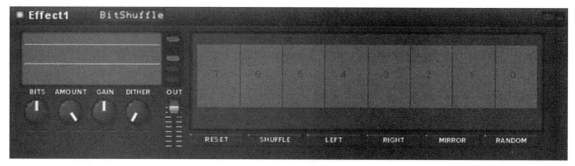

Figure 8.8   The BitShuffle module in KarmaFX Synth Modular.

Compression

Compressors were originally used to prevent a signal overloading an input, and indeed, compressors still are used for this purpose. In essence, a compressor is an automatic gain control: When a signal gets to a certain level (the threshold), the compressor restricts how much louder the signal can get (see Figure 8.9).

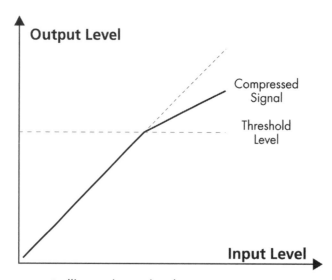

Figure 8.9   A compressor controlling an input signal.

In practice, you're quite unlikely to want to use the compressor as a volume control. Instead, you can use it for the effect that it will have on your sound. The main audio changes that a compressor can introduce are:

■ Making a sound fatter and/or smoother

■ Enhancing the perceived loudness of the sound (without increasing its volume)

■ Giving the sound more punch

The disadvantages of using a compressor are that the resulting sound can tend to dominate a mix. With more extreme compressor settings, the sound will usually have a more uniform level and will fill a broader frequency range. Both of these factors can make it harder to mix a highly compressed synthesizer sound. Another downside of compressor abuse is that the resulting sound tends to be less interesting—the delicate harmonic shifts of a patch tend to get covered up because all of the harmonics take a similar level.

The main controls that most compressors have are:

- **Threshold.** The Threshold control sets the level at which the compressor will start to have effect. In other words, sounds that are louder than the threshold level will be compressed. If you set this too high, then the compressor will not have sufficient effect. If you set this too low, then all of your sounds will be compressed, which may make your sounds become flat and lifeless.

- **Ratio.** The Ratio control sets the amount of level reduction above the threshold. A ratio of 1:1 gives no compression, and a ratio above 10:1 gives extreme compression, or limiting (in other words, the volume is limited to the threshold). You will probably find a happy medium somewhere between those two extremes. (Usually the range between 2:1 and 4:1 will give good results.)

- **Attack.** The Attack control sets the time, after reaching the threshold, over which the compressor will start to have effect. This can be useful for letting peaks through so that the sounds don't become too "squashed." However, if you're letting peaks through, you need to make sure these don't overload and cause distortion.

- **Release.** The Release control sets the time, after falling below the threshold, over which the compressor will cease to have effect. Generally, you would want to set the shortest release time possible; however, this may give unwanted audio side effects. For instance, you may get "pumping" sounds.

- **Level.** The Level control—or as it is sometimes called, the make-up gain—comes at the end of the compressor's audio path. This sets the output level of the unit and can compensate for any level reduction due to compression.

Take a look at Figure 8.10, which shows how a compressor can affect the level of a signal. Note that this illustration does not show the effect of make-up gain.

In addition to the main controls, some compressors include a number of specialized controls and features:

- **Link.** With a link control, you can link together two compressors so the behavior of one mirrors the other. This is particularly useful if you're trying to ensure that you treat the left and right audio channels in the same way. (If you apply different settings to the left and right, then you can find odd audio effects when listening in stereo.)

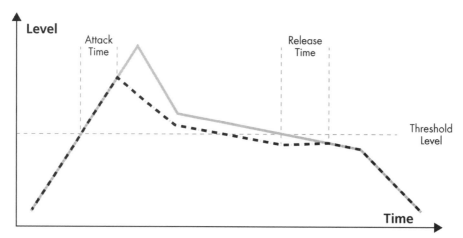

Figure 8.10 The effect of compression on an audio signal. The gray line is the original signal; the dotted black line is the output after compression.

- **Side chain.** For most compressors, the compression is based on the incoming signal. However, you can also compress the signal but base the compression on another audio source—the other audio source would be the side-chain signal. You don't hear the side chain; it is just used to determine the compression on the audio that you are listening to. This facility is often used in radio, where the level of the music will be reduced when the DJ talks—in this case, the side chain is the DJ's voice.

- **Knee.** The graph shown in Figure 8.9 illustrates a *hard-knee* compressor. This is where the level reaches the threshold and is then compressed. With a soft-knee compressor, the effect of the compression is gently introduced, so compression happens before the threshold. With the knee control, you can adjust the range over which the compression is introduced, giving a smoother and less noticeable form of compression.

You can find a compressor in Zebra 2 (see Figure 8.11), VAZ Modular (see Figure 8.12), and KarmaFX Synth Modular (see Figure 8.13).

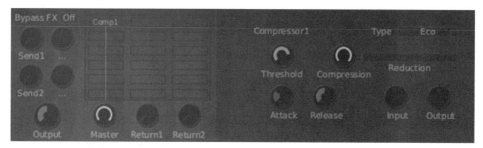

Figure 8.11 The compressor in Zebra 2.

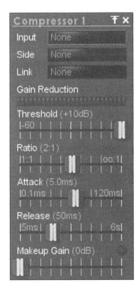

Figure 8.12   The compressor in VAZ Modular.

Figure 8.13   The compressor in KarmaFX Synth Modular.

EQ

The purpose of equalization is to make certain elements of the sound spectrum louder and other elements quieter. In that respect, an EQ unit has many similarities with filters (which is not surprising, since EQ units are effectively specialized filters). You can use EQ creatively or surgically. However, remember that you still need to get your sound to sit in a mix, so go carefully with the EQ. Make sure you are not using the EQ to try to cover the faults of poor programming.

Parametric EQ

The most flexible form of EQ is the parametric EQ (see Figure 8.14). With parametric EQ, you can set:

- The frequency to be boosted or cut.

- The amount of boost or cut.

- The bandwidth of the boost or cut. The bandwidth determines how wide the boost or cut is, much like a constantly variable slope control for a filter.

A parametric EQ unit will give you control over those three elements. Some parametric EQs have several bands so you can perform more detailed EQ tweaks. In the world of modular synthesizers, if your EQ unit doesn't offer enough bands, you can always add another module.

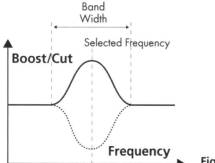

Figure 8.14   A parametric EQ unit.

There are a number of parametric EQ units in the featured synthesizers:

- The EQ unit in Zebra 2 (see Figure 8.15).

- The EQ module in VAZ Modular (see Figure 8.16). There is also a single-band version of this (not illustrated).

- The Parametric Filter in KarmaFX Synth Modular (see Figure 8.17), which blurs the distinction between a filter and EQ.

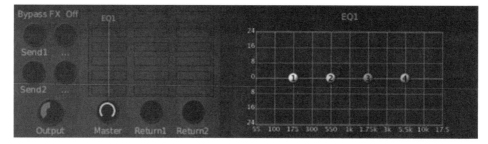

Figure 8.15   The EQ unit in Zebra 2.

Figure 8.16   The EQ module in VAZ Modular.

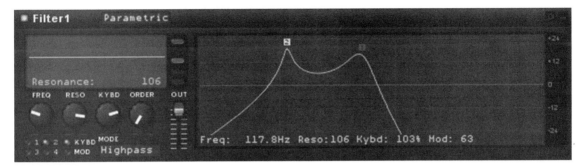

Figure 8.17 The Parametric Filter in KarmaFX Synth Modular.

Shelf EQ

A slightly more tailored form of EQ is the shelf EQ. A shelf EQ will cut or boost:

- The whole signal above a specified frequency in the case of a high shelf (see Figure 8.18)

- The whole signal below a specified frequency in the case of a low shelf (see Figure 8.19)

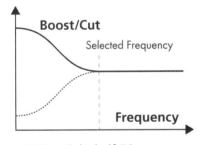

Figure 8.18 High-shelf EQ.

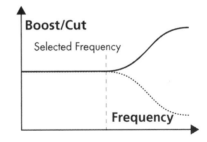

Figure 8.19 Low-shelf EQ.

With shelf EQ you usually get control over the frequency (above or below which the signal is cut or boosted) and the amount of cut or boost. Sometimes you also get control over the slope in the same way that a parametric EQ gives you control over the bandwidth.

The parametric units in Zebra 2, VAZ Modular, and KarmaFX Synth Modular all have the facility to designate bands as shelving bands (which gives you some control over the slope). In addition, the KarmaFX Synth Modular offers a specialized Shelving EQ module (see Figure 8.20), as does Zebra 2 (see Figure 8.21), giving this as an option in its VCF module.

Graphic EQ

A less flexible but much quicker form of EQ is graphic EQ. With this, the number of bands, the frequency of the bands, and the bandwidth are predetermined; you get control over the amount of cut or boost.

Figure 8.20 The Shelving EQ module in KarmaFX Synth Modular.

Figure 8.21 The Low-Shelf EQ module in Zebra 2.

KarmaFX Synth Modular has a 10-band and a 31-band graphic EQ (see Figures 8.22 and 8.23).

Figure 8.22 The 10-band EQ unit in KarmaFX Synth Modular.

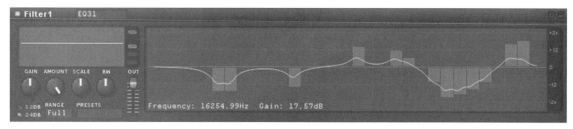

Figure 8.23 The 31-band EQ unit in KarmaFX Synth Modular.

Delay

Delay effects fall under three main groupings:

- Echo-type effects, where you can clearly hear the delayed signal, and the delay will often be used for rhythmic purposes.

- Modulation-type effects, where a short delay time is used, and you cannot separately identify the delay signal. However, the delayed signal is then often modulated to create a thickening effect.

- Reverb-type effects, where there are many short delays, giving the effect of a much longer decay time but without the echoes being individually identifiable.

In many ways, these latter effects types are subgenres of delay effects. However, there are many specialized units, so I am splitting the units over three sections (with echo-type units being dealt with in this section). As you will see, many (but not all) straightforward delay units can be used to create reverb-type effects and modulation effects, so please don't see the categories I have put the units into as limitations.

The most common controls that all of the delay units have are:

- **Delay type.** Some units allow you to select different types of delay and other modules offer several options within the same module. You should also remember that as we are working in a modular environment, several delay lines can be hooked together to create the same audio results that may be created by more specialized units, and equally, the routing options can be used to split a signal for different processing. The following list notes some of the main ways you can structure a delay line. Some of these options may not be immediately available in all of the synthesizers (unless you want to start hooking up modules).
  - **Mono delay.** A mono delay adds a simple delay to the input signal. The same effect can be achieved if the delay time is equal for both channels in a stereo delay.
  - **Stereo delay.** With a stereo delay, there are two separate delay lines, which may (or may not) have different delay times. Conventionally the delay lines are hardwired left and right.
  - **Cross delay.** Like a stereo delay, a cross delay has two channels. However, the output from the first delay is fed into the second and the output from the second is fed into the first. This can give the effect of spreading the delays across the stereo spectrum or ping-ponging the delays between the two channels.

There are, of course, many other structures. These are just a few ideas to get you going.

- **Delay time.** The delay time controls the time until the first delayed signal is heard. (Each subsequent delayed signal will be delayed by a similar value.) This time can be set:
  - As an absolute value—for instance, 0.5 seconds.
  - As a tempo-related value expressed as a fraction of the beat. So for instance, a delay could be set at 1/4, in which case the delayed signal would be delayed by a quarter note. The advantages of this approach are that it is easy to set the tempo to create a rhythmic effect, and the delay time will change if the track's tempo changes. There are specialized tempo-synched units available, or you can often attach the necessary tempo feed in the modular environment.

- **Feedback.** Feedback controls how many times each delay repeats. (Quite literally, it controls how much of the delayed signal is sent back to the input.)

- **EQ or Filtering.** Delay lines will often include some EQ or filtering to help shape and control the delayed signals. Typically, these controls will be used to cut the high-frequency elements of the delayed signal to make the sound duller, resulting in a more natural-sounding echo, or to cut the low frequencies, thereby thinning out the delay so that it is not so obtrusive.

- **Modulation.** The modulation control allows you to change the pitch of the delayed signal. The next section ("Modulation Delay Effects") shows how this functionality can be used.

- **Mix.** A mix control will allow you to mix dry and delayed signals. Quite often, it is preferable to set the mix control to 100% wet and to then mix the separate dry and wet signals later in the audio chain.

All of the featured synthesizers have delay units (and VAZ Modular also has a dedicated tempo-synchronized delay unit). These are shown in Figures 8.24 to 8.28.

Figure 8.24 The Delay unit in KarmaFX Synth Modular.

Figure 8.25 The Delay unit in SynthEdit.

Figure 8.26 The Delay unit in VAZ Modular.

Figure 8.27 The Tempo Delay (tempo-synchronized delay) unit in VAZ Modular.

Figure 8.28 The Delay unit in Zebra 2.

Modulation Delay Effects

The modulation delay effects all work in a similar way:

- There is a dry signal.

- The dry signal is delayed—this is a short delay that cannot be perceived as a separate event.

- That delayed signal has its pitch modulated by a low-frequency oscillator.

- The dry signal is then mixed with the delayed/pitch-modulated signal to give a fuller/warmer/ richer/whooshier (insert whatever description you want) sound.

Most of the units have controls very much like the delay units, but they all have a built-in low-frequency oscillator to modulate the pitch of the delayed signal.

- **Delay.** Although the delay time of the delayed signal may be imperceptible, it has a significant effect on the sound, hence this control.

- **Feedback.** The feedback control sets the number of times the delayed signal is repeated. This has an effect on the perception of the "depth" of the effect.

- **Rate.** The rate controls the speed of the low-frequency oscillator, which modulates the delayed signal.

- **Depth.** The depth control adjusts the extent to which the low-frequency oscillator modulates the pitch of the delayed signal.

- **Tone.** Tone controls (which can include filters) adjust the tone of the delayed signal, taking away any sharpness to the sound and any metallic ringing.

- **Mix.** The mix control adjusts the balance between the dry and delayed signals.

There are three main types of modulation delay units.

- **Phasers.** As well as delaying the signal, some phasers run the delayed signal through a notch filter.

- **Flangers.** Words cannot readily describe the difference between the sound produced by a phaser and the sound produced by a flanger; however, to my mind, a phaser gives a more nasal sound, whereas a flanger gives a more whooshy-type sound. Flangers and phasers are often used on percussion sounds and with plucked-type sounds (such as guitars and electric pianos). The sound is very distinctive and is hard to use in a subtle way, so you are not likely to want to use the effect too frequently.

- **Chorus.** A chorus can produce a lush/smooth sound, but at extremes it can sound like vibrato played too fast or just bad tuning. Used in moderation, the effect can either add sparkle or thicken up a sound without noticeably changing the sound's characteristics. As an example, it is quite common to use a chorus with bass guitar sounds to provide a more rounded and brighter sound.

There's quite a choice of modulation delay units in the featured synthesizers.

- KarmaFX Synth Modular has a chorus unit (see Figure 8.29) and a phaser (shown in Figure 8.30).

- VAZ Modular offers a chorus (Figure 8.31), a flanger (Figure 8.32), and a phaser (Figure 8.33).

Figure 8.29 The Chorus unit in KarmaFX Synth Modular.

Figure 8.30 The Phaser module in KarmaFX Synth Modular.

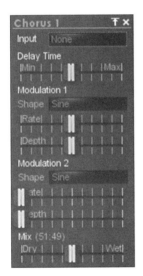

Figure 8.31 The Chorus unit in VAZ Modular.

Figure 8.32 The Flanger unit in VAZ Modular.

Figure 8.33 The Phaser unit in VAZ Modular.

- The Zebra 2 ModFX (see Figure 8.34) is one unit, but you have three choices for its functionality: the chorus (which produces chorus/flanging effects), the phaser (which phases...), and the phorus (which is somewhere between a phaser and a chorus/flanger).

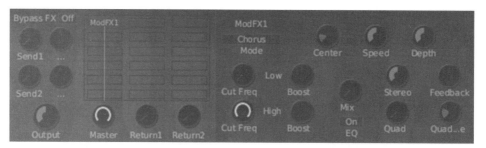

Figure 8.34 The ModFX unit in Zebra 2.

Reverb

Reverb can give a sound some spatial context.

Some reverb units act like delay units with a short delay time. Some are more complex and split the reverb into two parts, which you can separately control:

- The initial early reflections

- The longer reverberation tails

With reverb units, there is significant interaction between the controls, so even more than normal it is necessary to balance several parameters when shaping the sound. The most common controls offered on reverb units include:

- **Reverb type.** Often, you will be given the choice of a range of spaces that the reverb unit is simulating. These can range from small rooms to large halls. The reverb type will often have a significant effect on how the other controls work. (For instance, if you are using a large-hall algorithm, then you won't be able to simulate a small room by turning down the room size.)

- **Pre delay.** This controls the time between the original signal sounding and the reverb taking effect. Smaller values give the perception of a smaller room, while longer delays give the perception of larger rooms.

- **Size (room size).** This controls the size of the room being simulated by the reverb unit. Usually, this control has the same effect as a decay control and affects the length of the reverberation; however, some units offer separate size and decay controls to give greater control over how long the reverberation will sound.

- **Damp.** Damping works by cutting the higher frequencies in the reverb signal. One of the reasons why electronic reverb sounds artificial (in other words, clangy and metallic) is because it has too much high-frequency information. The damping control can help to create a more realistic simulation.

- **Width.** This often controls the stereo width of the reverb.

- **Diffusion.** Some reverb algorithms include parameters to control the diffusion of the sound. This tends to have an effect on how smooth the effect sounds and whether any stereo image is maintained in the reverberation.

- **Tone.** Most reverb units have some tone control, ranging from a simple tone knob to a number of filters to subtly shape and control the reverb.

- **Mix.** The mix control balances the level between the dry signal and the reverb.

There are three reverb units in the featured synthesizers.

- The KarmaFX Synth Modular Reverb module (see Figure 8.35) offers a wide range of controls.

- The Reverb unit in VAZ Modular (see Figure 8.36) only has one main control: reverb time (and there is a mix control, too).

- The Reverb facility in Zebra2 (see Figure 8.37) is another highly sophisticated reverb unit.

Figure 8.35 The KarmaFX Modular Reverb module.

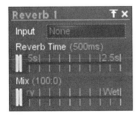

Figure 8.36 The VAZ Modular Reverb module.

Figure 8.37 The Reverb unit in Zebra 2.

I think it's time to start building some sounds.

9 Creating Sounds

Conventional synthesizers—or if you prefer, non-modular synthesizers—generally give you a fixed number of modules and a fixed audio path within which those modules are deployed. You may have some routing options—for instance, you may have a number of filters through which the sound can be directed, or you may have some modulation choices—but on the whole, the synthesizer is "fixed." And that design of synthesizer is the most popular design.

This fixed-architecture approach is popular for a variety of reasons:

- It's fast. You don't have to load up the modules—you just start crafting sounds.

- It's easy. You don't have to hook up the modules.... (And, generally, the synthesizer will make a noise immediately.)

- It's straightforward to get a grasp on the instrument. You don't have to hook up the modules....

Okay, you get the idea. However, one thing these synthesizers lack is flexibility. I'm not talking about the possibility to make tweaks here and there or switch an oscillator in or out, but the facility to go wild and do exactly what you want. For instance, if you want 10 oscillators, there only a few non-modular synthesizers that will be able to help you.

However, there's another consideration when you get into the world of modulars: architecture. With a non-modular synth, you get what comes and work within those constraints. With a modular, you start from a blank page and build. Apart from the limits of your CPU, the only constraint on your creativity is your imagination. Ironically, when you remove all limitations, people often get scared or lose the desire to be creative; hence, you will often find people replicating classic synthesizers with modulars. While this may be interesting, if this is what you want to do, then I suggest you go buy a software re-creation of the original hardware.

Synthesizer Architecture: Initial Considerations

The architecture of a sound requires thought in a number of areas:

- The intended end sound (obviously)

- The modules that are used

- How the audio path is connected

- How the modules are then controlled

Perhaps one of the toughest issues to consider is when to bring the elements on the audio path together and when to keep them apart. You might want to bring the sound together at an earlier stage in order to reduce the number of modules:

- This simplifies the operation of the sound because there are then fewer things that need to be controlled. If the whole path passes through a common set of modules, then you only need to change the settings of these common modules once. If the modules are duplicated, then the settings need to be adjusted in several places.

- A reduced number of modules will also make it easier to see and understand the key elements that control the sound. This means you won't be left twisting knobs without being able to hear the effect of the change.

- Fewer modules will also lead to less strain on your CPU.

You might want to keep the audio separate and only bring it together immediately before the output in order to ensure that each element of audio is separately processed so that the end sound can be maintained. For instance, you may:

- Have a higher-frequency element that will get lost if it goes through a low-pass filter too early in the audio chain

- Have several different elements that each need to be processed in a different manner

Sonic Considerations

Beyond the practical aspects of how you construct a sound in terms of which modules get connected, there are the sonic possibilities. For instance, you're no longer limited to one or two filters—you can have as many as you want. For instance, you could:

- Put four 24-dB filters in series to create a 96-dB filter that has an extreme cut-off slope.

- Put three 12-dB filters in series—thereby creating a 36-dB filter—but then boost the resonance in each and set the cut-off frequencies to different levels. This would give three separate resonance peaks, creating a sound that could not be created with a conventional filter. You may be able to do something similar if your synthesizer has a separation feature, but if you do this process manually, then you will have precise control over each module (and hence will be able to set the cut-off frequency and the amount of resonance in each filter in the chain).

As I have mentioned already—and I will mention again before the end of this book—sound design and synthesizer architecture are chicken-and-egg issues. The placing of an element within a structure will have a fundamental effect on the sound created. Take a distortion unit and a filter:

- If the distortion unit is placed before the filter in the audio chain, then the filter will work to adjust the tone of the distorted signal. This will work to smooth out the distortion, thereby making the distortion unit have less effect on the overall sound (although it may still give a significant change in the tone).

- If the distortion unit is placed after the filter in the audio chain, then the distortion unit will distort the filtered sounds. The filter will have a significant effect on the incoming signal, affecting both its tone and its level (since the volume of a signal drops as the filter cuts progressively more of the signal). Therefore, as the filter works on the signal being fed into the distortion unit, the quality of the distortion—in terms of both the amount of distortion and the harmonics that are affected—will change.

The placement of these two elements is a simple and straightforward issue. The sonic results could be significant. Let's take this idea a bit further and look at *some* of the possibilities.

Filter Configuration and Signal Routing Options

So far in this book we have focused on sounds that have been created using a sound > filter > amplifier audio path; see Figure 9.1. Then take a look at Figure 9.2, where I've shown this patch set up in VAZ Modular.

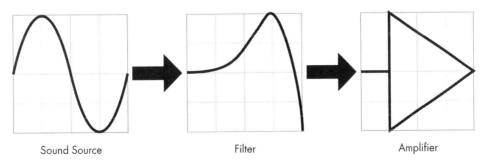

Sound Source   Filter   Amplifier

Figure 9.1 The sound > filter > amplifier audio path.

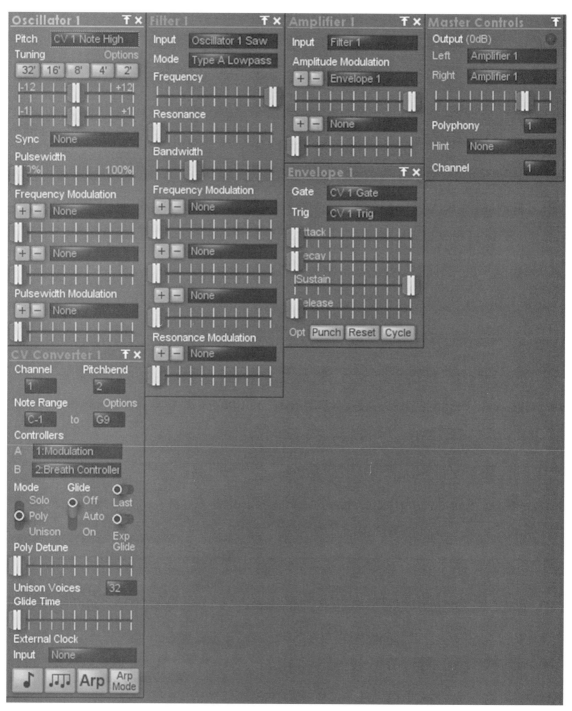

Figure 9.2   A basic sound created in VAZ Modular. For this patch you will see that an envelope has been attached to the amplifier unit, but there is no filter envelope.

Let's take this idea a step further and replace a filter with two filters and a distortion unit (and as I've started with VAZ Modular, I'll use a waveshaper to create the distortion). As you can see from Figure 9.3, we now have options.

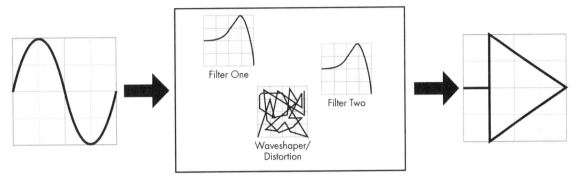

Figure 9.3   Replacing a single filter with two filters and a signal modifier suddenly gives a lot of options.

Obviously, there are a lot of options around the filters, in terms of both their cut-off slope and their types (low-pass, high-pass, and so on). However, for the moment, let's not think about those things. Instead, let's look at how we can hook up the new modules.

Straight Series

One straightforward way to hook up the modules is shown in Figure 9.4.

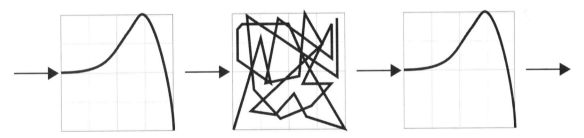

Figure 9.4   Hooking up the three new modules in series.

With this option:

1. The input signal from the oscillator flows into Filter 1, where the sound is processed.

2. The processed sound then flows into the waveshaper. Since the sound has previously been filtered, some of the rough edges may have been knocked off. This may—I repeat, *may*—in certain circumstances mean that the waveshaper is perceived as being slightly more gentle in its effect.

3.   The wave that comes out of the waveshaper is then fed into Filter 2. This is an opportunity for any edges added by the waveshaping to be smoothed out a bit.

Straight Series with Feedback

I'm going to introduce a new idea here that doesn't need a new module: feedback.

Feedback allows some of the output signal to be fed back into the audio chain. This is can help to dirty or thicken up a signal—it can also give wild results, so it should be used with caution.

This option takes the previous configuration and feeds the output signal back into Filter 1; see Figure 9.5.

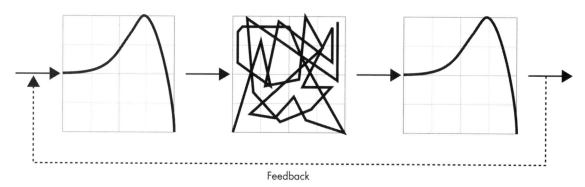

Feedback

Figure 9.5   The three modules arranged in series but with some feedback added to enrich the sound.

Take a look at Figure 9.6, which shows how this arrangement could be set up in VAZ Modular.

You will notice that this arrangement seems to have considerably more modules than the simple setup shown in Figure 9.2. Obviously, there are more modules—in particular, the second filter and the waveshaper. However, immediately before Filter 1 you will see a mixer and a gain control.

■   The purpose of the mixer is to join the raw wave output from the oscillator and the feedback signal into a single audio flow, which can then be sent to Filter 1.

■   The gain control is intended to keep a lid on the feedback so it can be used subtly or in a highly aggressive manner.

Filtered Feedback

In addition to controlling the gain of the feedback, the tone of the feedback can be controlled, as you can see in Figure 9.7.

This arrangement offers some interesting possibilities for shaping the feedback signal, and because some of the more offensive/uncontrollable elements in the feedback can be filtered,

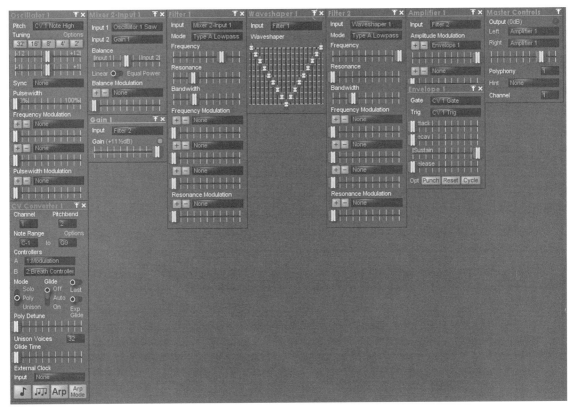

Figure 9.6   Setting up the straight series with feedback arrangement in VAZ Modular.

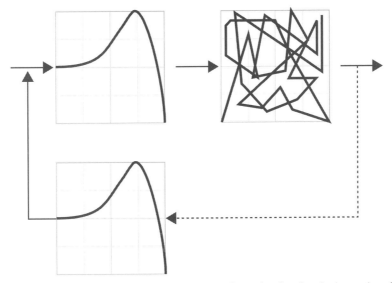

Figure 9.7   Controlling the tone of the feedback by sending the feedback through a filter.

you can use more feedback than if you were only dealing with unfiltered feedback. In particular, with some of the higher-frequency elements filtered, you could allow more "growl" to get recirculated.

You will also notice that the waveshaper is connected directly to the output. You may find that the right tone is coming straight out of the waveshaper, but then again it may be too harsh. If you want to tone it down a bit, you can—we're using modular synthesizers here—just attach another filter.

Parallel Filters

With the parallel filters arrangement, the output from the oscillator is fed directly into the wave-shaper and then the output from the waveshaper is split and fed into both Filter 1 and Filter 2, which are arranged in parallel (see Figure 9.8).

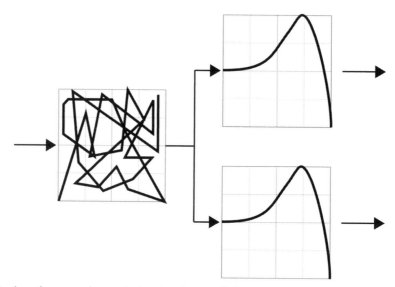

Figure 9.8   Filtering the waveshaper twice, but in parallel.

This option allows the waveshaper output to be filtered twice. However, since the filters are arranged in parallel, this means that filters can output completely different sounds, giving further interesting tonal possibilities.

Half Waveshaping

In this last permutation I'm going to look at (and it's the last one I'm putting forward—not the end of the possible permutations that are available):

- The oscillator's output is split so that it can be processed independently by each of the filters.

- Filter 1's output is then processed through the waveshaper.

- The output from the waveshaper and the output from Filter 2 are then mixed.

- This mix is sent to the output, and a feed is also fed back into the start of the chain.

The parallel processing offers dual tone options, but the mix/feedback combination allows some room to cross-pollinate the separate audio signals. Figure 9.9 shows the configuration.

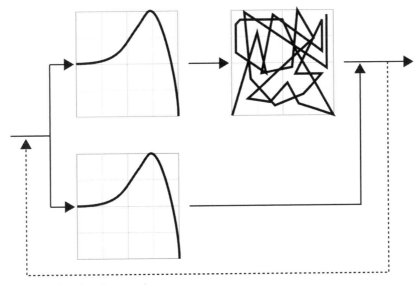

Figure 9.9   Half waveshaping in practice.

CPU Considerations

As well as thinking about the sonic possibilities, it's worth also considering the impact of your decision on your CPU. You don't need to get too hung up about this issue (unless you are using an underpowered computer). However, there is no point in wasting cycles that could be used elsewhere.

You will find that certain modules tend to use more CPU than others—for instance, depending on the particular module, filters and reverb units tend to be quite hungry. These are not the only culprits, but they are typical of the kind of units that can chew up your CPU—but also where you can make some efficiency savings.

Here are a couple of thoughts that you might want to ponder. While these comments specifically refer to filters and reverb units, they may equally be applied to other similar units. Take a moment or two to look at your designs and identify any inefficiency or wastage. (For instance, does that 35th oscillator *really* add to the sound?)

- You probably only need one reverb unit per sound. Even if you have several different elements within a particular sound, there is unlikely to be much to be gained (sonically) by adding a separate reverb unit for each sound. Equally, you should consider whether it might be more efficient to use a reverb unit outside of the synthesizer so that the reverb could then be shared between several different audio sources, thereby achieving yet more efficiency.

- Although it is tempting to construct mega-filters and to use the steepest slopes, do you really need this filtering? Very often, when sounds are constructed in isolation, you will be able to hear the subtle nuances of a filter, and the difference between a 36-dB and a 24-dB cut-off slope will be obvious. However, when you listen to a part within the context of a track, these small differences are often lost and can sometimes work against a sound.

Design Philosophy

Later in this chapter, we are going to look at some practical examples of sound design, but before we get there I want give something of an overview of the whole process.

The following comments are my personal opinions and should not be taken as facts. If you disagree with me, then your opinion is probably correct—I cannot know the context in which you will be using your sounds, so it would be presumptuous of me to suggest that I could ever know better. So if you disagree, that is fine with me as long as you've made a clear and conscious decision.

Programming with a Purpose

There may be many reasons to design a sound. For me, the most compelling reason for building a patch is the need to find a specific sound that works for a specific track (or a specific sound that is *needed* in some other specific context, such as a movie). If you stumble across a sound that you think is interesting, it doesn't really mean much unless you can then use that sound appropriately. While you may program "just for fun"—and I'm not going to knock that as activity or as a learning exercise—the remainder of this book is predicated on the assumption that you will have a specific goal when creating any sound.

Only you know how and where a sound is going to be used. And while it is something of a chicken-and-egg conundrum, I always find that it is more difficult to program the nuances of a sound without having a rough MIDI part playing. In practice, if you separate the arrangement of the part from the programming of the sound, you will always be at a disadvantage because you will not be able to hear the context in which the sound is being used, hence you will not have that immediate feedback as to whether the sound works, and if so, how well it works.

By equal measure, I would encourage you to try sounds in a different context from the one for which they were originally intended. For instance, many bass patches make great stab sounds. Don't do this as a last-ditch measure when nothing else works, but rather as an exercise to find how different sounds can work in a different context.

Many people will also encourage you to "just experiment" with programming. Personally, I dislike the notion behind this comment. I'm not saying that experimentation is bad or that you shouldn't try things, and as you will have noticed throughout this book, I have suggested that you go away and play. My only argument here is that the "just experiment" philosophy is used by those who can't be bothered to learn how to use a tool properly. Equally, this argument is used by developers who can't be bothered to explain to people how to use a tool properly or who have developed a tool that may be interesting but is ultimately without purpose.

So sure, experiment, but be ready to program with a purpose when you need to.

Arrangement of the Track

There are many ways to get to a sound—most obviously, use a preset or use a commercially available sound bank. These are valid ways of getting a sound, so why would you bother programming your own sound?

As I have already mentioned, there is one simple reason why you would program your own sounds—and within the scope of programming, I would include tweaking a sound from another source—and that is to get the right sound for your production.

When you are mixing a track, each instrument needs its own space, or else the mix is likely to get cluttered, indistinct, or just generally bad. You may have the best bass, pad, stab, and lead sound available in your synth, but do these elements all fit together? Does your bass muffle the kick drum? Do the bass and the stab occupy different sonic ranges? Does the stab stand out over the pad and does it then clash with the vocal?

These are all elementary problems associated with the mix that are often addressed with equalization or more radical surgery at the end of the production process.

Even if the sonic ranges occupied by your synthesizer parts aren't the problem, have you found the right sound for your track? Does the bass fit that pumping rhythm you've worked so hard at? Does that lead cut the top of your head off, or is it just a flaccid preset that seemed all right when you sequenced the riff? Does that stab really lock in with the bass to give a perfect performance, or is it an unequal match for that bass? And what about that pad? Does it sound like something from a 1970s string machine? Or worse still, does it sound like a cheap and nasty piece of software when you want it to sound like a 1970s string machine?

Can't I Just Go and Buy Something?

A simple question that is often asked is, "What is wrong with commercial banks and the banks that come with my synthesizer?"

As simple question deserves a simple answer: There is nothing wrong with presets. The only downside to presets is that they're just not designed to fit your specific track, and you may not immediately know how to control them. For instance, you might sweep the filter when it may be more appropriate for the sound you are after to sweep the depth of the envelope modulation of the filter.

People (including me) use presets for many reasons:

- Some are excellent, and they save programming time (so you can make music).

- They sound good.

- The results are better than you can program yourself.

- The style is outside of your usual programming style.

- The presets give you inspiration.

As I said, I use presets and will continue to use presets in addition to programming my own sounds. However, it seems that you're being very hopeful that you could take a sound that has been programmed in a vacuum (in other words, the sound was programmed by someone who knows nothing about your track), *and* that the sound will then be used in the context of a mix, *and* that it will work perfectly.

I can believe that a patch programmed out of context might be right for your track. However, I find it hard to conceive that it would fit the mix perfectly *and* would fit the playing style of the MIDI track, where it will be responding to velocity and other playing techniques.

I think you also need to consider the purpose of factory presets and what sound designers have to do to persuade people to purchase a bank of patches. Presets that come with a synth have one purpose—to display the capabilities of that synth. This is a sensible thing to do and is exactly what I would do if I were in the business of making synths.

However good the presets are, however well they demonstrate the synth in question, they are not necessarily right for your track. So what do you do? Most people consider buying some presets from somewhere else. Which presets do they choose? Usually the ones that sound most flashy—not necessarily the ones that fit with the track they are trying to construct.

If you have a choice between bad programming done by yourself and a good preset, then the good preset should win every time. Sound programming should *never* detract from the music and the music-making process. You should also remember that there is no rule that the sound design has to be undertaken by the creator/producer of a composition. It is a perfectly valid decision to use external sound design, provided the result works for the track.

Finally, please don't form the view that I think you have to program your own sounds to create a musically valid piece. I'm just as critical of the use of presets you have created yourself if they are inappropriate for a track.

Principles of Sound Design

Unfortunately, there is no magic formula to creating a sound on a synthesizer. However, I would suggest a few basic steps before you jump in:

- Get as familiar as you can with the synthesizer you are using.

- Have a definite aim in what you're trying to program—don't just fiddle with the knobs and hope something useful comes along.

- Understand what each module does and the function of each knob on the modules.

Once you have these basics sorted, I suggest a multi-stage approach:

- **Start simple.** Don't try to build the whole sound immediately—build in steps and slowly add elements to embellish the sound. Understand the signal flow in your creation and how each element interacts (and especially look out for the interactions you were not expecting).

- **Get something that is "all right."** In other words, get a sound that is functional and is reasonably close to where you want to end up—you should be able to get to this point quickly.

- **Undertake the detailed tweaking.** This is the time to make sure the patch is exactly right for your needs—this will be the time-consuming part of the programming.

- **Only add what you need.** Only add—and only keep—a module (or a routing) if you understand what its function is within the context of the sound. If it no longer has a function that has a material effect on the sound, then junk it. Keep reviewing and keep culling redundant modules.

When it comes to getting something that is "nearly" right, I see no reason not to use a preset, although the subsequent editing may take longer because you will have to familiarize yourself with the workings of the patch.

Main Food Groups

When I program sounds from a blank sheet, I tend to start by thinking in terms of the main food groups.

Most sounds can be characterized by two key elements—their brightness and the envelope (primarily the attack time of the envelope, but often you need the decay time and the sustain level to be right for the contrast of the attack to be clear). Once these two elements have been addressed, any tonal nuances after that may be affected by a range of factors.

Brightness

If you are trying to categorize the brightness of a sound, it will generally fall within one of four descriptions:

- Very bright

- Bright

- Dull

- Very dull

You can try to subdivide further, but realistically, it is already quite difficult to try to find the line between these four categories.

Attack

If you try hard, you can find four categories of attack time:

- Fast—percussive (for instance, a xylophone hit or a guitar string being plucked)

- Fast—but not percussive (for instance, an organ)

- Medium

- Slow

Again, you can try to subdivide the categories further, but it is a fairly pointless exercise.

Getting the Combination Right

Once you understand what you want in the way of brightness and envelope, getting the right sound depends on the right elements being drawn together. For instance, the following sections describe some combinations you may want to look at.

To Get Brightness

Consider the oscillator (or oscillators) and filter combination. If they don't work together, you will get a shrill sound or a thin sound or a dull sound, but never a bright sound. For instance, if you are creating a sound based on a square wave, you may find it preferable to choose a 12-dB filter. A 24-dB or 36-dB filter may work, but to my ear they ultimately rob many square waves of much of their character, which you may want to keep if you are trying to create a bright patch.

Equally, you may want to consider a non-subtractive means of sound generation. For instance, FM synthesis can give you very bright sounds, and as long as you control the sound, it won't become harsh.

To Get Richness

One of the key elements to a rich sound is its movement. You can achieve this with careful selection of your sound source (which will usually involve several slightly detuned oscillators and perhaps some delicate use of a sub-oscillator, or maybe several similar oscillator/filter combinations, each giving a subtly different sound). Alternatively, you can just slap on loads of chorus. My preference is the former option.

Of course, the other way to keep a sound moving is to use modulators—in particular, LFOs and envelopes (or maybe both together).

To Get Attack

Most obviously, it is important that the envelope opens quickly to get some attack in a note. Depending on the tonal quality you are after, it is often important that the note then decays quickly to the sustain level—this will give you a percussive envelope reminiscent of a plucked guitar string or similar.

However, to ensure that the attack is emphasized, another significant factor is the waveform. Some waves can sound slower than others. For instance, all other factors being equal, a square wave can sound like it has a faster attack than a sine wave. In general, bright sounds (especially distorted bright sounds) are perceived as having more attack. Again, you might want to look at FM sounds for their attacking qualities.

To Get Warmth

A warm sound is subtly different from a rich sound; often it is much less bright. Warmth is also a comparative term—if a colder sound starts a patch and is then washed over by a warm sound, the contrast can give the listener the illusion of warmth.

Any warm sound will probably have a slow attack and a slow release. There must be thickness to the sound, which will often come from a number of oscillators. As noted earlier, one of the key elements of a warm sound is the changing tone that can be achieved with another oscillator or a different filter with an even slower envelope. In a modular setup, it is a simple task to create a patch where one sound washes over a second (totally separate) sound.

To Get Punch

It is hard to get some punch into a sound without adding too much brightness. First you need a fat sound source, then you need a fast attack (but often not too fast), and finally you need a hefty filter. The filter can be modulated with the envelope so that the attack is emphasized but the brightness is controlled.

Playability

Any patch has to be highly playable. The playability of the patch is one aspect that separates average sounds from professionally produced sounds. Use your knowledge of how the sound will be deployed to set the modulation sources.

For instance, if the sound is going to be played by a live musician, then you might ensure that velocity has an effect and that the modulation wheel and expression pedal both offer a wide range of control. However, if the MIDI track controlling the sound is going to be programmed, then you might want to make sure that external controllers, such as track envelopes, can have a significant effect. So for instance, you may add an additional filter that has little effect in the normal course but can be readily controlled by a track envelope.

Building Blocks

There are perhaps two approaches to getting an initial sound. So far in this book we have looked at the first approach: Get a basic setup and work with it. Mostly we have taken a basic oscillator/ filter combination and worked from there.

The oscillator/filter combination is a useful "block"—in other words, a sound source that can be combined with other elements to form more complex architectures to make more interesting sounds.

However, the oscillator/filter combo is not the only sort of block you could work from, and this is where we move to the other approach to finding an initial sound: creating sounds without a filter. We've looked at several ways of creating sounds without filters—in particular, additive and FM. These are both good options with great scope for creating a broad sonic palette, which can then be controlled over time with a wide range of modulators. And, of course, these approaches can also both be used in conjunction with subtractive synthesis techniques.

However, there is a far more straightforward approach to creating new tones: oscillator combining. In other words, taking two (or more) oscillators and creating a new tone. We looked at oscillator combining briefly in Chapter 4—now I want to think a bit about how those combinations could be applied. The key here is not to simply think of combinations as an end in and of themselves—instead, think of them as building blocks that can then be combined with other building blocks, each block fulfilling a different role within a sound.

At its most basic, you can combine two oscillators with the same waveform (see Figure 9.10). Slightly detuning one wave creates a thickening to the sound and gives a sound that is fuller and richer than you may expect with two oscillators.

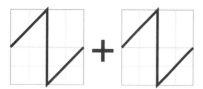

Figure 9.10 Two slightly detuned oscillators with the same waveform selected will give a thickening to the sound.

Two slightly detuned oscillators is the plain vanilla of the synthesizer world—it serves a function, but there is more to life. Also, from a sonic perspective, it is something of a compromise. If you want a fat sound, then a multi-voice oscillator is likely to give you the sound you want more swiftly. But if you stay with two oscillators, you will find that you can create a more powerful unit by adding a sub-oscillator—in other words, an oscillator pitched one or two octaves below the pitch of the main oscillators (see Figure 9.11).

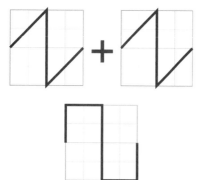

Figure 9.11 Using a sub-oscillator can add weight to a two-oscillator combination.

You may also find that a different waveform works well as the sub-oscillator wave. For instance, if you have two sawtooth waves, a square wave will often work well as a sub-oscillator. However, when you select your sub-oscillator wave, you should consider what you are trying to achieve. Usually there are two aims:

- Are you trying to simply add weight/depth to the existing sound?
- Are you trying to change the tone of the existing sound?

Both of these approaches are valid, and they are not mutually exclusive. However, rather than just twist knobs and hope, you might want to think about what you are trying to achieve. If your aim is to add weight but not to change the tone, then very often all you need is a sine wave (which will reinforce the low end). However, if you also want to reshape the tone, then try out some other waves.

Using the same wave as the main oscillators will not guarantee that you will not change the tone. Indeed, very often this additional lower oscillator will have a significant effect on the sound if it uses the same waveform. (Equally, a sine wave is not always a benign addition.)

As with the two-oscillator combination, you could combine a sub-oscillator with a multi-voice oscillator—this is a very quick and dirty way to create a simple synthesizer. By the way, as a general rule, I don't like using multi-voice oscillators as sub-oscillators—I find it simply ends up giving too much of a thick and indistinct low end. Instead of hearing a nice, clean bass, all I hear is mush, so I stick with single-voice sub-oscillators.

Of course, you don't have to keep the two oscillators at broadly the same pitch. You can combine oscillators at different pitches to create new sounds. For instance, you could combine oscillators where one is an octave higher than the other (see Figure 9.12) or where one is two octaves higher than the other (see Figure 9.13). If you're going to take this approach, then it is often a good idea to synchronize the oscillators (so that the phase of both waves remains consistent)—the alternative is that the phase relationship between the two oscillators changes, giving an inconsistent sound source.

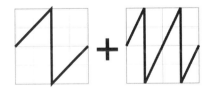

Figure 9.12 You can combine oscillators where one is an octave above the other...

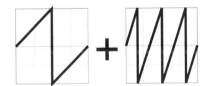

Figure 9.13 ...and you can combine oscillators where one is pitched two octaves above the other.

Of course, even though the illustrations only show sawtooth waves, you can always combine different shapes of waves, and you're not limited to octave separations—you could have single semitone variations (although these are rarely pleasant). However, you're quite likely to find something that works if the separation forms part of a chord; typically, these will all work well:

- A minor third—three semitones up

- A major third—four semitones up

- A perfect fourth—five semitones up

- A perfect fifth—seven semitones up

However, you probably don't want to try all of these possible inversions at once.

As you can imagine, when you start combining waves, you get a lot of different permutations very quickly, and many of those permutations are not very useful ("useful" in this context meaning "could be applied in a real-world situation," not simply whether it works in a conventional musical context).

When you are considering whether a combination works in a musical sense, you may come down to a choice between two main options. Which one works for you will depend on what result you're looking for and how the sounds are then treated (in terms of filtering and other processing):

- **A single cohesive tone.** In many ways, the most successful result of joining two waves together will be a completely new sound (which may or may not bear any sonic resemblance to its parents). Generally, you will find that if the pitch difference between the two waves is an octave or less, then you have a greater chance of obtaining this elusive, cohesive new tone.

- **Two separately identifiable elements within a new tone.** Often—particularly when there is a wide pitch variation (usually over two octaves) between your sound sources—you will hear a new sound, but you will also be able to identify a separate higher-pitched element, too. Sometimes this combination of sounds will work, and other times you will be disappointed. Often these combinations break down during filtering (tending to sound like the lower-pitched voice).

- **Two waves that just don't work together.** Okay, I know I said there were two options, but there is a third—and perhaps the most obvious—end product of grouping two waves together: failure. In other words, all you can hear is the two separate sound sources. If this happens, then unless your aim in programming has been to hear two separate sound sources, the combination has not moved you forward (in a sonic sense).

Building Sounds

The remainder of this book is dedicated to sound building (note sounds, not FX units). Primarily, I'm going to look at making the sounds, but as an integral part of that exercise, I'm going to discuss some of the architecture. As with the approach I adopted earlier in the book, my aim is for you to understand the process by following what I am doing. Accordingly, there are no downloadable patches to accompany this chapter—it's more important that you learn to use your ears and hear what's going on than it is to precisely replicate sounds by loading presets.

I'm mostly going to use VAZ Modular and Zebra 2 to create the sounds here. I could have used any of the four synths, but those two give the best screenshots, and so, for no other reason, I will use those. You can apply all of the principles in this sound-building section to KarmaFX Synth Modular or to SynthEdit. The principles also apply to a wide range of other synthesizers.

It may sound heretical, but some of the sounds I am going to build could be replicated on a standard fixed-architecture synthesizer—this chapter is about making sounds, not doing wild and wacky things just for the heck of it. But one issue to remember is that with the sounds I am building here, I am selecting from a much wider choice of modules than would be available for fixed-architecture synths—so for instance, I have a wide choice of oscillators and an even wider choice of filters. The permutations of these choices give me far more sonic options than would be available with a conventional synthesizer.

And then, of course, even if I am building something comparatively conventional, because we are in the modular world I do still have the option to connect up some other modules and do something wacky.

One thing that I do ask you to remember while we are looking at these sounds is that everything is out of context here. All of the sounds are being built without reference to how they would fit into a song. Therefore:

- We are likely to try to make the sounds as "good" as possible, so that they shine when heard on their own, and as a consequence...

- If/when the sounds are heard in the context of a track, they may not work.

As a last point before we start looking at synthesizer programming, could I respond to one of the comparatively frequent requests that I receive—that I should re-create specific sounds? Most commonly, it is suggested that I demonstrate how to re-create the individual instruments within an orchestra. I'm not going to do this, but please let me explain why I am dodging that bullet (and why you may find that exercise less than fruitful).

- First off, it is really difficult to reproduce the sound of a real instrument. I think you could dedicate a whole book (literally) to reproducing one instrument.

- Part of the reason for the complexity of real instruments is the variations. Take a violin as an example: A player can change the tone by moving where a string is bowed (if it is bowed), by changing how the string is bowed, by playing the note on a different string, with different pressure holding the string, by changing the force with which the string is struck, and so on.

- Once each of the nuances of the broad tone palette has been replicated by a synthesizer, then there is the issue of playing the sounds. This gets you into a world of patch changing/ cross-fading and hideous MIDI programming. Added to this, to reproduce the sound of an orchestra, at a minimum, each instrument part would have to be played. That's a heck of a lot of synthesizer programming and a lot of MIDI programming, and you would then need a significant amount of computer grunt to run enough synths for each sound nuance.

So in short, it's really difficult to program these sounds, and more to the point, if it were possible to program such a sound to a sufficient degree of reality, then there probably isn't a computer powerful enough to run all of the necessary synthesizer instances—and even if there were, no one has the time to program these things. At the end of the day, it would be much easier to hire an orchestra or use one of the massive sound libraries.

I don't want to discourage any creative endeavor, but as a suggestion, you might want to focus your sound creation in other areas.

Anyway, that's why I don't try to replicate real instruments. Now let's move on and create some synthesizer sounds.

Noisy Synth

The first sound I'm going to create is built on the filtered noise principle that we looked at earlier in the book. However, I've added one or two twists to make it a bit more interesting and a bit more playable—in particular, this has a much more subtle and controllable tone. I've made this sound in VAZ Modular—you can have a look at the finished product in Figure 9.14.

Now let me try to explain what I have done and why I've done it.

As you can see, the sound source is the Noise Source module. I've set the noise Color slider midway between Pink and Red—this gives a (comparatively) dark-sounding noise. I then set the Color Modulation to be controlled by incoming velocity, but the polarity has been reversed. This means that as the incoming MIDI velocity increases (in other words, a key is struck harder), the tone changes, becoming brighter.

The noise is then fed into a filter. In this instance, I chose Filter R. Well, I say *chose*...it was actually the first filter that I clicked on, and I liked the sound so I stuck with it. I chose the 1-Pole Low-Pass filter, which is a 6-dB filter with resonance, and pulled the cut-off down a bit. I then also pushed up the Resonance (so the slider was about halfway). To finish this block, I then set the pitch (CV1 Note Low) as a modulation source for the filter's cut-off frequency and pushed the slider to the maximum. This means that the cut-off frequency tracks the (lowest) pitch played on the keyboard. As with the earlier sound, this patch allows you to "play" pitched noise. However, the quality of that noise can be changed with MIDI velocity, thereby giving us many more subtle played tones.

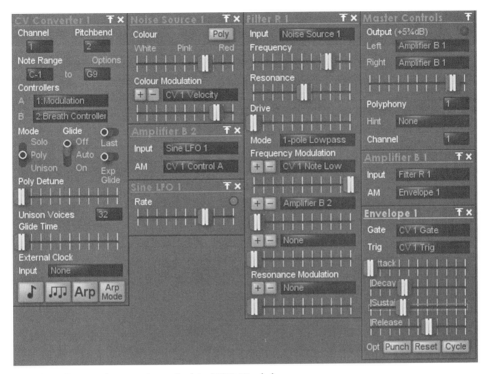

Figure 9.14   A noisy synth sound created in VAZ Modular.

The filter then runs into the amplifier—I selected the Amplifier B model, which has its amplitude modulated by Envelope 1. The envelope has been set with:

- A very fast attack time

- Quite a quick decay time

- A moderately low sustain level

- A comparatively long release time

Let me explain my logic here.

The decay time, working in conjunction with the low sustain level, gives an emphasis to the initial attack of the volume envelope (which is what this envelope controls). This gives the volume envelope a "plucked" character.

This plucked character is less noticeable at higher velocities when the noise source is brighter. However, at lower velocities—when there is a darker sound feeding into the audio chain—the initial impact gives a more interesting sound.

The envelope is completed with the comparatively long release time. This gives some sustain to the notes over the decay phase and almost sounds like an echo (almost).

To add a bit more control for the player, I added an LFO. In this case, I used the Sine LFO (because I only needed a sine wave). The LFO was fed into an amplifier (again, Amplifier B), and CV1 Control A was set to modulate amplitude. The CV1 Control A slot is linked to the modulation wheel, and so with the amplifier, this means that the amount of modulation put out by the Sine LFO can now be controlled by the modulation wheel.

The output from the second amplifier (in other words, the LFO modulation) was then connected to the second frequency modulation slot on the filter, so the LFO could mess with the filter's cutoff. If you look at Figure 9.14, you will see that the slider associated with this modulation has been moved only slightly, even though the modulation is controlled by the modulation wheel. The reason for this was that I wanted a very subtle sound—if the slider is moved any farther, then it is possible to get really wild sounds, and I wanted to exclude those possibilities.

Finally, I decided to keep this as a monophonic sound. This is not an everyday sound that would have a place in any track. It is a very specific sound that would have highly limited uses, and when it is used, the sound would work as a specific feature (probably embellishing a melody line). By contrast, setting this patch to play chords would just give an uncontrolled noise that would have little use.

Those were the choices I made for this sound. If you disagree—and I encourage you to disagree— then please feel free to tweak it or design your own sound.

Organ-Like

After my rant about re-creating real instruments, it might seem a bit odd to be starting with something that sounds like it could be an emulation of a real instrument.

Let me explain myself.... This sound is not intended to re-create a particular sound. Instead, we are going to take some of the principles of an organ and give them our own unique twist. In so doing, we're going to create something that can create organ-like sounds but, in addition, will create something that a conventional organ may not be able to readily replicate.

With classic organs (check back to Figure I.1 for a picture of a software implementation of one of the classics), the sound source is (in effect) a group of sine waves. In many ways, organs were the first additive synthesizers. Unlike an additive synthesizer, however, there is a limited range of sine waves (nine in total) in an organ, and their pitch relationship is fixed—all the player has control over is the relative volume of those sine waves. The fixed-pitch relationships of the nine sine waves are:

- One octave below the fundamental

- A fifth (seven semitones) above the fundamental

- The fundamental

- An octave above the fundamental

- One octave plus a fifth above the fundamental

- Two octaves above the fundamental

- Two octaves plus a major third above the fundamental

- Two octaves plus a fifth above the fundamental

- Three octaves above the fundamental

So here's what we're going to do: We're going to take eight sine waves (we'll use eight because we have some eight channel mixers in VAZ Modular), and we're going to feed them into two eight-channel mixers. One mixer will then be fed to the left output and the other to the right. We can then use each mixer to dial up our organ sound—in other words, the organ sound will be created and controlled in the mixers. This immediately gives us a twist on the original hardware organ (and I'm not counting ignoring a sine wave as a twist) in that there will be two parallel sound sources—the left mix and the right mix.

Not only will there be different sounds to the left and right, but since we will be adjusting the mix by hand, it will be almost impossible to perfectly replicate one mix on the other side. This means that there is the possibility of the sound shifting between the speakers as we deal with very similar, but different, sounds. This could give us some interesting effects.

Anyway, that's the theory—let's start making the sound. If you take a look at Figure 9.15, you will see where we are heading.

The core of the sound comes from the eight Sine Oscillators. Unlike its hardware equivalents (or its software incarnations), this organ is missing the ninth sine wave. In this case, it is missing the highest sine wave, which would be tuned three octaves above the fundamental. The remaining oscillators have been tuned as follows:

- Sine Oscillator 1, Tuning $16' + 0$ (one octave below the fundamental)

- Sine Oscillator 2, Tuning $8' + 7$ (a fifth above the fundamental)

- Sine Oscillator 3, Tuning $8' + 0$ (this is the fundamental)

- Sine Oscillator 4, Tuning $4' + 0$ (one octave above the fundamental)

- Sine Oscillator 5, Tuning $4' + 7$ (one octave and a fifth above the fundamental)

- Sine Oscillator 6, Tuning $2' + 0$ (two octaves above the fundamental)

- Sine Oscillator 7, Tuning $2' + 4$ (two octaves and a major third above the fundamental)

- Sine Oscillator 8, Tuning $2' + 7$ (two octaves and a fifth above the fundamental)

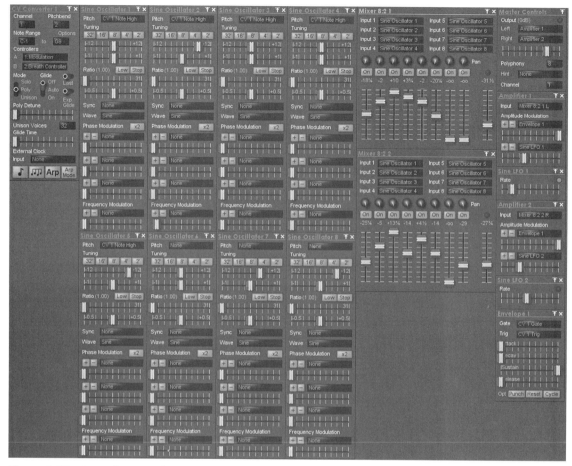

Figure 9.15 A mock organ (with a twist or two) created in VAZ Modular.

The phases of these waves are left free running.

As you can see from the tuning, the wave combinations give you some interesting possibilities. For instance, if you select Oscillators 6, 7, and 8, then you will create a major chord (to which you could add a bass note by pushing up Oscillator 4).

The oscillators are then fed into two mixers. With each mixer, Oscillator 1 is attached to Input 1, Oscillator 2 to Input 2, and so on. Because we're working in the world of modulars, we could create as many of these mixes as we want—I have chosen to create two.

In Mixer 1 the sounds are all panned to the left, and in Mixer 2 the sounds are then panned to the right. The left output from Mixer 1 is then attached to Amplifier 1, and the right output from Mixer 2 is attached to Amplifier 2. Amplifier 1 is then attached to the left channel of the Master Controls, and Amplifier 2 is attached to the right channel, so the different mixes are panned hard left and hard right, respectively.

If you look back to the mixers, you will see that under the pan knobs there are orange On buttons (and I do realize you won't be able to pick out the color if you are looking at the gray-scale Figure 9.15). If you push up the sliders, then these On buttons give you a very quick way to switch on and off each of the oscillators so you can get a general sense of the impact of each sine wave on the overall sound.

By the way, if you do push up all of the sliders, then you will get some nasty distortion due to the overloading of the mixers. As a result, you will see that I have pulled down the overall level slider in each mixer (located on the right of each mixer)—this keeps things within reasonable bounds.

Earlier in this chapter (in the "Building Blocks" section), I mentioned the notion of bringing together several sounds to create a whole new sound and, ideally, a cohesive new tone. This creation is a great example of that principle in practice. As you push up the sliders, you will be mixing up to eight different sound sources. The result is not a sound that sounds as if it was generated by different oscillators—instead, it sounds like one oscillator with different waves.

Take some time to play with the mixers and listen to the range of tones you can create. Most of the sounds will have an organ-like quality (which isn't really that surprising), but many will have a more synthetic tone. If you're not sure where to start, then set everything to zero, push up the fundamental and the fundamental plus one octave (Sliders 3 and 4), and go from there. While these two sine waves will give a basic sound, that sound is a good foundation from which to listen to the effects of, and interactions with, other elements.

When it comes to creating sounds, I suggest you exercise some caution with Sine Oscillator 1 (which works as a sub-oscillator). This can add a lot of low-end volume that may not be immediately noticeable. However, its effect, if not used judiciously and if there's a lot of other stuff going on, can be to muddy up the tone. Used with caution, it works well.

You will probably find that the sliders controlling the oscillators tuned to octaves (Sine Oscillator 1, Sine Oscillator 3, Sine Oscillator 4, and Sine Oscillator 6) will (generally) be the easiest sliders to control when you are trying to change the tone. The other sliders control sine waves that are harmonically related and that—at extremes—will create chords. If you create chords with the individual waves, then you may hear dissonance when you play chords (as you will, in effect, be overlaying several chords).

As I've already mentioned, each of the mixers has its own dedicated amplifier. The volume level of both amplifiers is controlled by the same envelope: Envelope 1, which has been set to give a basic organ shape to the sound (in other words, attack time set to zero, sustain level set to the maximum, and release time set to zero). This means that you hear a sound when a key is struck, and when a key is released, the sound dies immediately.

Each of the amplifiers is also modulated by its own low-frequency oscillator. (In both cases I have selected a Sine LFO module.) Unlike the envelope, there are separate LFOs for each amplifier—the frequency of each LFO and the depth of each LFO are then set differently for each amplifier. While the settings are quite subtle—they are intended to give a gentle wobble to the respective volume levels for each side—this combination adds to the shifting nature of each sound. Each side of the audio panorama now has different sounds, and the volumes constantly change. This adds a lot of movement to a sound that is effectively a bunch of sine waves.

Now, of course, you will see that there are many other options we could consider here. For instance, instead of creating one sound for the left channel and another for the right, we could overlay the sounds and set them to be mixed on the basis of incoming MIDI velocity. This would give us a velocity-responsive organ where the tone changes according to the playing style. That is something else you couldn't do with the original hardware (or with most conventional fixed-architecture synthesizers).

Equally, there are options you could consider to further replicate the behavior of hardware organs. For instance:

- There is a distinctive key "click" with hardware organs. This was an original design fault, but it stayed because people liked the sound. You could easily replicate this sound, perhaps with a noise source.

- You may also want to think about reproducing the swirling effect created by Leslie speakers, which helped to give organs their classic tone.

As always, the choices are yours to make.

Pseudo Echo

Here's something a bit different. This sound is a pad that is intended to do two things:

- Sound something like an echo
- Be a bit "sparkly" when the keys are released (but not before)

In case you're sitting there wondering "Why?!?," let me explain. I want the echo effect so that the pad has more rhythm—I don't want something flat and featureless. And the sparkly thing is to sound pretty but not get in the way of the rhythm.

Take a look at Figure 9.16 to get an idea about what is involved in this sound. As you can see, there are not many modules, but the modulators go off the page.

The basis of the sound is a sawtooth wave (in this case I chose Saw Soft and loaded it into Osc1) running through a low-pass filter (in this case I chose LP 12dB and loaded it into VCF1). So far, so average.... However, I wanted to create an echo-type effect while sustain notes are held. There were two elements to this effect:

- First, there is a repeating quality to the sound—I didn't want a consistent sound, but instead was after a stuttering-type effect. To create this effect, I set up LFO1 to (negatively)

Figure 9.16   The Pseudo Echo patch created in Zebra 2.

modulate the output volume of Osc1. I set LFO1 with a square wave, and with the negative modulation, this meant that through half of each wave cycle (when the wave was at its maximum), the volume would be pushed to zero, and hence there would be silence. The LFO was tempo-synched at a rate of 1/8.

■   Second, to mimic an echo, I needed the sound to get duller over time in the way that an echo can do. I did this by controlling the filter cut-off with an envelope (Envelope 1). The filter was set with the Cut-Off quite low (in other words, most of the signal was filtered out), and the Resonance was set just under halfway. Then the envelope controlling the filter's cut-off was set as follows:

• Attack: The attack time was zero (in other words, fast) so that the envelope's effect was immediate.

• Decay: The decay time was long so that the envelope would slowly close the filter, giving a very gentle reduction in tone.

- Sustain: The sustain level was just under half—I set it to a level where the sound was quite dull but still distinct with the Resonance setting.
- Release: The release time was set to the maximum so that the filter would slowly close after a note is released. This would give a further dulling of the sound, but without totally closing the filter (which would cut the sound completely).

In addition, I didn't want the filter to be static once the envelope had stopped moving because it had reached the sustain level, so I added two more tweaks:

- First, I set LFO2 with a Random Hold wave with its frequency set to 1/4 to modulate the filter's cut-off. The effect of this was quite subtle, but it was enough to keep changing the character of the filter...but only slightly.

- Second, I set LFO3 with a square wave with its frequency set to 1/4 to modulate the filter's resonance. This modulation was set through the ModMatrix. Again, it is a subtle setting that gives the filter some movement, ensuring that the sound is not static when the envelope controlling the cut-off frequency reaches its sustain phase.

The final step in this part of the sound is the volume envelope. This was set by selecting Envelope 4 instead of Gate (above the audio channel's volume control). Given the effect of the filter on the volume, this envelope is less important, except in one area, where it is crucial. The settings for the envelope were:

- Attack: The attack time was set to zero so that the sound could be heard immediately.

- Decay: The decay time was moderate (the knob was turned to nearly 3 o'clock). This gave a gradual decay to the sustain level.

- Sustain: The sustain level was fairly high. (Again, the knob was turned to around 3 o'clock.)

- Release: The release setting is the crucial setting for this envelope. Without a suitable release stage, the release stage created in the filter will be prematurely cut. Therefore, the release time was set to a fair length. However, the release time was not as long as that set for the filter envelope—there is an element of the filter envelope's movement that will never be heard (because the filter is so far closed), so I wasn't worried about the volume envelope cutting this.

So that's the main body of the sound; let's move on and look at the sparkles. At this stage you may find it easier to work on the sparkles in isolation. To do this you can switch out the existing modules by double-clicking on them in the grid. This will remove each module and any associated modulators from the rack.

The intention behind this part of the sound is to give a quite bright sound during the release phase of the sound. Because this is not a "flat" pad, I wanted something that was quite animated—almost like a musical version of fairy dust. This moving, fairy-dust sound is created through the interaction of two elements.

The basis for this sound was created in Osc2, into which I loaded the Bells Flipper wave, or rather, the Bells Flipper waveset. This is a collection of single-cycle waves, each having a bell-like tone. Audition them (using the Wave knob on the oscillator), and you will hear some interesting and bright tones. I didn't just want one sound, I wanted several, so I set the LFO G1 to (fully) modulate the Wave choice. In the LFO, I chose a Random Hold wave and set the sync to 1/4. I also balanced the Amplitude knob in the LFO to about halfway, as this seemed to give a good shift through the waves.

However, although I like this sound, it wasn't giving me that sparkling sort of tone I was after; it was simply shifting the waveform giving a continuous tone. To get the sparkle, I needed to add a bit of a stutter in the same manner that I did for Osc1 earlier on. This time I called up LFO G2 and set it to (negatively) fully modulate the Volume of Osc2. In LFO G2 I then selected a square wave and set the Rate to 1/16.

This second LFO gives the oscillator its stutter. If you turn down the effect of LFO G1 (which sweeps through the waveset), you will hear a consistent tone, but with stuttering. If you turn LFO G1 back up so that there is sweeping through the waveset, you will hear that with every other stutter, there is a different wave selected. The combination of the two gives an interesting effect—it's almost as if the wave is talking.

This is an interesting sound, but I wanted to tame it a bit, so I pushed it through the VCF2 filter. In the filter I selected a band-pass filter—BP RezBand—and dialed a Cut-Off frequency that was quite high (so the effect of the filter was gentle) and added some resonance. (I set the Resonance control to about one-quarter—you could dial a much higher setting to give a more nasal tone.)

The effect of the filter is to make the sound of these sparkles a bit thinner. I also wanted to add a bit of movement to the filter, so I set LFO G1 (which already controls the waveset sweep) to also modulate this filter's cut-off. This modulation means that the filter will jump about a bit—however, the effect is quite subtle and is more in the nature of gently changing the tone. Also, because the wave is changing when the filter cut-off is changing, the effect of the LFO is less obvious. If you remove the LFO, then the sound has less subtle shades and colors.

The filter also serves another useful purpose: to silence these sparkles until the release stage. This result is achieved by putting Envelope 3 into the second modulator and setting it to negatively fully modulate the filter. The envelope was then set like an organ:

- The attack time was set to zero.

- The sustain level was set to the maximum (and hence the decay time was irrelevant).

- The release time was set to zero.

As the envelope worked negatively, its effect was to set the cut-off value to its lowest level, which has the sonic effect of closing the filter and hence cutting the sound. However, when the filter reverts to its usual setting—which it does when the note is released—then the sound will be heard.

Now, if you've been following this sound closely, at this stage you will be hearing nothing and you may be rather confused. If this is you, follow these steps:

1. Turn off the second audio channel. Next to the output routing (which shows Main) there is a button. If you click on the button, it will show red, and the audio channel will be closed.

2. In the first audio channel (where hopefully you have switched off the other modules by double-clicking on them), add a Channel Mix module.

3. Right-click on the Channel Mix module in the grid (it will show as Mix1) and select Side Chain 2. You should now see a line drawn from VCF2 to the Mix1 module. The audio output from VCF2 is now mixed with the output from the first oscillator and will be subject to the volume envelope on this audio channel.

Now when you play a note you will hear nothing. However, when you release the key, you should hear the sparkle effect during the release stage of the note.

To complete this sound:

1. Drag VCF1 so it is after the Mix1 module in the audio chain (in other words, it is below the module in the grid). This doesn't have a huge effect on the tone of the sparkles, but it does rein them in slightly. More importantly, it allows some of the volume-reducing effect of the VCF1 module to also be applied to the sparkles, giving them that decaying echo quality.

2. Switch on the Osc1 and VCF1 modules.

Now when you play the sound, you will hear the stuttering echo while the keys are held, but when you release the notes, the sound will continue *and* the sparkles will be added in. If the transition to the sparkles is too abrupt, you will find that the sparkles can be faded in by increasing the release time in Envelope 3.

I'm biased; I quite like this sound. I also have the advantage that I designed it for another piece I am working on, so I have an idea of how it could work for me.

But would it work for you? Would it work in the context of a track for you? Obviously, I don't know. Maybe yes or maybe no. If it doesn't work, then don't use it—either tweak it until it does work or create something from scratch that does.

Human Choir

Hopefully you can guess what my inspiration was for the Human Choir sound. The purpose of this sound is to use something approaching the human voice as the jumping-off point for the sound and then to move on from there.

If you take a look at Figure 9.17, you will see that the sound only has a few modules—and those appear at first glance to be doubled. However, there are subtle differences. You'll also note that the XY pad has been hooked up—the reason for this is to give the player some real-time control over the sound.

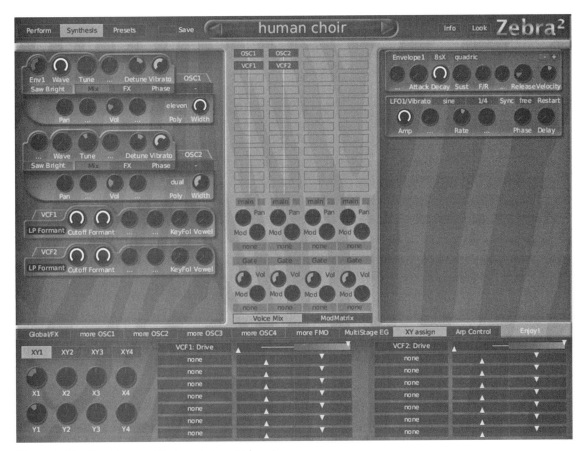

Figure 9.17 The Human Choir patch in Zebra 2.

The sound starts in Osc1 where the Saw Bright waveset has been loaded. The Wave knob has then been set to the maximum amount—so by default, the last wave in the set will play—but Env1 has also been set to negatively modulate the waveset position. In other words, when Envelope 1 is at its maximum value, the first wave in the series will play.

Envelope 1 has been set with the attack time, sustain level, and release time all at zero. However, the decay time has been set to the maximum. This means that working in conjunction with Osc1, when the note is triggered, the first wave in the series will be played (because the envelope will be at its maximum value). As the note is held, it will decay to zero (the sustain level). As the note decays, it will cause Osc1 to sweep through the waveset that has been loaded. This will result in a subtle shift in tone as the note sustains.

The multi-voice mode has been selected for the oscillator. In this case, there are 11 voices—the detuning is not too extreme, but the width control has been set to the maximum. There is also a fair amount of vibrato added. (The knob has been turned to about 1 o'clock.) However, in the context of this sound, the vibrato is not too intrusive when you listen to the end result.

The second oscillator, Osc2, has a similar setup, but there are some differences:

- The Saw Bright waveset has been loaded, but the first wave has been chosen, and the waveset is not swept.

- Multi-voice mode has been engaged, but only two voices selected. The detuning is slightly more subtle, although there is more vibrato. The Width control is at the midway point.

- The Tune knob has been adjusted to drop the pitch by an octave.

You will also see that the volume of each of the oscillators has been dropped, and the global volume was similarly cut. The reason for this was the high output levels from the filters.

There are two filters in this sound—their settings are exactly the same:

- The selected filter is LP Formant. This is a formant filter that is designed to reproduce some of the characteristics of the human voice. As such, it has a number of resonant peaks that cause volume spikes, which is why the volume has been cut so severely.

- The Cut-Off has been set to the maximum, so the low-pass bit of the filter does nothing.

- The Resonance has been set to the maximum—this sharpens up the formants and gives a more pronounced effect.

- The Vowel settings have both been set to zero. However, we will mess with these settings in a moment.

I could have used one filter for this sound—the basic sonic results would have been the same. However, I decided to use two so that I could control the filters in real time and get a different sound out of each of the oscillator/filter combinations. In addition, because each of the oscillators was set up differently, the oscillator/filter combinations react to changes in different ways.

The control I set up was one XY pad. I set:

- The X axis to control the Vowel settings in Filter 1, which passes the nine-voice oscillator
- The Y axis to control the Vowel settings in Filter 2, which passes the two-voice oscillator pitched an octave below the other

This gives huge levels of control and very broad tonal possibilities. In particular, it is possible to combine different vowel sounds at different octaves to give sounds that cannot readily be created by humans.

I finished the sound with a tweak you may not be expecting: I engaged Legato mode. This does three things for me:

- First, it sets the sound so that only one note at a time can be played. This may seem odd for a choir-type sound where you may expect chords. However, chords gave too much mush and didn't sound particularly pleasant, so I didn't want that option.
- By only playing one note at a time, the volume is kept in check. With chords it was even more likely that the output would be overloaded.
- Legato mode also means that the envelope controlling the waveset sweep does not get reset if the previous note is still held when the next note is struck. This allows the pitch to change without leading to a change in tone.

Set up this patch for yourself and try it. In particular, listen to the tones you can find with the XY pad.

Rough and Ready FM

FM synthesis allows you to create some "wooden" tones (in the sense of tuned wooden percussion). My aim with the Rough and Ready FM sound was to create a sound using that tone but to add broader range to the sound, maybe even getting closer to a bell-like sound in certain circumstances. Take a look at Figure 9.18 to see the finished sound (or at least those modules from the finished sound that can be seen).

This is the first sound in this chapter created purely with FM principles (although there is a minor amount of filtering), so let me walk you through the sound in a bit more detail.

The sound is created with FM synthesis techniques using the four FMOs (frequency modulation oscillators). These are arranged in a parallel-carrier configuration—one modulator driving three carriers—effectively working as three modulator/carrier groupings running in parallel. The basis of the sound is created by FMO1 frequency-modulating FMO2.

The Tune knob in FMO1 was set to 31—in other words, 31 semitones, or two octaves plus seven semitones above the base pitch. This oscillator works as the modulator for all of the carriers, but for the moment, let's keep our focus on its relationship with FMO2, which keeps its base pitch.

Figure 9.18 Rough and Ready FM setup in Zebra 2.

If FMO1 were to simply modulate the frequency of FMO2, then the resulting sound would be quite high-pitched and buzzy.

So instead, I set the depth of frequency modulation to be controlled in FMO2 by an envelope: Envelope 1. I gave the envelope depth a modest setting in the oscillator and then set the envelope as follows:

- Attack: The attack time was set to zero (so the note started immediately).

- Decay: The decay time was quite swift.

- Sustain: The sustain level was fairly low. This meant that with the quick decay, there was a bell-like chime at the start of the note. Also, like a bell, the sound then rings at the sustain level—this setting does have considerable effect on the tone.

- Release: The release time was kept at zero (so the note ends immediately when a key is released).

As well as the envelope, the other key factor controlling the amount of frequency modulation, and therefore the tone, is the Velocity setting in FMO1. This is set to a modest level, but it does give some tonal touch sensitivity to the sound—most importantly, at lower velocities, it gives me the slightly wooden tone that I am after. Clearly, this touch sensitivity will also apply to the other modules that are frequency-modulated by this oscillator.

So far we have created a note that sounds and then sustains infinitely. Although we have only created a metallic sound so far, you will remember that my aim was more of a wooden tone—and a key characteristic of wooden tones is that they decay. I could have effected that decay with an envelope, but instead I chose to use a filter because that gives a more natural decaying characteristic. It's also easier to program. If I had wanted to program this effect using FM, then I would have needed two envelopes:

- One to control the decay of the carrier

- Another to control the decay of the modulator so that the tone gets duller as the sound decays

The flip side of taking this easier route is that I have less control over the tone as it decays. Within the context of this sound, that is a compromise I can live with.

To create the filter decay, I selected the VCF1 filter and loaded the LP Xcite filter (a 24-dB low-pass filter). I then set:

- The Cut-Off to zero, completely cutting all sound.

- Resonance to zero—I don't care about resonance in this sound.

- Envelope 2 to modulate the Cut-Off, and the Modulation Depth knob was set to the maximum (so the envelope directly controls the filter cut-off).

The envelope then has a very straightforward setting:

- Attack: The attack time was set to zero so the filter is immediately fully opened (so on the initial strike, the unfiltered sound is heard).

- Decay: The decay time was set to the maximum.

- Sustain: The sustain level was set to zero, so at the end of the decay time, the filter will be fully closed.

- Release: The release time was set to a moderate level. It may seem odd to set this, but there is a good reason. If the release time is set to zero, then the filter closes with a bit of a thwack, giving a thump at the end of the note. This was not an effect that I liked, nor one that I wanted. By slowing the release time, the filter closes silently, which is the result I wanted.

We've now created one of the three elements. Let's move on to the second element in the sound, which is created by the interaction of FMO1 and FMO3. Before we start working on this element, I suggest you mute the audio channel we have just created. That will allow you to hear this new sound. I'm not often keen on creating elements separately, since it can then be difficult to mix the parts together to form a cohesive sound. However, with this element I am trying to create something quite delicate, so we'll mute the main part, but we will need to listen closely when the final sound is created. By the way, we're muting the audio channel and not the modules because I need one of the modules (FMO1) to help create this sound.

If you look back at Figure 9.18, you will see that FMO3 is located in the second audio channel; however, FMO1 is still able to act as the modulator. To sort this routing, right-click on FMO3 and select Input 1—you will then see a routing "wire" attach from FMO1 to FMO3.

FMO3 is tuned up seven semitones, so it is a major fifth higher than FMO2. When the two oscillators play together, this gives a "power fifth" type of chord sound, which isn't really what we're after. However, when we look at the frequency modulation, we can see that FMO1 is pitched two octaves above FMO3, which gives a useful relationship for creating FM sounds. As you will hear before too long, when both carrier oscillators are frequency-modulated, the pitch relationship between them is not obvious in the same manner that it is if you play the oscillators without frequency modulation.

In this combination, the modulator is pitched quite high by reference to the carrier (two octaves above). This gives great scope for a whole range of metallic tones. Unfortunately, that's not what I was after—I wanted something more wooden. And that's where an envelope came to my aid.

I set Envelope 3 to modulate the frequency modulation depth of FMO3. The Depth knob was set to the maximum, and the envelope was set as follows:

- Attack: The attack time was set to zero.

- Decay: The decay time was fast—not zero, but still very quick.

- Sustain: The sustain level was set to zero. The effect of this setting is that the whole envelope is governed by the decay time setting.

- Release: The release time was set to zero.

- Velocity: The Velocity knob was set to the maximum. This means that the effect of the envelope is controlled by incoming MIDI velocity—with higher velocity, the envelope has greater effect.

As you can see, the envelope has been set to give a "blip," and the magnitude of that blip is controlled by MIDI velocity. However, while that may not appear to be a particularly significant setting, the effect on the tone is interesting. Instead of a metal sound, there is a wooden sound—it is hard to describe in words (especially as it varies with velocity), but it is somewhere between a wooden xylophone and a pan pipe being gently blown. If you select Filtered FM as the FM type on FMO3, then you will get an even smoother, more wood-like tone.

At the moment, this sound will sustain indefinitely. I will address that later, but for the moment, mute the second audio channel, and let's look at the third element, which is going to add some bass to the sound.

The bass sound is created by FMO4, and as with the other modules, this is frequency-modulated by FMO1. To create the bass tone, the pitch of this oscillator has been dropped by setting the Tune knob to −12. (In other words, the oscillator is one octave below the pitch of the main oscillator, FMO2, and three octaves and seven semitones below the modulating oscillator, FMO1.)

As with FMO3—but to a greater extent due to the even larger pitch difference—there is scope to create a range of metallic tones with this carrier/modulator pitch relationship. So again, as with the other carrier oscillators, I haven't set the FM depth on the oscillator; instead, I've used an envelope. For this oscillator, I've used Envelope 1, which is the same envelope that controls the FM depth on FMO2, but this time the maximum extent of the modulation is slightly less. This gives a warmer tone—more of a gentle, deep metallic buzz. (Think of a metallic didgeridoo, and you'll be starting to get the idea.)

However, you will remember that Envelope 1 had some velocity scaling, so if you hit a key hard, then the sound will get much brighter. In addition to this tonal velocity scaling, there is some velocity scaling in the oscillator, so it will become louder with increased velocity.

Anyway, that's the third element, so now we're ready to put the pieces together. Turn down the output volume and then switch on the other two elements. The sound that we have now created is quite robust—it is interesting, but it doesn't quite have the controllable subtlety and nuance I was aiming for. Also, you will notice that if you hold a note, it will sustain indefinitely.

To rectify the situation:

1. Mute the second and third audio columns in the grid.

2. Move the VCF1 module several slots down in its column in the grid (so it is closer to the bottom of the audio chain).

3. Insert two Mix units into Column 1 between FMO1 and VCF1. (This should have no effect on the sound.)

4. Right-click on the Mix1 module you have just loaded and select SideChain 2. This will route FMO3 to Mix1 (and the connection wire should show).

5. Right-click on the Mix2 module you have just loaded and select SideChain 3. This will route FMO4 to Mix2 (and the connection wire should show).

With this new arrangement, you will notice some subtle differences:

- First off, the sound is much quieter, so please feel free to tweak the output volume.

- The initial impact of the notes is similar; however, as you sustain a note, because all of the oscillators now pass through the low-pass filter, the tone is cut.

- Also, the filter cuts the volume, so the notes no longer sustain indefinitely.

Hopefully, you will be able to find the broad range of tone—from something quite woody to something quite metallic at the other end. However, the sustain notes still sounded a bit static to me, so I decided to add some vibrato.

I didn't want the vibrato to have immediate effect. Instead, I wanted it to gently fade in, so I used an envelope (in this case, Envelope 4). I used the envelope to fade up the amount of vibrato in FMO1 (the modulator oscillator)—as the modulator wobbles, so the pitch of the whole patch wobbles.

I hooked up the vibrato control through the ModMatrix, where I set:

- FMO1: Vibrato as the target

- Env4 as the source

The knob controlling the amount of modulation was then set to the maximum. I then set the envelope:

- Attack: The attack time was quite long—nearly set to the maximum. This setting ensures that there is no vibrato effect when short notes are played, but when sustained notes are held (as they begin to decay), the vibrato effect kicks in.

- Sustain: The sustain level was set to the maximum (so the decay time setting was irrelevant).

- Release: The release time also has no effect on the sound.

One last tweak was to set the oscillators to stereo mode and move their positions within the stereo spectrum. I didn't do anything scientific—I just twisted the knobs until I became aware of the elements being balanced in different positions.

Now that the sound is finished, you will notice how the three elements blend. While there are different tonal nuances from each element, you cannot individually identify each part. To take this further, switch FMO3 in and out. (You can do this by double-clicking on it in the grid.) You will notice that its sound is not particularly prominent, but it does add midrange warmth to the sound. Just for the heck of it, listen to each element in isolation, and then switch all of the elements back on. Can you separately identify one element? I couldn't, but your ears may be better than mine. Assuming that, like me, you can't individually identify the separate elements, then you can regard this patch as a successful blend of three elements.

Then again, you may prefer the sound we achieved when the second and third elements did not pass through the filter. If this is your preference, please feel free to go ahead and re-patch the sound to get it to a place where you feel happy with it.

Bass

It would be remiss of me to write a book covering sound and not to include a bass sound. It would be even more remiss of me not to include a monster sound that you can twist in interesting ways. Take a look at Figure 9.19 to see the Bass sound.

Figure 9.19   Bass in Zebra 2.

If you are in any way unsure about the power of your speakers, then turn down the volume. This sound is going to use a few techniques that will blow your voice coils if you're not careful (or if you push things just a little bit further than I am suggesting).

The aim of this is to create a bass sound (obviously), but one that is controllable so we can move from something very thick and highly dominant to a somewhat more delicate, less obtrusive sound. Beyond that, I also wanted to be able to transition between the sounds in a moderately smooth manner. Well, that was the aim....

Let's start with the thick element. This is built around Osc1, into which I have loaded a Saw Bright wave. To make things a bit thicker, I selected multi-voice mode (Quad—which is hidden in Figure 9.19) and pushed the Detune knob enough to get a pretty thick and bassy sound. On its own this could be used as a bass sound (indeed, many do use similar sounds as such); however, the sound was a bit one-dimensional. I also wanted something with more kick (hence my suggestion to turn down the output).

The real kick to this element of the sound is created with two filters: VCF1 and VCF2. Load them up so that VCF1 comes before VCF2, and let's move on.

First, turning to the second filter in the chain, VCF2, we're going to use this as a (fairly) conventional low-pass filter to give the sound some squelch and also to cut some of the higher-frequency elements. The filter I selected was LP OldDrive, which gave a nice sound. I then used Envelope 1 to control the cut-off frequency to give some shape and a bit of spit. The settings I dialed were:

- Cut-Off was cut quite heavily and set at around 10 o'clock. This only allowed the very lowest frequencies through (and then they were quite muffled).

- Resonance was set quite high, at about halfway. This boosted the sound, but still all that could be heard was a muffled sound (albeit somewhat louder). At this point, the sound was more like a bad electronic kick drum (or perhaps a good electronic kick drum if you were after something really muffled and indistinct).

- The next step was to set Envelope 1 to modulate this filter and push the Depth knob to the maximum. With the sustain level set to the maximum, this fully opened the filter, so I pulled the sustain level down (to about 10 o'clock) where the sound sounded right to me.

- I set the attack time to be quick but not immediate. The attack is not sufficiently slow that you can hear the filter move, but instead there is something of a buzz generated at the very start of the note. This buzz worked well with the notion of a very fat, dominant sound.

- The decay was also quick—quick enough to give a bit of squelch. Again, the setting was a balance—it was quick enough to get some squelch, but not so long that the squelch became slow or became too much of a noticeable feature. Setting the decay time with sounds like this is very much a matter of taste, and individual tastes will vary. Equally, you may have to balance the decay time and sustain level settings to get the combination right.

- The release time was pushed off zero so that the filter's closure would not be heard.

- Lastly, a small amount of velocity scaling was set so that the effect of the envelope—and therefore its effect on the filter, and hence the resulting sound—could be controlled by incoming MIDI velocity information.

At this point, the patch had a fairly good sound, but I wanted to add some low-end grunt. My aim here was to make the sound stronger and more solid in the low end—not to fundamentally change the tone. There are several options for this sort of sonic operation:

- **Add another oscillator.** Adding an oscillator will certainly fatten a sound. However, it would change the nature of the whole sound, which was not what I wanted to do.

- **Add a sine wave.** Adding a sine wave is essentially a subset of the "add another oscillator" option. It was an option I thought about, but it didn't give me the level of control I wanted.

- **Boost the low-end EQ.** Boosting the low-end EQ would certainly give a kick to the sound, but it could also make it muddy and wouldn't serve to focus on the note being played.

I didn't want to follow any of these routes. Instead, I used a high-pass filter—in other words, a filter that cuts the low end of the spectrum—and this is where VCF1 is called into action.

Now…intuitively, you wouldn't choose to use a high-pass filter to create a low-end sound. But let me explain. I chose the HP 12dB filter and set the Cut-Off control to zero, so in effect the filter had no effect because its cut-off frequency was lower than the lowest frequency. (In other words, anything that was being filtered would be out of range.) I then made two significant tweaks:

- I pushed the Resonance control up, setting it to about 10 o'clock. The effect of this is to boost the sound around the cut-off frequency. This means that the filter will work to boost the lowest frequency allowed to pass by the setting of the cut-off frequency, but will cut anything below that.

- I then set the KeyFol knob to the maximum. This directly links the Cut-Off knob's setting to the incoming pitch of the note. In effect, therefore, the cut-off frequency will follow the note being played—as a result, the boosted note (due to the resonance boost) will be the note played.

These two tweaks mean that only the played note is boosted. This gives emphasis to the boosted note while keeping the rest of the sound clean. In this way, the filter is working like an EQ unit that is tracking each played note. Again, I set the resonance to my taste—you may want more or less boost to the note's fundamental.

That is the fat element of the sound completed. As I have pointed out in a few places, there are many places where you can adjust the sound to your liking, and you can make as many choices as we look at the second element of the sound. However, whatever choices you make, at some point you are going to need to get these sounds to work together (at least to a certain extent), so feel free to follow your own path, but do keep the final goal in mind.

Anyway, mute the sound we have created, and let's move on to make the other element. For this sound, I loaded Osc2 and VCF2 into the second audio channel in the grid. (You'll see what I did with VCF3 shortly.) This filter/oscillator combination is very similar to the combination of Osc1 and VCF2—the waves are the same and the filters are the same. The settings, however, do vary.

In the oscillator, only a single wave was used, and the Wave knob was pushed to just under halfway. This immediately gave a less aggressive sound. The filter was also set very differently:

- The Cut-Off was set to zero, so no sound would pass through.

- The Resonance was modest—set to about 10 o'clock.

- The Envelope (in this case, Envelope 2) was set to just before 3 o'clock (about 2:30).

The combination of these three settings—in conjunction with the envelope—gives a more restrained, gentler sound. The envelope (Env2) was then set as follows:

- Attack: The attack time was quick, but as with the first filter envelope, it was slowed slightly to give a bit more "quack" at the start of the sound.

- Decay: The decay time was set to just under halfway. This is nearly slow enough to hear the filter moving. It gives the impression of a slightly spongy sound.

- Sustain: The sustain level was set to a moderate level to ensure that—in conjunction with the decay time—there was not a "plucked" effect when a note was struck. It was also set at a level such that when the sound reached the cut-off frequency, it would be low and so in effect the note would be filtered out.

- Release: The release time had no effect on the sound!!

- Velocity: The velocity was set at a modest level to allow a certain amount of tone control through varying incoming MIDI velocity. Although it is set at a similar level to the velocity control of the other filter envelope, this setting seems to have far more effect on the tone for this element of the sound.

I mentioned the notion of giving the sound some quack. Now, it would be misleading to suggest that this sounds anything like a duck, but the end result does have something of the quality of a duck.

The next step was to bring the sounds together. I did this by opening a ChannelMix module in the first audio chain and setting its SideChain as Channel 2. I then unmuted Channel 1 and muted Channel 2 so that the whole sound was mixed in one audio channel. With the Channel Mix module, the Mix knob will now control the respective levels of the two elements. I set the sounds in the respective elements to give a fairly consistent sound change as the Mix setting is adjusted from one extreme to the other. You might want to tweak your sounds if the transition is too lumpy.

The final element in the sound chain is VCF3. The sound of the two mixed elements passes through this filter. I set this with the HP 12dB filter—in other words, another high-pass (low-cutting) filter.

The main purpose of this high-pass filter was not to shape the tone as an integral part of the tone. Instead, it was there to give the player some control over the sound—in particular, to allow the player to thin out the sound. In order to give the player some control, I attached the Cut-Off to the Y axis of the XY pad. Having made the attachment, I went to the XY Assign pane and set the control as follows:

- The minimum setting (in other words, the setting when the Y controller is at the bottom of its pane) was set to zero (far left).

- The maximum setting (in other words, the setting when the Y controller is at the top of its pane) was set to halfway.

- The red/yellow bar was then dragged fully to the left (so the bottom arrow was at its minimum and the top arrow at its maximum). By dragging the bar, the Cut-Off knob on the filter module was moved to the maximum.

With these settings, as the XY pad central button is pushed up, the high-pass filter has more effect, thinning out the sound.

I then set the X axis of the same XY pad to control the mix between the two elements in the Channel Mix module. The setting here is simple; the minimum arrow is set to the minimum, and the maximum arrow is set to the maximum, with the red/yellow bar set in the middle. This means that as you move the XY button from left to right, you transition from Sound 1 (the fat sound), through a 50/50 mix, to Sound 2 (the thinner quack bass).

This nearly gave me the sound I wanted, but I still needed one last tweak.

I set the X controller to adjust the envelope depth setting in VCF2 (which is the low-pass filter giving the squelch to the first oscillator). This change is equivalent to reducing the envelope depth after the X control has passed the midway point. The net effect here is that the level of the first oscillator is being reduced, *and* the sound of that oscillator is being softened because the effect of the envelope is being reduced. To my ear—and as always, feel free to disagree—this smoothes the transition from the brighter sound to the softer sound.

To set this control in the XY pad, I attached the VCF2: ModDepth1 destination to the X controller and then set:

- The minimum arrow (the bottom arrow) to the halfway point

- The maximum arrow to the 25% mark (so the maximum is less than the minimum)

And that's it! Go play and enjoy a very variable and controllable bass.

Synth Brass

This Synth Brass (see Figure 9.20) sound is the last sound in this book and is something of a trip back to the 1970s.

Figure 9.20   Synth Brass in Zebra 2.

However, while it may not be the most modern sound you will hear, this sound uses many of the features of Zebra 2 to give us some control and variation over our sound. Unlike sounds created on synthesizers in the 1970s, we don't simply have one sound here—instead, we have three that are blended, and of course, there is an element of player control.

The first element of the sound is created by a combination of Osc1 and VCF1. The aim here was to create a lower-register synth brass type of sound, which has the characteristic of being slightly overblown—in other words, there is the effect of imprecise blowing. This is intended to be a bit sloppy and not to give a tight brass sound. To my ear it sounds best at lower registers and doesn't work too well with very fast playing (not least since the sound would be inconsistent with that style of play).

The sound is created by a combination of the Saw Bright wave and the LP 12dB filter, which has its Cut-Off controlled by Envelope 1. This combination was then set as follows:

- The Cut-Off control was set to about 10 o'clock. This muffled the sound, leaving only the faintest trace of a low-frequency noise to pass.

- The Resonance was moved slightly. The intention here was to add a touch of brightness; however, if anything more had been added, the effect would have been noticeable.

- The envelope depth was set to about 2 o'clock (so it has some effect, but not as much as it could have).

- The KeyFol knob (which controls the extent to which the filter opens up with higher playing) was set to about 9 o'clock. The combination of the envelope and the key following gives some brightness to the sound, but the character was set with the envelope.

- The attack time knob in the envelope was set to about 10 o'clock. This is perhaps the most important setting for achieving that slightly overblown sound. If the attack time is too fast, then the sound will have too much bite (and will lose some of that real brass vibe), but if the attack is too slow, then the whole brass tone disappears.

- The decay time was swift. This helps emphasize the "spit" at the start of the brass.

- The sustain level was set to somewhere past halfway. There were two purposes in this setting. First, it gave some effect to the decay time, meaning that the initial spit could be heard. Second, it was set at the point where the tone of the sustaining sound was right—in other words, it was set at the point where the filter tone was right.

- The release time has little (if any effect) on this sound, so set that knob where you like.

- Finally, the Velocity knob was set so that there is some response to incoming MIDI velocity data (with the effect that the tone can be controlled—to a limited extent—by MIDI velocity).

The sound that has just been created is going to be focused on the lower end of the keyboard, and I'll talk about hooking that up after we've created the other layer. At the higher end of the keyboard, we're going to create a sound that is controllable between two extremes:

- At one extreme, the sound will be a brighter, more immediate version of the sound that we have just created.

- At the other extreme, the sound will be a much harder sound.

These three elements are then going to be mixed together to create a playable instrument where the tonal shifts are seamless. So let's move on and created the brighter, more immediate version of the sound we have just created.

We're going to create this sound with a combination of Osc3, VCF2, and Envelope 2, using nearly identical settings to the ones we have used for the existing combination. I suggest you mute the current channel and create the new combination in the second channel.

The key differences are:

- The Resonance is higher, being set at around 10 o'clock. This helps give more brightness.

- The envelope has a greater effect—again, potentially giving more brightness, but also giving more effect to the movement of the envelope.

- The attack time in the envelope is faster, so the overblown effect is not heard—instead, there is more of an immediate brass sound.

- The decay time is slower (although still quite swift). With the additional resonance boost, this gives a more noticeable effect to the movement of the filter cut-off by the resonance.

- The sustain level is lower. This has two effects.
  - First, it gives more emphasis to the attack/decay portion of the note.
  - Second, it allows the tone of the note to be adjusted (by effectively controlling the cut-off frequency during the sustain period). In this case, the sustaining tone is close to—but noticeably different from—the sustaining tone in the Osc1/VCF1 combination. To my mind, this tone is slightly brighter and a touch more nasal.

- With this combination, the release time does matter—if it is set to be too short, then there is a noticeable sound when the filter closes, so I pushed the Release knob to a position where there was no noticeable effect.

The third element to the sound is created with Osc2 and is also based around a Saw Bright wave. To create this sound, drag Osc3 to the third channel, mute it, and then insert Osc2 before VCF2. By the way, there is no sonic reason for this change—indeed, by replacing Osc3 with Osc2, the sound should remain the same. All I'm doing here is following a process so that what you create looks like Figure 9.20.

The purpose of this third element, as created with Osc2, is to create a more cutting tone. This is not necessarily a brighter tone, but definitely a more dominant tone. The next challenge that then occurs is how to deploy this tone. However, I'll leave that until after we have created the sound.

I did two very simple things to noticeably change the sound of Osc2:

- First, I pushed up the Sync knob (on the Phase pane of the oscillator). This gives a much brighter, more cutting sound. I set the knob to just past 9 o'clock, where I felt I had the right balance of tone, weight, and cut.

- Second, I dropped the pitch of the oscillator by an octave. This change gave the sound more authority. Due to the Sync effect, the octave drop sounded more like a change in tone and less like a drop in pitch (and hence the sound lost none of its aggression).

While this does sound quite radical (in some ways), please do remember that the point of this element is to use it as a different tonal shade within the context of a whole sound. The aim is not to use it on its own. Anyway, we now have three sound elements:

- **The flabby brass.** This is a combination of Osc1 and VCF1.

- **The brighter, faster brass.** This is a combination of Osc3 and VCF2.

- **The low but dominant brass.** This is a combination of Osc2 and VCF2.

However, you will have noticed that these are three elements, and some parts aren't even hooked up yet. Before we get going, let me try to explain my grand scheme for how these pieces will fit together in the overall sound.

- The flabby brass will be spread over the lower ranges of the keyboard. This will be cross-faded with the sounds across the higher ranges. This cross-fading will be achieved by some pitch-related control.

- The other two elements will be spread over the higher ranges. Both will cover the same range; however, there will be some cross fading. This time, we will cross-fade from one sound to the other based on velocity, so at higher velocities, the lower but more dominant brass sound will predominate, but at lower velocities, the brighter, faster brass will come to the foreground.

To hook up the modules:

1. Un-mute Channel 1.

2. Mute Channel 2 and Channel 3.

3. Open a Channel Mixer (Mix1) in the first audio channel. However, place it a couple of slots down in the grid. (I put it in the sixth row.)

4. Connect VCF2 to the Mix1 module. (Right-click and select SideChain 2.) The "wire" connecting VCF2 to Mix1 should show in addition to the wire connecting VCF1 to Mix1.

5. In the second audio channel, move the VCF module down a few slots. (I put it in the fourth row.)

6. Open a second Channel Mixer (Mix2), but this time in the second audio channel immediately before VCF2.

7. Connect Osc3 to the Mix2 module. (Right-click and select SideChain3.) The wire connecting Osc3 to Mix2 should show in addition to the wire connecting Osc2 to Mix2.

This completes the audio routing; now we need to add some control, so I turned to the ModMatrix.

You will see that the Mix1 module balances the flabby sound that we want over the lower key region with the combined elements for the higher region. In effect, therefore, when I play the lower ranges, I want the Mix knob twisted to the left, and when I play keys in the higher ranges, I want the Mix knob twisted to the right. Clearly this is not practical, so I set the knob to the mid position and hooked up some control in the ModMatrix, where I set:

- Target: Mix1 Mix
- Modulator: KeyFol, and I pushed the knob to the maximum

This gives a smooth and automatic pitch-related transition from one sound to the other. However, I did feel one minor tweak was in order and pulled down the volume of Osc1 so that it was balanced with the combination of the other oscillators.

The second part of cross-fading relates to the two elements created by Osc2 and Osc3, which are then both fed into VCF2. The intention here is to add some velocity cross-fading; however, you will remember that there is also some velocity scaling on the envelopes, so we already have some tonal flexibility with velocity changes. The change controlled by Mix2 is intended to enhance and extend that effect. Indeed, it will work quite well because as the sound gets brighter (due to the filters being modulated), we can bring in the more dominant sound, which, you will remember, is an octave lower. Hence, with increased velocity we will get a brighter, fuller sound (rather than a thinner sound).

The mix between Osc2 and Osc3 is controlled by Mix2. We just need to control that mix with velocity, and our work is done. To do this, I turned to the ModMatrix again and set it (in the second slot) as follows:

- Target: Mix2 Mix
- Modulator: Velocity

In the Mix2 module, I set the Mix knob to the maximum. This meant that the default sound was the softer sound created by Oscillator 3. In the ModMatrix, I set the Modulation Depth knob to about 9 o'clock so that velocity will negatively modulate the Mix setting—in other words, as velocity increases, the mix will increasingly favor Oscillator 2 (the darker, more forceful tone).

And to me, that was a perfect Synth Brass sound with three distinct elements that blended together so that you can't hear the joins. That's enough reading. Put down this book, switch on your synthesizers, and get to making music.

Index

A

A: Attack Time control, 34–35, 201, 204
ADC (analog-to-digital converter), 17–18
Additive module (KarmaFX Synth), 159–162
additive synthesis
    basic description of, 124–125
    difficulties with, 128
    principles of, 126–128
    sawtooth wave, 126–127
    square wave, 126
    triangle wave, 127
ADSR (attack time, decay time, sustain level, release
      time), 73, 201–204
aftertouch, as modulation source controller, 50
Aftertouch plug, 243
aliasing, 21
all-pass filter, 172, 180
All-Pass filter (KarmaFX Synth), 195
amplifier, 45, 236–238
Amplifier module
    KarmaFX Synth, 236
    VAZ Modular, 237–238
analog distortion, 257–258
analog-to-digital (ADC) converter, 17–18
AND gate, 248
And mode, 247
ASIO (Audio Stream Input/Output), 20–21
ASIO4ALL, 20–21
Attack control, 261
attack time, 33–34
attack time, decay time, sustain level, release time
      (ADSR), 73, 201–204
AU (Audio Units) format, 5
audio conversion, 17–18
audio drivers, 20–21
Audio Out plug, 89
audio path
    basic description of, 23
    hooking up in KarmaFX Synth modular, 78–79
    hooking up in SynthEdit, 86–89
    hooking up in VAZ Modular, 66–72
    hooking up in Zebra 2, 58–59
    sound sources, 45
    in subtractive synthesis, 24
    SynthWiz Simple Synth, 53
Audio Stream Input/Output (ASIO), 20–21
Audio Units (AU) format, 5
automation
    drawing, 229–231
    functions, 226
    preparation for, 227–229
    record, 229

B

backgrounds, 99–102
band-pass filter, 171, 179–180, 192
band-reject filter, 171, 180
bandwidth filter parameter, 174
bass
    bass sound, 313–317
    soft bass sound, 39–40
Bend Range plug, 243
bipolar envelope, 208
bit depth, 16–17
brass sound, 318–322
brightness, sound, 287–288

C

Cakewalk, 9
*Cakewalk Synthesizers: From Presets to Power
      User*, 158
Cantible host, 9
Cantible Lite website, 9
carrier:modulator ratio, 133–134
cascades, 131
Ceiling module, 249
channel, MIDI, 6–7

Channel Mixer, 240
Channel plug, 243
Channel setting (CV Converter), 245
ChannelMix module, 239
Chaser 8-Way module, 238
choir sound, 305–307
chorus effects, 270–271
Comb filter
    KarmaFX Synth, 195
    VAZ Modular, 190–191
    Zebra 2, 182–183
comb filter, 172
combining oscillators, 116–118
combining sound
    doubling oscillators, 113–115
    reasons for, 112
compression, 260–262
computer
    hard disk space, 2
    keyboard, 2
    memory, 3
    music-making requirements, 1–3
    problems, 1
    processor power, 2
Connect dialog box, 87
connection, MIDI, 6–7
container properties, 103–104
control elements, 46–47
control messages, 50
control voltage, 69, 242
Controllers setting (CV Converter), 245
control/modulation path, 23
conversion, audio, 17–18
Core Audio, 20
Cosmo B Oscillator (VAZ Modular), 150–151
Cosmo Z Oscillator (VAZ Modular), 150
CPU consumption, 52, 283–284
cross delay effects, 267
cross-modulation filter (XMF) (Zebra 2), 180–181
curves, envelope, 207
Cut-Off Envelope, 35–37
cut-off frequency filter parameter, 173, 176–177
Cut-Off Frequency slider, 31–32
CV Converter module, 71–72, 244–245

D

D: Decay Time control, 35, 202, 204
D: Delay Time control, 204
DAC (digital-to-audio converter), 18
DAHDSR envelope, 204–205
damping, 272
decay time, 34

delay effects
    chorus, 270–271
    cross delay, 267
    delay time controls, 267
    feedback, 268
    flanger, 270
    modulation control, 268
    modulation delay, 269–271
    modulation-type, 266
    mono delay, 267
    phaser, 270
    stereo delay, 267
delay, mix control, 268
deployment, sample
    key ranges, 123–124
    multi-sample versus single-sample, 122–123
    single-cycle and longer waves, 122
    velocity ranges, 124
depth/amount control, LFOs, 212–213
design. See sound design
Detune knob (Zebra 2), 137
detuning oscillator, 115
diffusion, 272
digital distortion, 258–259
digital-to-audio (DAC) converter, 18
DirectX (DX/DXi) format, 5
distortion
    analog, 257–258
    digital, 258–259
Divide module, 249
doubling oscillators
    hard sync, 114–115
    multi-oscillators, 115
    oscillator detuning, 115
    phase and polarity, 113–114
downloading SynthWiz Simple Synth, 3, 9
drawing automation, 229–231
drive filter parameter, 174, 178
DX/DXi (DirectX) format, 5

E

echo sound, 300–304
effects. See FX units
envelope
    ADSR, 201–204
    bipolar, 208
    curves, 207
    DAHDSR, 204–205
    discussed, 25
    FM sound control, 132
    followers, 209–210
    key tracking and, 208–209

LFO *versus*, 210–211
as modulation source, 49
multi-stage, 205–207
piano note example, 199–200
retrigger, 235
samples and, 208
volume envelope example, 200–201
EQ (equalization)
graphic, 265–266
parametric, 263–264
shelf, 265
Exp Glide mode, 245

F

Fade 1/2 by 3xC mode, 241
fat sound, 110
feedback, 268, 280, 282
filter
303, 175, 194
all-pass, 172, 180
band-pass, 171, 179–180, 192
band-reject, 171, 180
bandwidth parameter, 174
comb, 172
cut-off frequency parameter, 173, 176–177
defined, 45
drive parameter, 174, 178
Filter S, 175
formant, 172, 179
high-pass, 170–171, 179, 192
KarmaFX Synth filter modules, 192–196
key tracking and, 176–177
low-pass, 31, 169–170, 178–179, 192
as modulation destination, 51
Moog, 175, 193–194
notch, 171, 180, 192
oscillator/filter combination, 289–292
parallel, 282–283
peaking, 171–172
resonance parameter, 173, 176–177
slopes, 174–175, 177
SVF, 175
SynthEdit filter modules, 196–197
VAZ Modular filter modules, 183–192
Zebra 2 filter modules, 178–183
Zolzer, 175, 193
Filter block (SynthWiz Simple Synth), 31–32
filter configuration and signal routing, 277–283
filter cut-off control (SynthWiz Simple Synth), 54
Filter K (VAZ Modular), 186
Filter R (VAZ Modular), 186–188
Filter S filter, 175

Filter S (VAZ Modular), 188–189
filter sweep, 36
filtered feedback, 280, 282
filtered noise sound, 41–43
flanger effects, 270
Fletcher, Tobias, 9
Floor module, 249
FM (frequency modulation) synthesis
carrier:modulator ratio, 133–134
cascades, 131
operators, 128–129
parallel carriers, 129–130
parallel modulators, 130–131
ring modulation, 134–135
simple FM, 129
sound control, 131–133
tuning challenges, 133–134
FM Oscillator (Zebra 2)
basic description of, 142–143
FM modes, 144–145
main controls of, 144
More FMO sub-page, 145
followers, envelope, 209–210
formant filter, 172, 179
Formant filter (KarmaFX Synth), 195–196
format
AU, 5
DX/DXi, 5
RTAS, 5
stand-alone, 5
VST/VSTi, 4, 13–14
forum, 1
free/low-cost host, 9
free-running phase, 114
frequency analyzer, 251–252
frequency, LFOs, 211–212
frequency modulation (FM) synthesis
carrier:modulator ratio, 133–134
cascades, 131
operators, 128–129
parallel carriers, 129–130
parallel modulators, 130–131
ring modulation, 134–135
simple FM, 129
sound control, 131–133
tuning challenges, 133–134
FX tab (Zebra), 139
FX units
basic description of, 255
compression, 260–262
delay
chorus, 270–271
cross delay effect, 267
delay time controls, 267

FX units (*continued*)
    feedback, 268
    flanger, 270
    mix control, 268
    modulation control, 268
    modulation delay, 269–271
    modulation-type effects, 266
    mono delay, 267
    phaser, 270
    stereo delay, 267
    distortion
        analog, 257–258
        digital, 258–259
    equalization, 263–266
    insert FX, 256
    reverb, 272–274
    send FX, 256

G

gate, 73–74
Gate control, 243
Gate Logic module, 246–247
GeoBlend wave-shaping mode, 142
GeoMorph wave-shaping mode, 142
Glide controls (CV Converter), 245
glide time, 235
Glide Time mode, 245
global controls
    pitch bend range, 235–236
    polyphony, 233–234
    portmento, 234–235
graphic EQ, 265–266

H

H: Hold Time control, 204
half waveshaping, 282–283
hard disk space, 2
hard sync, 114–115
hard-knee compressor, 262
harmonics, 125
    additive sawtooth wave, 126–127
    additive square wave, 126
headphone, 2
high-pass filter, 170–171, 179, 192
host, 4, 8
    Cantible, 9
    free/low-cost, 9
    Project5, 9, 13–14
    SAVIHost
        basic description of, 9
        running SynthWiz Simple Synth under, 10–11

    setting up audio under, 11–12
    setting up MIDI under, 12–13
    Tobybear MiniHost, 9
human choir sound, 305–307

I

input
    MIDI, 6
    SynthWiz Simple Synth, 54
input/output, 241–246
insert FX, 256
installation, SynthWiz Simple Synth, 9–10
interface, MIDI, 6
Inverter
    SynthEdit, 249
    VAZ Modular, 247

K

KarmaFX Synth
    303-Like filter, 194
    Additive module, 159–162
    All-Pass filter, 195
    Amplifier module, 236
    attaching modulators in, 80–81
    Comb filter, 195
    discussed, 3
    filter modules in, 192–196
    Formant filter, 195–196
    hooking up audio path in, 78–79
    LFOs in, 214
    loading modules in, 76–78
    Moog filter, 193–194
    Noise module, 163
    Osc 1 module, 155–156
    Osc 2 module, 156–158
    patch construction with, 75–82
    Patch Properties box, 82
    Sampler module, 158–159
    saving sound in, 81–83
    SVF filter, 192–193
    VAZ Modular comparison, 75
    Zolzer filter, 193
key pitch, 47
key ranges, 123–124
key scaling, 132–133
key tracking
    envelopes and, 208–209
    filters and, 176–177
    as modulation source, 49–50
    range limiting, 97–98
    SynthEdit, 94–96

Key Tracking slider (SynthWiz Simple Synth), 37
keyboard
    MIDI, 5–6, 49
    piano-style, 2
KeyScale knob (Zebra 2), 141
knee control, 262

L

latency
    audio conversion, 17–18
    dealing with, 19
layers, 7–8
legato mode, 235
Level control, 261
level meter, 94, 250–251
LFO (low-frequency oscillator), 128–129
    depth/amount control, 212–213
    envelopes *versus*, 210–211
    frequency/speed control, 211–212
    in KarmaFX Synth, 214
    monophonic, 213–214
    phase control, 213
    polyphonic, 213–214
    random wave shape, 211
    sawtooth wave shape, 211
    sine wave shape, 211
    square wave shape, 211
    in SynthEdit, 216–217
    triangle wave shape, 211
    uses for, 210
    in VAZ Modular, 214–215
    in Zebra 2, 215–216
link control, 261
logic gates, 248
loops, 120–121
Low Pass plug, 89
low-frequency oscillator. *See* LFO
low-pass filter, 31, 169–170, 178–179, 192

M

Master Controls module (VAZ Modular), 68
mathematical functions, 248–249
memory, 3
MIDI
    channel, 6–7
    connection, 6–7
    control messages, 50
    input devices, 6
    interface, 6
    keyboard, 5–6, 49
    layers, 7–8
    MIDI Learn, 226

MIDIUnLearn, 226
    out port, 5
    setting up under SAVIHost, 12–13
    splits, 7–8
MIDI Data plug, 88
MIDI In module, 242–243
MIDI to CV unit, 242
MIDIData module, 242
MIDITrig module, 242
MinMax modules (VAZ Modular), 247
Mix tab (Zebra 2), 138–139
Mixer 2-Input module, 239
Mixer 3-Input module, 239
mixers, 238–240
Mode switch, 245
modulation
    defined, 33
    effect of key pitch on sound, 47
    effect of time on sound, 48
    effect of velocity on sound, 47
    FM (frequency modulation)
        carrier:modulator ratio, 133–134
        cascades, 131
        operators, 128–129
        parallel carriers, 129–130
        parallel modulators, 130–131
        ring modulation, 134–135
        simple FM, 129
        sound control, 131–133
        tuning challenges, 133–134
    PWM (pulse-width modulation), 111
    ring, 134–135
modulation control sources, 48–50
modulation destinations
    basic description of, 50
    filter, 51
    pan, 51–52
    pitch, 51
    pulse-width, 51
    volume, 51
modulation elements, 46–47
modulation envelope controls, 56
modulation envelopes, 54–55
Modulation Mixer, 240
modulation path, 23
modulation sources
    aftertouch, 50
    basic description of, 49
    envelopes, 49
    key tracking, 49–50
    MIDI control change, 50
    modulation wheel, 50
    pitch bend, 50
    velocity, 49
    XY controllers, 50

modulation wheel, 50
modulators
    attaching in KarmaFX Synth, 80–81
    attaching in SynthEdit, 90–91
    attaching in VAZ modular, 73–74
    attaching in Zebra 2, 59–61
    parallel, 130–131
modules
    loading in KarmFX Synth Modular, 76–78
    loading in SynthEdit, 84–85
    loading in VAZ Modular synthesizer, 64–66
    loading in Zebra 2, 58
mono delay, 267
Mono Mode, 243
Mono Note Priority mode, 243
monophonic LFOs, 213–214, 234
Moog filter, 175, 193–194
More FMO sub-page (Zebra 2), 145
MSEG (multi-stage envelope generator), 206
MultiOscillator controls (VAZ Modular), 149
multi-oscillators, 115
Multiply module, 249
Multi-Saw Oscillator controls (VAZ Modular), 150
multi-stage envelope, 205–207
multi-stage envelope generator (MSEG), 206
Musical Instrument Digital Interface. See MIDI

N

NAND gate, 248
Noise module
    KarmaFX Synth, 163
    Zebra 2, 145–146
Noise Source module (VAZ Modular), 151–152
noise wave, 31, 112
NOR gate, 248
notch filter, 171, 180, 192
note off message, 49
note on message, 49
Note Range setting (CV Converter), 245
Nyquist point, 21

O

One-Pole filter (VAZ Modular), 184
operators, FM sound, 128–129
OR gate, 248
Or mode, 247
organ-like sound, 296–300
Osc 1 module (KarmaFX Synth), 155–156
Osc 2 module (KarmaFX Synth), 156–158
Osc module (Zebra 2)
    basic description of, 136–137
    FX tab, 139

GeoBlend mode, 142
GeoMorph mode, 142
KeyScale knob, 141
Mix tab, 138–139
More Osc settings, 141–142
Phase knob, 141
Phase tab, 140–141
SpectroBlend mode, 142
SpectroMorph mode, 142
Sync switch, 141
wave selection, 138
Oscillator module
    SynthEdit, 164–165
    VAZ Modular, 147–148
oscillator/filter combination, 289–292
oscillators
    combining, 116–118
    discussed, 25
    doubling
        hard sync, 114–115
        multi-oscillators, 115
        oscillator detuning, 115
        phase and polarity, 113–114
    LFO, 128–129
oscilloscope, 252–253
out port, MIDI, 5
output, 54, 241–246
Output Level section
    output meter, 29
    SynthWiz Simple Synth, 37–38
output meter, 29, 57
Output plug, 89
overdrive units, 258

P

pad-type sound, 40–41
pan, 51–52
Pan knob (Zebra 2), 139
parallel carriers, 129–130
parallel modulators, 130–131
parametric EQ, 263–264
partials, 125
patch construction
    empty patch option, 76
    with KarmaFX Synth Modular,
        75–82
    simple effect option, 76
    simple patch option, 76
    simple sampler option, 76
    with SynthEdit, 83–94
    with SynthWiz Simple Synth, 53–58
    with VAZ modular, 63–74
    with Zebra 2, 58–62

Patch Properties box (KarmaFX Synth), 82
peaking filter, 171–172
phase
    oscillator, 113–114
    sampling and, 121
phase control, 114, 213
Phase Distortion module (SynthEdit), 165–166
Phase knob (Zebra 2), 141
phase synchronization, 114
Phase tab (Zebra 2), 140–141
phaser effects, 270
Pink Noise wave, 31
pitch, 51
pitch bend
    as modulation controller and source, 50
    ranges, 235–236
Pitch drop-down list (VAZ Modular), 146
Pitch message, 49
Pitch plug, 89, 243
Pitchbend setting (CV Converter), 245
pitched noise sound, 42
playability, sound design, 289
pluck-type sound, 39–40
plug-in. See host
polarity, 113–114
polarity reversal, 114
Poly Detune setting (CV Converter), 246
polyphonic LFOs, 213–214
polyphony, 233–234
portamento, 234–235
Portamento Time mode, 243
presets, 285–286
processor power, 2
Project5 host, 9, 13–14
Project5 Power, 9, 227
pulse wave, 31, 111
pulse-width, 51
pulse-width modulation (PWM), 111

R

R: Release Time control, 35, 202, 205
RAM (random access memory), 3
Ramp wave, 30, 111
random access memory (RAM), 3
random wave, 211
range limiting, 97–98
Ratio control, 261
Rausch, Klaus P.
    Sample This!, 120
Read This First file, 9
Real-Time AudioSuite (RTAS) format, 5
record automation, 229

reedy sound, 111
Release control, 261
release time, 34
resonance boost, 32
resonance control, SynthWiz Simple Synth, 54
resonance filter parameter, 173, 176–177
retrigger envelope, 235
Retrigger mode, 243
reverb effects, 272–274
rich sound, 288
ring modulation, 134–135
rough and ready FM sound, 307–313
RTAS (Real-Time AudioSuite) format, 5

S

S: Sustain Level control, 35, 202, 205
Sample module (VAZ Modular), 152
sample rate, 16–17
Sample This! (Rausch), 120
Sampler module (KarmaFX Synth), 158
sampling
    basic description of, 118
    defined, 119–121
    deployment
        key ranges, 123–124
        multi-sample versus single-sample, 122–123
        single-cycle and longer waves, 122
        velocity ranges, 124
    envelopes and, 208
    loops, 120–121
    multi-sample, 121
    phrase, 121
    re-creation of musical instrument, realistic example
        of, 120
    sampled waves as sound source, 120
    single cycle, 121
    single shot, 121
    sustain loop, 121
Save as VST dialog box, 105–106
Save Preset dialog box, 66
SAVIHost
    basic description of, 9
    running SynthWiz Simple Synth under,
        10–11
    setting up audio under, 11–12
    setting up MIDI under, 12–13
saving
    in KarmaFX Synth, 81–83
    in SynthEdit, 83–84
    in VAZ Modular, 74
    in Zebra 2, 62–63
saw wave, 30

sawtooth wave
    additive, 126–127
    basic description of, 110–111
    LFOs, 211
Scale Sum By Const mode, 241
Scaler (VAZ Modular), 248
scaling
    key, 132–133
    velocity, 132
Seib, Hermann, 9
Select MIDI Devices dialog box, 12
Select Wave Devices dialog box, 12
self-oscillate, 32
send FX, 256
Shaper controls (Zebra 2), 181–182
shelf EQ, 265
side chain control, 262
signal routing and filter configuration, 277–283
simple.dll file, 9
Sine Oscillator (VAZ Modular), 152–153
sine wave, 30, 109–110, 211
single cycle, 121
single shot, 121
site. See website
slopes, filter, 174–175, 177
soft bass sound, 38–39
sonic sound, 276–277
sound
    architecture of, 276
    attack time, 288
    bass, 313–317
    brass, 318–322
    brightness of a, 287–288
    combining
        doubling oscillators, 113–116
        oscillators, 116–118
        reasons for, 112
    echo, 300–304
    effect of key pitch on, 47
    effect of time on, 48
    effect of velocity on, 47
    fat, 110
    filtered noise, 41–43
    human choir, 305–307
    organ-like, 296–300
    pad-type, 40–41
    pitched noise, 42
    pluck-type, 39–40
    reedy, 111
    rich, 288
    rough and ready FM, 307–313
    soft bass, 38–39
    sonic, 276–277
    squelch, 43–44
    static, 40

    swelling string, 203
    synth brass, 318–322
    warm, 289
    wooden, 111, 307–313
soundcard, 2
sound design
    brightness of sound, 287–288
    building blocks, 289–292
    correct combinations, 288–289
    oscillator/filter combination, 289–292
    playability, 289
    presets, 285–286
    principles, 286–289
    programming with purpose, 284–285
    rich, 288
    track arrangement, 285
    warm sound, 289
sound source, 45, 120
SoundFont Oscillator module (SynthEdit), 166–167
speaker quality, 2
SpectroBlend wave-shaping mode, 142
SpectroMorph wave-shaping mode, 142
speed, LFOs, 211–212
splits, 7–8
splitters, 238
square wave
    additive, 126
    basic description of, 111
    LFOs, 211
squelch sound, 43–44
SSS Emulation, 25–26
static sound, 40
Steinberg website, 4
step generators, 217–220
stereo delay, 267
303 filter, 175, 194
Subtract modules, 249
subtractive synthesis, 24
Sum Modulation mode, 241
sustain level, 34
sustain loop, 121
SVF filter, 175
    KarmaFX Synth, 192–193
    VAZ Modular, 189–190
swelling string sound, 203
Sync switch (Zebra 2), 141
synth brass sound, 318–322
SynthEdit synthesizer
    attaching modulators in, 90–91
    Connect dialog box, 87
    default values, 98
    destination connections, 91–92
    direct text entry, 29
    discussed, 3
    exporting VSTi from, 102–107

filter modules in, 196–197
filter, volume and envelope controls, 91
hooking up audio path in, 86–89
interface building, 98–102
Inverter, 249
key tracking, 94–96
Level Adjuster module, 249
level meter, 94
LFOs in, 216–217
loading modules in, 84–85
logic gates, 248
mathematical functions, 248–249
Oscillator module, 164–165
patch construction with, 83–86, 88–89, 91–94
Phase Distortion module, 165–166
range limiting, 97–98
response to MIDI data, 85
saving in, 83–84
SoundFont Oscillator module, 166–167
VCA module, 237
Volume slider controls, 94
synthesis
   additive
      basic description of, 124–125
      difficulties with, 128
      principles of, 126–128
      sawtooth wave, 126–127
      square wave, 126
      triangle wave, 127
   subtractive, 24
SynthWiz Simple Synth
   audio path, 53
   basic description of, 3–4
   Cut-Off Envelope, 35–37
   downloading, 3, 9
   Filter block in, 31–32
   filter cut-off control, 54
   inputs/outputs, 54
   installation, 9–10
   Key Tracking slider, 37
   modulation envelope controls, 56
   modulation envelopes, 54–55
   Output Level block, 37–38
   output meter, 29, 57
   patch construction with, 53–58
   resonance control, 54
   running under Project5, 13–14
   running under SAVIHost, 10–11
   sections of, 26, 28
   sliders, 29
   volume control, 57
   Volume Envelope, 33–35
   waveform options in, 30–31
   waveform selector, 27–28

T
Threshold control, 261
time, effect on sound, 48
Tobybear MiniHost, 9
track arrangement, 285
triangle wave
   additive, 127
   basic description of, 31, 112
   LFOs, 211
trigger, 73–74
Tune knob (Zebra 2), 137
tuning challenges, FM synthesis, 133–134
tuning controls (VAZ Modular), 146–147
Type A filters (VAZ Modular), 185
Type B filters (VAZ Modular), 185–186
Type C filters (VAZ Modular), 186
Type D filters (VAZ Modular), 186

U
Unison Voice setting (CV Converter), 246

V
VAZ Modular synthesizer
   Amplifier module, 237–238
   attaching modulators in, 73–74
   audio connection, 66–67
   basic description of, 63
   Comb filter, 190–191
   Cosmo A Oscillator, 150
   Cosmo B Oscillator, 150–151
   CV Converter module, 71–72
   discussed, 3
   Filter (all-purpose filter), 184–185
   Filter K, 186
   filter modules in, 183–192
   filter options, 183
   Filter R, 186–188
   Filter S, 188–189
   Gate Logic module, 246–247
   hooking up audio path in, 66–72
   Inverter, 247
   KarmaFX Synth comparison, 75
   LFOs in, 214–215
   loading modules in, 64–66
   Master Controls module, 68
   MinMax modules, 247
   MultiOscillator controls, 149
   Multi-Saw Oscillator controls, 150
   Noise Source module, 151–152
   One-Pole filter, 184

VAZ Modular synthesizer (*continued*)
    Oscillator module, 147–148
    patch construction with, 63–74
    Pitch drop-down list, 146
    response to MIDI data, 70
    Sample module, 152
    saving sound in, 74
    Scaler, 248
    Sine Oscillator, 152–153
    SVFilter, 189–190
    tuning controls, 146–147
    Type A filters, 185
    Type B filters, 185–186
    Type C filters, 186
    Type D filters, 186
    Vowel filter, 191–192
    Waveshaper filter, 192
    Wavetable Oscillator, 153–154
    WTVoice module, 154
VCA module (SynthEdit), 237
VCF module (Zebra 2), 178–180
Vector Mixer, 225
velocity
    effect on sound, 47
    as modulation source, 49
    ranges, 124
Velocity plug, 243
velocity scaling, 132
Vibrato control (Zebra 2), 137
Virtual Studio Technology (VST/VSTi) format, 4,
        13–14
visualization modules
    frequency analyzer, 251–252
    level meters, 250–251
    oscilloscope, 252–253
    volt meter, 250
volt meter, 250
volume, as modulation destination, 51
volume control (SynthWiz Simple Synth),
        57
Volume Envelope
    Attack Time control, 33–34
    Decay Time control, 34
    Release Time control, 34
    Sustain Level control, 34
    SynthWiz Simple Synth, 33–35
Volume knob (Zebra 2), 139
Volume slider controls, SynthEdit, 94
Vowel filter (VAZ Modular),
        191–192
VST Plug-Ins dialog box, 14
VSTi, exporting from SynthEdit,
        102–107
VST/VSTi (Virtual Studio Technology) format, 4,
        13–14

W

warm sound, 289
Wave knob (Zebra 2), 137
wave shapes
    noise wave, 112
    pulse wave, 111
    ramp wave, 111
    random wave, 211
    sawtooth wave
        additive, 126–127
        basic description of, 110–111
        LFOs, 211
    sine wave, 109, 211
    square wave
        additive, 126
        basic description of, 111
        LFOs, 211
    triangle wave
        additive, 127
        basic description of, 112
        LFOs, 211
waveform options, in SynthWiz Simple Synth, 30–31
waveform selector (SynthWiz Simple Synth), 27–28
Waveshaper filter (VAZ Modular), 192
waveshaping, 282–283
Wavetable Oscillator (VAZ Modular), 153–154
WDM (Windows Driver Model), 20
website
    Cantible Lite, 9
    Steinberg, 4
White Noise wave, 31
Windows, ASIO for, 20–21
Windows Driver Model (WDM), 20
wooden sound, 111, 307–313
WTV module (VAZ Modular), 154

X

XMF (cross-modulation filter) (Zebra 2), 180–181
X-Mix module, 238
XOR gate, 248
Xor mode, 247
XY pads
    basic description of, 221–222
    destinations, assigning, 222–224
    ranges, 224–225
    Vector Mixer, 225

Z

Zebra 2 synthesizer
    attaching modulators in, 59–61
    Comb filter, 182–183

Detune knob, 137
discussed, 3
ease of use, 58
filter modules in, 178–183
FM Oscillator
    basic description of, 142–143
    FM Modes, 144–145
    main controls of, 144
    More FMO sub-page, 145
hooking up audio path in, 58–59
LFOs in, 215–216
loading modules in, 58
Noise module, 145–146
Osc module
    basic description of, 136–137
    FX tab, 139
    GeoBlend mode, 142
    GeoMorph mode, 142
    KeyScale knob, 141
    Mix tab, 138–139

More Osc settings, 141–142
    Phase knob, 141
    Phase tab, 140–141
    SpectroBlend mode, 142
    SpectroMorph mode, 142
    Sync switch, 141
    wave selection, 138
Pan knob, 139
patch construction with, 58–62
Save Preset dialog box, 66
saving sound in, 62–63
Shaper controls, 181–182
Tune knob, 137
VCF module, 178–180
Vibrato control, 137
Volume knob, 139
Wave knob, 137
XMF (cross-modulation filter), 180–181
Zolzer filter, 175, 193